Making Difference in Medieval and Early Modern Iberia

MAKING
DIFFERENCE

in Medieval and Early Modern Iberia

JEAN DANGLER

University of Notre Dame Press

Notre Dame, Indiana

Manufactured in the United States of America

Library of Congress Cataloging-in-Publication Data
Dangler, Jean.
Making difference in medieval and early modern Iberia / Jean Dangler.
    p.   cm.
Includes bibliographical references and index.
ISBN 0-268-02575-4 (cloth : alk. paper)
ISBN 0-268-02576-2 (pbk. : alk. paper)
1. Spanish literature—To 1500—History and criticism.   2. Literature
and society—Spain.   3. Spain—Intellectual life—711–1516.   I. Title.
PQ6058.D36   2005
860.9'002—dc22

                                             2005025254

∞ *This book was printed on acid free paper.*

Contents

Acknowledgments

Six or seven years ago, in an undergraduate course on medieval Iberia, a student asked me why the Arabic and Hebrew poetry of al-Andalus (which we read in Castilian translation) was important to the study of "Spain." It was the perfect moment for a discussion about the fundamental question of how we see and understand the medieval Iberian past. I now invoke this question toward the beginning of all my classes. Since then, and throughout the preparation of this book, I have wondered about my own insistence on devising ways to understand Iberia's complex, multicultural networks. I have realized for some time that growing up in Hawaii shaped my being and perception. But only recently have I connected the richness and diversity of my birthplace to my work in the Iberian past and to my resolve in making meaning from the variety of texts and communities that composed medieval Iberia. I am grateful for that relationship.

Many people provided me with companionship and comfort during the writing of this book. I thank Michael Solomon for his friendship and for his unrelenting support of my ideas and research, as well as for his kind words in moments of adversity. I am also grateful to Carlos J. Alonso for his continued guidance and reassurance in the profession. I would like to acknowledge Lisa Dillman, Kristin Naupert Briega, Alejandro Rupert Moreno, María José Serrano Cejalvo, and Shonna Trinch for their invaluable friendship and contributions to my work. My gratitude to my partner, Ainslee Beery, is unwavering.

Research and preparation for this book were facilitated by grants from the Department of Modern Languages and Linguistics at Florida State University, and from the College of Liberal Arts and Sciences at Tulane University. The writing of chapter 3 was aided by an American Summer Faculty Fellowship from the American Association of University Women. Portions of chapter 2 were published in "Subject Crossings in Andalusi Lyric," *Revista de estudios hispánicos* 38 (2004): 303–16, and material from chapter 3 appeared in "Conversion and Diversion in Iberian Cutting Poems," *Hispanic Review* 72.4 (2004): 491–503.

I dedicate this book to the memory of my aunt, Carolyn L. Dangler, who taught me to travel, to bodysurf, and to seek things.

Making Difference in Medieval and Early Modern Iberia

Introduction

Rapacious politics and media representations today suggest that the hierarchical colonial relation between dominating Westerners and subordinated "others" from the South and East is an intrinsic, enduring part of human history. It is as if powerful nations had always created hierarchies of dominance and subjection to denigrate people of color, the poor, and foreigners. But otherness and alterity, that is, the way that difference is created between subjects and things, were not always forged in order to elevate certain groups over others. In multicultural medieval Iberia, which maintained varying relations between Muslim, Christian, and Jewish communities, differences between subjects and things were not always made as they are nowadays. While medieval people clearly saw one another as different, powerful groups did not automatically seek to expunge other subjects, because medieval alterity did not center on hierarchies of value between esteemed and denigrated peoples. Rather, two prominent tenets, multifaceted subject formation and the embrace of contrasts and the negative, distinguished medieval alterity from modern notions of otherness. Medieval subjectivity was not always marked by essential qualities of character but was mutable and shifting, while the adverse often was esteemed in the making of meaning and the forging of the social order. The negative and adverse do not solely refer to unseemly qualities, such as ugly or bad, but they also signify absence, silence, and emptiness.

I have identified these tenets based on numerous medieval discourses and be-lieve they underlie many medieval texts even if they are not explicitly stated as such. They manifested in the everyday social order, and they girded epistemological and ontological models that integrated rather than expulsed the divergent. Although it is difficult to determine whether they preceded the epistemological and ontological models or vice versa, it is evident that the tenets pervaded many areas of medieval life and thought.

Alterity changed greatly in the fifteenth century when the incipient Castilian nation-state demanded more stratified hierarchies of worth between subjects and things. Diverse people no longer formed part of an interdependent whole but instead were attributed favorable or derogatory values that determined their inclusion or ex-clusion from powerful, dominating groups. These shifts were exemplified by serious political and social events at the end of the fifteenth century, which included the con-version and expulsion of Jews and the dissolution of the last Iberian Muslim kingdom in Granada in 1492. As this book will show, four Iberian discourses evidenced the me-dieval tenets and later reinforced changes in the principles of alterity: (1) *muwashshah/ jarcha* poems from al-Andalus, (2) Andalusi "cutting poems" (*cartas de tijera*), (3) medi-cal literature about the body, and (4) discourse about the monster. Early modern modifications to these discourses illustrated the shifts in alterity and in prevailing cultural values.

This argument may apply to other areas of the medieval world, but medieval Iberia is ideal for a study of alterity because it was a multicultural territory of Mus-lim, Jewish, and Christian communities. Geographic, cultural, political, and economic negotiation and contact were constant between Christian kingdoms in the north and the Islamic domain called al-Andalus toward the south, which Muslims ruled from 711 until 1492. Medieval Iberia was not hierarchical and homogeneous, but culturally heterogeneous and politically vacillating. Absolute categories and boundaries about language, ethnicity, gender, and geography often prove inaccurate for the medieval peninsula, where rigid classification was not a cultural value. Intercultural contact and exchange were conspicuous parts of medieval life in al-Andalus and in northern Christian kingdoms, a fact that lends itself to a variety of questions about how to char-acterize medieval Iberia and its inhabitants. The diversity of Islamic and Christian kingdoms and the fluid borders between them give the medieval peninsula a supple character that defies absolute definition.

The intricate, variable arrangement of Iberian society demands sophisticated dis-cussions that extend beyond the concepts of *reconquista* (reconquest) and *conviven-cia* (cohabitation). Until recently these terms dominated scholarly dialogue due to the renowned debate between Américo Castro and Claudio Sánchez Albornoz, who during the 1940s and 1950s sought to link medieval culture and history to an ostensibly modern Spanish national character. Castro held that medieval Iberia was a tolerant place of *convivencia* where Christians, Muslims, and Jews lived together harmoniously. He suggested that modern Spanish identity was ethnically and culturally formulated on the substratum of al-Andalus, which he aimed to show by revealing how medieval Castilian artifacts, such as the *Libro de buen amor* (*Lba*), were indebted to Andalusi linguistic and cultural influences.[1] In contrast to Castro's ideas about *convivencia,* Sánchez Albornoz elided Andalusi influence altogether in his belief that contemporary Spanish identity derived from the Visigoths, who ruled the peninsula prior to the Muslim arrival in 711. Sánchez Albornoz linked Spanish identity to northern European and Roman roots and largely disregarded almost eight centuries of Muslim rule.[2]

Castro and Sánchez Albornoz's debate coincided with a traditional focus on the *reconquista* as a nationalist ideological tool to reinforce the predominance of Christian kingdoms over supposed Muslim invaders. The reconquest ideology depicts the Islamic dominance of the peninsula as illegitimate, even though preceding Visigothic forces occupied Iberia also without prior claims to power, and it portrays Christians as poised to regain peninsular control, starting with Pelayo's battles from Covadonga in 719. This idea of the reconquest as a massive, intractable wave of Christian forces that rolled southward from Asturias in the north has been debunked as historically incorrect.[3] Historians have sought more precise historical accounts in order to avoid portraying medieval Iberia as a monolith that bears a natural connection to fixed, modern-day "Spanish" identity. For example, David Nirenberg argues that medieval Iberia was marked by a constant shift between coexistence and conflict that made it both tolerant and tranquil, as well as violent and conflictive.[4] John V. Tolan calls for historical analysis according to specific time periods and social contexts. In his study of medieval European portrayals of Muslims, he shows that medieval Iberians depicted Muslims in various ways that depended on concrete historical contexts and the motivations of individual writers.[5]

Medieval Iberia's historical revision coincides with the need to find new meanings for medieval Iberian alterity. Modern concepts of otherness and cultural difference have been molded by such groundbreaking works as Edward Said's *Orientalism,* which showed that the Eastern other was a simultaneously exotic and dangerous European construct from the colonial era. European colonizers controlled Western perceptions of Islamic and Asian societies through ambivalent portrayals that revealed a coinciding attraction and repulsion of the other. Thus the modern other is a person whose subjugation always depends upon a contrast to a superior, dominant self. While scholars such as Homi K. Bhabha have demonstrated that colonial relations were more permeable than this paradigm allows, the archetypal model of the powerful white subject and the marginal dark other continues to inform in a profound way modern ideas of otherness.[6]

The modern paradigm of dominance and disempowerment contrasts with medieval Iberian concepts of otherness that were founded on ideals of negotiation, balance, and integration. Mark D. Meyerson has questioned the tacit application of "marginality" and "otherness" to medieval Iberia because he objects to the frequent assumption that Christians and Jews in al-Andalus and Jews and Muslims in Christian domains were excluded from spheres of power. Meyerson argues that people from so-called marginal groups often wielded political influence and frequently were not subordinate to numerically larger groups.[7] He also finds the modern concept of the other unconvincing because it does not recognize the other's potential force: "[T]he legal, literary, and polemical texts in which the 'other' was constructed often were produced because the 'other' had become too familiar and hence too dangerous, because the 'other' was not 'other' at all."[8] Meyerson urges scholars to focus more on specific relations of power and powerlessness in concrete social milieus instead of depicting medieval Iberian relations according to modern divisions between dominant groups and disempowered others.[9]

In accord with Meyerson's suggestion, this book diverges from the assumption that medieval society created others as we do today. It implicitly calls into question studies such as Joan Young Gregg's, which points to devils, women, and Jews as medieval society's main others.[10] Young Gregg portrays medieval marginalization and otherness as monolithic, while scholars such as Meyerson call for more nuanced approaches to the issue. In *Other Middle Ages,* Michael Goodich mentions the fluidity of the medieval margins and the frequent difficulty of categorizing people, although he discusses the marginal largely from the point of view of the church and the clergy. This is particularly evident when he emphasizes the Eucharist as the unifying symbol that rallied Christians and pitted them against nonbeliever "others."[11] Unfortunately, this generalization about the effects of the Eucharist illuminates little about how difference was conceived in a complex setting such as medieval Iberia.

The medieval other was neither transhistoric nor transgeographic but differed according to time period, geographic location, and an author's purpose. Similarly, alterity was not homogeneous in the Middle Ages, since medieval people produced difference between subjects and things for a variety of reasons, including denigration. What distinguishes medieval alterity from modern otherness is the predominance of the two tenets that had largely disappeared by the sixteenth century, that is, multifaceted subject formation and the embrace of contrasts and the negative. Although medieval people did not forge differences between subjects and things solely according to these two principles, they were embedded in medieval thought and practice in ways they were not in early modern society. For example, Catherine Brown and James F. Burke recently demonstrated the wide-ranging significance of contraries in medieval Iberian identity, rhetoric, law, and teaching. They show that rather than reject or marginalize variance, medieval writers and artists from numerous disciplines embraced it because it was crucial for the making of meaning.[12]

My book extends Brown's and Burke's discussions beyond Romance discourse to show the pivotal role of the equivocal in a variety of Arabic, Jewish, and Romance fields, including aesthetics, theology, and entertaining literature, and it theorizes about the importance of the adverse in the making of difference in everyday society. Until about the fifteenth century, coexisting contraries within a subject or on a manuscript folio often were culturally esteemed and constituted a significant feature of alterity. Contrasts not only had a symbolic, ideological, and cognitive value, but were central to making difference in the ordinary world. The merit of the equivocal and adverse was tangible in Iberia's fluid social composition, and the discourses that are analyzed in this book reinforced the cultural significance of contingency and permeability.

Complex historical shifts from approximately the late fourteenth century on changed the tenets of alterity, as early modern society created unprecedented ruptures between cultural groups and attributed to them varying degrees of esteem or antipathy. While divisions between subjects were evident in medieval Iberia as well, efforts to separate people did not predominate as they did under the early modern aegis of the nation-state. The Castilian polity of the Catholic Kings (1479–1516) relied on the collusion of a variety of participants from society's educated ranks who could disseminate the state's homogeneous values. As I will show in chapter 1, poets, physicians, theologians, and literary writers contributed to the establishment of the state by often rejecting variance instead of embracing it in their texts.

Although the early modern changes in alterity crystallized in the creation of the Castilian polity, they also corresponded to a more elusive shift in how early modern people often perceived the world around them. Michel Foucault suggests that where many medieval subjects saw mutual relations in diversity, early modern people witnessed division and duplicity. In his study of Miguel de Cervantes's *El ingenioso hidalgo don Quijote de la Mancha* (1605, 1615), Foucault shows that don Quijote exemplifies this change because he seeks in the ordinary world a direct parallel to the chivalry novels he so voraciously reads. Quijote is one of the last medieval readers and interpreters of the world: "His whole journey is a quest for similitudes: the slightest analogies are pressed into service as dormant signs that must be reawakened and made to speak once more."[13] Quijote sees women servants as nobles and windmills as giants, while other characters deride his attempts to create in everyday society similarities with the conditions and inhabitants of his books. Foucault's reading of the *Quijote* indicates that medieval people saw a likeness in all diverse things, while early modern readers and writers classified and divided them. He believes that the change in perception produced a gap in meaning and signification: "[B]ecause of an essential rupture in the Western world, what has become important [in the early modern period] is no longer resemblances but identities and differences."[14] A plethora of events in the fifteenth and sixteenth centuries, including technological advances with the invention of the printing press, religious turmoil among Catholics, Protestants, and Muslims, and intensified political struggles for control conspired to create Foucault's "essential rupture" and to replace the medieval tendency toward similitude with separation and classification.[15]

Early modern Iberia manifested the new focus on division in the changes to the predominant tenets of alterity; subjects were increasingly defined by essential qualities, and contrasts and the negative were rejected rather than embraced. Shifts in alterity coincided with the modern creation of the other as someone to restrict and disempower, whom early modern authorities identified in women, Muslims, Jews, converts, and, later, indigenous people of the Americas. Diverse others no longer composed a varied societal whole; instead, they threatened the integrity of the Castilian polity. In trying to establish a circumscribed social order, early modern Iberian authorities imposed more rigid measures of social control, and a variety of writers bolstered those efforts with their books. Together they contributed to Iberia's transformation from a web of multiple medieval kingdoms and communities into a more hierarchical territory where the Castilian nation-state tried to efface difference.

Chapter 1 offers a fuller explanation of the tenets of medieval alterity and how they changed with the forging of the Castilian nation-state. It also shows that the early modern poets, physicians, cartographers, and literary writers who transformed the principles of alterity in lyric, medical treatises, and discourses on the monster constituted pillars of the Castilian polity. They bolstered the nation's focus on division and expulsion in order to forge and maintain the new social order, and they contributed to the invention of the early modern other as someone who threatened the integrity of the polity. In a similar way that the news media create and recreate images of the other today, early modern writers who were linked to the goals of the nation-state disseminated its values in their writings.

CHAPTER ONE

Identity and the Limits of Iberian Alterity

The Andalusi-Jewish intellectual and statesman Samuel Ibn Nagrila Ha-Nagid was revered for his scholarly and political accomplishments. Born in Cordova in 993, he learned Arabic, Hebrew, and Aramaic and extensively studied the Bible, Talmud, and Qur'ān, as well as Muslim jurisprudence. He lived in Granada for many years and became vizier of its Zirid ruler, dying there in 1056. Ibn Nagrila had close political and cultural relations with Muslims, since he was profoundly integrated into a multifaceted Andalusi society that was not marked by severe ethnic, religious, and linguistic divisions. Like other Andalusi-Jews of his time, Ibn Nagrila composed sacred and profane *muwashshah* poems in Hebrew, even though they were originally invented by Andalusi-Arab performers in Arabic.[1] The quintessential courtier-rabbi, Ibn Nagrila embodied the intricate meshing of Jewish, Muslim, and Christian cultures in al-Andalus and the generally diverse Iberian social organization.[2] His multicultural life was especially consistent with the character of al-Andalus, where cultural entwining among Muslims, Jews, and Christians did not seem to threaten discrete modes of identification or to destabilize particular Jewish, Christian, and Muslim identities. Secular and religious forms of identity were not necessarily at odds.[3] Al-Andalus was blended to such an extent that Moses Ibn Ezra (1055–1135) repeatedly spoke of the Hebrew Bible as a kind of "Jewish Qur'ān."[4]

Medieval Iberian Christian realms outside al-Andalus were also polyvalent even as late as the fifteenth century, as evidenced by the Castilian king Enrique IV, who admired life in Granada and forged amicable diplomatic relations with his Muslim neighbors. He maintained many traditional, heterogeneous practices at his court, such as the employment of Jewish doctors, tax assessors, and a judge, as well as of a *morisco* guard composed of Christian converts from Islam.[5] Even the Catholic monarchs Isabel and Fernando probably wore Muslim dress to the ceremony at the Alhambra where they accepted the capitulation of the last peninsular Islamic kingdom, Granada, to the Castilian crown. María Rosa Menocal suggests that their attire most likely reflected the vestiges of Iberian cultural meshing.[6]

Medieval Iberia frequently did not conform to modern concepts of identity and the social order, which are largely based on categorical divisions and national boundaries. For example, David Nirenberg finds little evidence of racial categories before the late fourteenth century, and argues that converts only began to be stigmatized as "racially impure" in the fifteenth century.[7] The lack of racial classification suggests that medieval Iberian alterity often was constituted differently than it is nowadays.

Beginning in the sixteenth century, imperial and colonial discourses and practice divided people according to ethnic, class, religious, and gender difference and created categorical structures of value that persist today in the era of globalization.[8] Modern concepts of difference between subjects often serve to marginalize and devalue specific groups, such as the poor, people of color, or women, and to esteem others. These divisions became increasingly heightened with the early modern forging of the Castilian nation-state, when institutions such as the church effectively consolidated their authority and power. Counter-Reformation efforts after the decrees at the Council of Trent (1545–1563) further entrenched the church and state in their dominant positions as designers of the social order. Official efforts to classify people according to economic, religious, ethnic, and other social divisions marked a change from more porous medieval alterity and subjectivity, which relied on the merging rather than the expulsion of diverse qualities and groups.

The two tenets of alterity that are identified in this book were not universal principles because medieval Iberians had at their disposal a number of ways to create difference. For example, textual genres such as epic and travel narratives are notorious for denigrating the other through their portrayals of Muslims, enemies, and foreigners. But many other works evidence the more flexible tenets of medieval alterity, such as the four discourses analyzed in this book. At approximately the same time that fifteenth-century political power began to consolidate in the building of the Castilian nation-state, these discourses indicate shifts in the formulation of alterity.

Medieval Iberian social and political conditions greatly varied from those of early modern and contemporary Spain and thus accommodated less hierarchical ranks of difference and alterity. Without a modern-style nation-state, Iberia was a multicultural territory of Muslim, Jewish, and Christian communities that were ruled by increasingly organized Christian kingdoms in the north and shrinking Muslim domains in the south. Muslims called their region al-Andalus, which they governed in varying political forms from 711 until the dissolution of the kingdom of Granada in 1492. Neither Muslim nor Christian rule was homogeneous during that period. After the fall of the caliphate at Cordova in 1008, previously centralized Muslim power was divided and diluted among the party-kingdoms, or *taifas*, that ruled al-Andalus from 1008 until 1086. Later fundamentalist Almoravids and Almohads from North Africa gained control and enacted social and religious reforms that reflected a growing Muslim intolerance of diverse cultures. Rules, laws, and social systems changed throughout the history of al-Andalus, but Muslim dominance and cohesiveness began to erode with the fall of the central caliphate at Cordova and the creation of the *taifa* kingdoms.[9] The erosion of the caliphate's power also corresponded to broad political changes in the Islamic world.[10]

The Christian north was equally mutable, since kingdoms with stable frontiers did not exist until approximately the thirteenth century.[11] Different Christian realms vied for power, as demonstrated by the offensive undertaken by the king of Navarre, García de Nájera, into the Ebro valley in 1045, where he had to battle against other Christians for control of Calahorra. A more decisive moment in the consolidation of Christian forces occurred in the twelfth century when Castile and Leon resolved their differences and began a united offensive southward.[12] With the aid of clerical and military orders, namely, that of Calatrava, they increased their territory until only the Muslim emirate at Granada remained in 1232. Yet the division of Christian power continued into the thirteenth century, when the Christian crowns of Aragon and of Castile and Leon divided their energies and the territory they were to control. As the crown of Castile and Leon drove Islamic forces southward on the peninsula, the Aragonese military moved eastward into the Mediterranean and conquered the Balearic Islands (1229 and 1235), Sicily (1282), Athens (1313), Sardinia (1324), and the kingdom of Naples (1442). These Christian crowns united only with Fernando and Isabel's marriage in 1469, and it was not until the eighteenth century that regional legal codes were condensed into one for all of Spain.

Just as these events suggest a variety of political permutations from 711 through 1492, social relations among Christians, Jews, and Muslims also were malleable and diverse. From the initial embrace of the North African forces by indigenous Iberians in the eighth and ninth centuries, to the institutionalized Christian attempts to regulate the peninsula in the later fifteenth and sixteenth centuries, cultural and political associations were complex and varied.[13] Absolute conclusions and generalizations about medieval Iberia are difficult to derive because of the peninsula's fluid political boundaries and cultural heterogeneity. Negotiation and exchange between different communities were unceasing realities of medieval Iberian life. One renowned example is the translation projects in twelfth-century Monte Cassino and Iberia, which initiated the transmission of ancient Greek and Latin texts to Christian Europe through Arabic translations and commentaries. The distribution of ancient medical, scientific, and philosophical works to the West by philosophers and physicians such as Aristotle, Galen, and Hippocrates is due to their preservation in Arabic manuscripts and commentaries from al-Andalus and other Muslim regions. Christian Europe gained access to a wide variety of previously unavailable Greek and Arabic thought and writings by way of these Arabic manuscripts.[14]

During the twelfth and thirteenth centuries in Christian Iberia, religious and royal authorities, such as the twelfth-century Archbishop Raimundo and the thirteenth-century king Alfonso X, el Sabio (1252–1284), actively supported and continued cultural efforts to translate many Arabic texts into Latin, and later into Castilian. These well-known cultural collaborations between Jews, Muslims, and Christians were realized at the Escuela de Traductores de Toledo (Translators' School of Toledo).[15] Cultural contributions were particularly important during the reign of Alfonso X, when the translation of scientific and philosophical texts was emphasized from 1252 to 1277 and the concentration on religious works was minimized. It is particularly notable that during this period Christian compilers and translators collaborated with Ibero-Jewish translators, who were fluent in Arabic and whose translating efforts were greater than those of their Christian assistants.[16] Jewish translators collaborated on a number of Alfonso X's scientific projects, such as the redaction of astronomical tables.[17]

Iberian cohabitation is particularly evident in Muslim-dominated al-Andalus, where cultural organization often revealed the integration of difference. For instance, Islamic law institutionalized the right of Jews and Christians to worship and practice their faiths and accorded them legitimate status as individuals and as members of a community. Muslim Andalusi society granted Christians the presence of bishops and priests to carry out baptisms and other ceremonies that Christian law prescribed.[18] The legally binding pact of Muslim protection of Jewish and Christian rights was called the *dhimma,* and Christians and Jews were called *dhimmī,* the protected ones, or tributaries. Restrictions on Andalusi Jews stipulated by the *dhimma,* such as wearing clothing distinct from Muslim garments or praying softly, were not widely enforced until the fundamentalist Almoravid and Almohad period at the beginning of the twelfth century.[19] Relations between Muslims, Christians, and Jews were not always static but also dynamic, as evidenced by Arab onomastic systems and tribal affiliations that allowed outsiders and converts to adopt new identities.

Intermarriage between Christians and Jews was common and suggests at times the permeability of Andalusi identity.[20]

The doctrinal religious debates that frequently took place throughout the Middle Ages between Christian, Muslim, and Jewish theologians represent a cultural exchange that was expected and sanctioned. Although decrees of tolerance varied among polemicists, leaders of all faiths engaged critically with the doctrine of other religions, and some theologians such as Ramon Llull learned Hebrew and Arabic to understand more fully the different religious principles and thereby contest them. Like other medieval writers of the dialogue tradition, such as the twelfth-century Peter Abelard, Llull demonstrated the worth of interreligious toleration in his *Liber de gentili et tribus sapientibus* (c. 1275) because he thought that unfettered exchange would potentially lead to universal religious accord. Llull's high regard for open, rational debate showed a concern for education rather than conversion, and it contradicts for modern scholars the idea of medieval Christianity as a homogenous monolith.[21] Llull's engagement with Arabic further attests to the language's prestige as the idiom of "high culture," which was also adopted by such scholars as Ibn Nagrila and the Jewish philosopher Maimonides.[22]

Medieval Iberian heterogeneity and integration are further evidenced in the political realm of al-Andalus, where Jewish administrators often held important and high-ranking positions in the courts of Muslim governors. For instance, the Jewish rabbi and politician Samuel Ibn Nagrila and his son Joseph both served as viziers to the Berber dynasty of the Zirid family who ruled Granada in the eleventh century. Ibn Nagrila was trained in Arabic, Hebrew, and Aramaic, he was well versed in Latin and the vernacular of al-Andalus, called Andalusi Romance, and he possessed profound knowledge of Arabic literature.[23] His wide-ranging expertise was not unusual for educated people of his day. Jewish courtiers such as the Nagrilas often gained favor both in Muslim and Jewish circles, suggesting their potentially far-ranging influence. But scholars have been careful to point out the occasional precariousness of political arrangements, since the high positioning of Jews could generate antipathy within the Muslim community, and, as Olivia Remie Constable argues, Jews were further at risk "in the absence of a strong royal patron." The insecure Jewish status is evident in the slaughter of thousands of Jews in Granada by the Almohads after Joseph's fall in 1066.[24] Another Jewish citizen held a prominent position in Muslim-dominated al-Andalus; Abū Fadl Ibn Hasday (1046–1100) was trained in Arabic science and philosophy and became chief of Saragossa, where he converted to Islam. It is possible that his conversion was due to complaints about his high political position.[25] Christians were also prominent in Andalusi politics, as evidenced by the participation of the Mozarab

bishop of Elvira, Racemundo (known in Arabic as Rabi Ibn Zayd), in diplomatic jour-
neys to Constantinople in 949, and to the court of Otto I in 955.[26]

Cross-cultural exchange was not only internal within al-Andalus, but the Andalusi
region had constant external communication with other European and Mediterranean territories. Unlike traditional views of the Iberian Middle Ages that suggest a
great economic and cultural divide between Muslims, Christians, and Jews, historians have shown that transactions among them were regular and dynamic. Although
Europe joined the global and Mediterranean economies long after the Islamic world,
it benefited from extensive economic commerce with Andalusi and Mediterranean
traders.[27] Andalusi commerce and Muslim trade in general were not isolated but
ranged from interaction with Christian kingdoms in the north to exchange with
traders throughout the Levant. In fact, until around the first half of the thirteenth
century, al-Andalus provided much of Christian Europe with a large number of lux-
ury items, such as paper, textiles, precious metals, and Eastern spices.[28] Andalusi Jewish and Muslim traders also played mediating roles in Mediterranean commerce between the north and east.[29]

Cultural exchange was constantly woven into the social fabric of al-Andalus. In his
study of cultural topics, which included the Spanish language and the fourteenth-
century *Libro de buen amor* (*Book of Good Love*), Américo Castro demonstrated the cultural meshing that characterized Iberian culture and society.[30] Other cultural exchanges included the poetic and literary genres and themes that Muslim and Jewish
poets shared, such as the hybrid lyric of the *muwashshah* and *zajal*. The *muwashshah*
was written in classical Arabic or Hebrew, and its final stanza, the *jarcha,* usually was
created in the Romance vernacular called Andalusi Romance. The *zajal* had the same
basic form as the *muwashshah,* but was composed in vernacular Arabic. Jews and
Muslims alike composed them, and they developed many of the same themes in their
works, such as wine, gardens, and the ubiquitous topics of love and death. Menocal
shows that the *muwashshah* and *jarcha* are composites that parallel the character of
Andalusi society as part of the East *and* the West.[31]

Language in al-Andalus further evidences intricate cultural connections. Communities were not organized around static linguistic categories and boundaries, but
they largely shared complex communicative modes. Consuelo López-Morillas suggests that Andalusi language was not a source of absolute cultural division because
oral and written communication took place within a multifaceted linguistic network. For instance, Andalusi Jews did not speak their own Arabic dialect as did Jews
of other regions in later time periods. Rather, Andalusi Arabic was common to Jews
and Arabs alike.[32] Moreover, the Andalusi Romance dialect did not deviate in its lin-

guistic structure from other varieties of Iberian Romance. Instead, its only distinctive feature was its recording in Arabic script. As López-Morillas shows, on a hypothetical linguistic map of Iberia at around the year 1000, Romance did not differ significantly from region to region. Castilian was the only variety whose linguistic features were sharply distinguished from the Romance of other Iberian locales, and Castile's political sway eventually led to the linguistic dominance of its language.[33] Until the Christian conquest of Muslim lands in the eleventh to thirteenth centuries, Christians in al-Andalus (Mozarabs) made Arabic their primary written language, evidence of linguistic and cultural linking. For Mozarabs, Arabic served as the prestigious written code that Latin did in other Christian communities, to the extent that Latin's disuse may have converted twelfth- and thirteenth-century Toledo into a center of Latin instruction to Mozarabs.[34]

Outside al-Andalus, cultural negotiation and exchange marked northern Christian regions. Scribes and translators at Alfonso X's late thirteenth-century Castilian court realized many projects in the vernacular, such as the legal codes of the *Siete Partidas* and the poetry of the *cantigas* (songs). Christian Iberia's relative cultural tolerance also extended to some of Alfonso X's policies on religion within his kingdom. For instance, his legal writings in the *Siete Partidas* prohibited the forcible conversion of Muslims and Jews to Christianity, indicating a partial acceptance of different religions in his Castilian domains. Although Muslims were rendered pejoratively in the legal codes (7.25), in "De los judíos" ("On Jews"), Jews were allowed more freedom than Muslims, namely in the licit existence of synagogues and the recognition of the Jewish Sabbath.[35] Muslim mosques in Alfonso's kingdoms belonged to the Christian king.

Although this example indicates that cultural acceptance was not absolute in medieval Iberia, other documentation demonstrates intensive cultural accord. Even in the later medieval period from 1350 to 1460, the historian Angus Mackay argues, at times the Castilian-Granadan frontier virtually ceased to exist.[36] Several cases from fifteenth-century Jaén demonstrate "contact" and "neighborliness" between Christians and Muslims when dealing with practical problems along the shared border.[37] Cultural assimilation increasingly eroded with the Christian expansion during the twelfth through fourteenth centuries, yet civil relations such as these suggest that Iberians did not always view the other as someone to deride and marginalize. While differences between subjects and things doubtlessly existed in medieval Iberia, they were not entirely intended to aggrandize certain groups and denigrate others. Medieval Iberia's permeable social organization allowed for principles of alterity that differed from dominant early modern tenets.

The Tenets of Medieval Alterity

Shifting political and social conditions in medieval Iberia were consonant with multifaceted subject formation and the embrace of contrasts and the negative. Although these tenets were not alone in determining medieval alterity, they pervaded medieval Iberian society. Even genres such as epic and travel narratives, which clearly dignified some individuals and deprecated others, frequently described different peoples in an ambivalent way. For instance, the anonymous epic *Poema de Mio Cid* (1207) depicts Muslims in a dual light as worthy of being conquered in Valencia but also as engaging in amicable relations with the Cid on other occasions. The Muslim's ambivalent, intricate portrayal may be explained by the fact that many medieval authors were tolerant of what they viewed as the virtuous pagan, even though their estimation sharply clashed with papal authorities.[38] But this explanation is not entirely accurate for medieval Iberia because al-Andalus became a target of papal crusades only in the late twelfth and early thirteenth centuries (1198–1216) under the authority of Pope Innocent III.[39] It is evident from this relatively late date and from the legitimate existence of the Andalusi political state until 1492 that Europe's general crusading efforts in the Middle Ages did not effect a complete Christian rejection of Muslims in multicultural medieval Iberia. The ambivalent features of Christian-Muslim relations in the *Poema de Mio Cid* more likely are due to commonly meshed Iberian cultural relations. Gregory S. Hutcheson concurs in his study of sexuality in narratives of *reconquista*, since he believes that heroic and epic texts demonstrated that the Muslim was integrated in a complex way into "the fabric of Iberia's history and identity."[40] The *Poema de Mio Cid* further evidences this blending in the derivation of the Cid's name from al-Sayyid, which is Arabic for "the lord." Moreover, the historical figure on whose life the poem is based, Ruy Díaz de Vivar, was not solely devoted to Christian kings for religious reasons, but fought in the service of both Christian and Muslim rulers.[41] Thus medieval alterity could be constituted in different ways and for a variety of reasons that reveal an array of cultural values about variation, from its rejection to its embrace.

Yet medieval artists and writers often illustrated the two main tenets of alterity in a variety of cultural production that included philosophical writing, entertaining literature, and iconography. They frequently demonstrated multifaceted subject formation through bodily images that depicted people not as essentially whole in their makeup, but as composed of shifting desires and contrasting qualities. Two medieval models of subjectivity demonstrate that individual identity was not based on static characteristics, but on elastic, mutable qualities. James F. Burke describes the first model, which posits the subject as an empty container whose basis consists of a longing for or a movement toward a desired object. According to this paradigm, subjectivity was constituted by the choices that one made between oscillating positive and negative objects of desire; one's identity changed according to varying choices and favored objects. In order to make apparent the conditions of the selection, the negative and positive elements (the profane and the sacred) were represented in textual discourse, along with a necessary link that demonstrated the interrelation between the two extremes.[42]

Medieval writers and artists sometimes illustrated this model through spatial imagery, particularly with images of inside/outside.[43] The self could be fashioned as an inner container to be permeated and affected by outer negative and positive qualities. Through teaching, medieval subjects learned to distinguish favorable elements from adverse ones. The spatial dimension of this inner/outer concept is apparent in a number of ways in the medieval period, from sacred and profane iconography in Romanesque cloisters to the texts and margins of medieval manuscripts. The mechanics of medieval manuscript culture indicate an interdependent relation between the central text and marginal notes and drawings rather than the exile of the marginal or profane.[44]

Evelyn Birge Vitz offers a second model of medieval identity construction in suggesting that medieval writers shaped individuals as fundamentally similar, yet different in their possession of the quantity of a certain quality. The fundamental medieval concern was the placement of subjects on a vertical axis that set individual worth as higher than that of others, but not apart from them, as on a horizontal line. Vitz indicates that medieval protagonists or heroes in narrative were defined by "the *quantity* of their 'qualities,' not by the *quality* of the 'qualities'—not by the particular form that these qualities take."[45] Thus worthy subjects remained above unworthy ones, but all human beings approximated one another on the same vertical axis, a placement that connoted their simultaneous likeness and difference.

In addition to these models, medieval subject formation was highly influenced by the medieval confidence in *assimilatio,* a notion that implied "ontological continuity" between language, subjects, and events. *Assimilatio* highlighted the likeness between things rather than their separation or the replacement of one with another. Burke explains this concept of similarity and correspondence as an active process whereby one thing "*becomes* or moves toward becoming" another. *Assimilatio* holds that "all facets of creation are aligned in a vast array of parallel systems that are hierarchically structured, and very real correspondences exist among the various facets of these systems."[46] *Assimilatio* highlights the placement of a subject or event within a particular system and in connection with other hierarchical systems, instead of focusing on independent identification and definition.[47] But the hierarchies do not demonstrate essential gaps between subjects, languages, and events. Rather, they indicate the fluid positions within systems, and they emphasize the process of becoming instead of the end result of the process.[48] In rhetorical terms, early medieval *assimilatio* underscores not the likeness of simile, but the correspondence and becoming of metaphor.[49]

Assimilatio and the two models of identity offer a framework for flexible, dynamic subject construction in the medieval period. The esteem for *assimilatio* allowed medieval writers to consider human fault and frailty as necessary parts of the regular order of the world.[50] Burke has argued that the mutable, contingent forging of the subject is one of the main reasons for the medieval juxtaposition of the sacred and profane in literature, art, and iconography, since both realms of value constituted individual identity.[51] These concepts are nowhere more apparent than in Juan Ruiz's fourteenth- and fifteenth-century *Libro de buen amor* (*Lba*), which recounts the amorous adventures of a lascivious archpriest. John Dagenais shows that the *Lba*'s implied ethical reader may choose between *buen amor* (good love) and *amor loco* (crazy love) according to the reader's circumstances and desire. The *Lba* does not divide carnal love from the sacred in an absolute hierarchy of value, but suggests that each has sanctioned functions depending on the reader's wishes. The work sometimes juxtaposes holy and profane love, but it also obscures them, leaving readers and listeners uncertain about whether love for women or for God constitutes good love. The *Lba* leaves this question to the reader and thus exemplifies the practice of ethical decision making that made up medieval reading and identity.[52]

Further kinds of evidence from medieval Iberia bolster the values embedded in these models and concepts about the resilience of medieval identity. For instance, sociological data from al-Andalus about onomastic systems and kinship affiliations show that individual Andalusi identity was not based exclusively on ethnic origin and religious association, but on permeable, interpersonal connections. One way that Arabs forged their identities was through an onomastic system that conserved genealogical traits of kinship. This system was transferred to al-Andalus and held that the surname (*nisba*) represented a crucial link because it could indicate the place of origin of one's family or the ethnic origin of one's tribe.[53]

For Andalusi converts to Islam, Arab surnames were signs of prestige, and converts adopted new last names according to the tribal groups that admitted them:

Como en el resto del mundo islámico medieval, la conversión a la nueva religión produjo, en al-Ándalus, la integración en las estructuras familiares y tribales de los árabes, que establecían lazos de "clientela" con los nuevos musulmanes. Éstos adoptaban el apellido del grupo tribal que los aceptaba en su seno y lo transmitían a sus descendientes.[54]

[As in the rest of the medieval Islamic world, conversion to the new religion produced in al-Andalus integration into the familial and tribal structures of the Arabs, which established links of "protection" for the new Muslims. These new Muslims adopted the surname of the tribal group that accepted them into their fold, and they transmitted it to their descendants.]

Thus the identity of converts was not based on birth origins, but on an affiliation with a particular tribe through the *nisba*. Manuela Marín demonstrates that the pacts of protection with certain tribes regularly were either lost over time or individuals deliberately omitted them so they would appear to possess a last name of authentic Arab origin.[55]

Another indication of the mutability of identification lies in the fact that, unlike Christian and Jewish cultures, Muslim society permitted the integration of non-Muslims through marriage. This sometimes contributed to the conversion of Christian women to Islam, as in the case of Sara, granddaughter of the Visigothic king Witiza, who married members of the Arab aristocracy on two different occasions.[56] Furthermore, social rank in al-Andalus was not always a fixed category, as evidenced by examples of slaves who rose to positions of influence and power through personal links of loyalty and patronage with Arab emirs and caliphs.[57] For instance, with the collapse of the caliphate in Cordova in 1008, several of the resulting *taifa* kingdoms, such as Denia and Badajoz, were governed by former "slaves," that is, Slavs and Berbers who had participated in the administration and army of the emirs at Cordova.[58] While their growing influence likely contributed to civil unrest prior to the caliphate's dissolution, their political sway also attests to their prominent social position.[59]

The elevation of these Andalusi "slaves" contests the assumption that medieval socioeconomic class determined identity in a rigid way. In order to understand how Andalusis may have viewed the subject, it is important to note that medieval Mediterranean slavery greatly differed from the exploitation and ownership that define modern servitude. This is evidenced by a case recounted in the Cairo *Genizah* (a collection of medieval writings by Jews found in Old Cairo) about the Indian "slave" Bomma, who traveled independently and carried out transactions throughout the Mediterranean on behalf of the twelfth-century Jewish Tunisian merchant Abraham Ben Yiju. Bomma and Ben Yiju were business partners and did not behave at all like masters and slaves in stereotypical modern portrayals.[60] This example and the privileges of

Andalusi "slaves" show that Mediterranean slavery was not a relation of bondage and abusive ownership, but a system of personal patronage that allowed individuals to escape social conditions acquired at birth. It emphasized the rights and obligations between people over "the establishment of abstract institutional frameworks" ("el establecimiento de marcos institucionales abstractos").[61] Thus the Andalusi citations reinforce the tenet of multifaceted subject formation because they demonstrate that Iberians did not always envision identity as fixed by absolute qualities and conditions, but as constituted by changeable associations.

These principles of flexible Iberian subjectivity are related to alterity's second tenet, the embrace of contrasts and the negative. The idea of "contrast" does not necessarily mean a binary comparison, but may comprise multiple, diverse elements. Furthermore, the term "negative" does not merely refer to pejorative features, such as bad or ugly, but has a philosophical and theological medieval meaning that frequently signifies deformation, absence, emptiness, silence, negation, or obscurity. Neither term is confined to esoteric realms of rhetoric or philosophy because they have palpable manifestations in medieval written and visual culture as part of the *via negativa* or the negative way, a sanctioned mode of representation and of deriving knowledge and meaning in the Middle Ages.[62]

As the discussion on Iberian subjectivity demonstrates, the *via negativa* played a crucial part in identity, since negative or profane elements were required for the malleable forging of the subject. Contrasts and the negative had legitimate, auspicious medieval value in models of subjectivity, as well as in a variety of discourses and visual imagery that ascribed them favorable worth rather than essential, disparaging value. Medieval Christian scholars and artists elaborated on ideas about negation that initially derived from the creation stories of Genesis. The tale that most readily showed the importance of the negative was Eve's conception as fulfillment of a lack. Her appearance illustrates the fundamental medieval belief that creation and human regeneration began in negation, which initiated and preceded presence and the affirmative:

> What prompts her creation is, in the final instance, the preceding perception of a need, a lack, an absence. This act of creation differs from the others by including negation and absence, by not being purely affirmative. Here the perception of absence clearly precedes presence and initiates the latter. Here God shows an awareness of the negative, associating it forever with solitude, absence, and need. This is more clearly a paradigm of human creation, where presence presupposes absence, and where the perception of absence insti-

tutes the creative act. For man, the primal lack is the absent other subject. Man stands in an emptiness which provokes the creation of Eve.[63]

Unlike modern, psychological interpretations of Eve's cultural meaning, Maire Jaanus Kurrik does not imagine her as lack, but as the affirmative product of creation provoked by Adam's deficiency, which is his negative emptiness and loneliness.

Negation and absence generated Eve's presence, a principle of creation that many medieval scholars and artists relied upon to produce their own work. They embraced the *via negativa* as a legitimate path toward affirmative fulfillment. For example, medieval topical theorists depended on the *via negativa* in their belief that the beginning locus of communication was an empty place. They thought that in order to make meaning coherent with language, a topical "place" had to be vacant.[64] This idea reappeared in varying forms through the early modern period, as evidenced by Sebastián de Covarrubias Horozco's etymology in 1611 for the Spanish words *loco* (crazy) and *lugar* (place) from the same Latin root, *locus, loci*.[65] For Covarrubias, one literally had to fill an empty head or place in order to "have sense."

The vacant place also is crucial to artistic creation in the Arabic tradition, as demonstrated by the importance of the negative in the classic *qaṣīda*, or ode, which often begins with an image of absence and loss upon finding the traces of an abandoned campsite.[66] This negative image played an important role in Andalusi-Arabic poetry as well, as evidenced by Ibn Shuhayd's (d. 1035) poem, which decried the ravaging of Cordova and the caliphate during the uprisings in the early eleventh century: "There is no one in the abandoned encampment to inform us of the beloved ones, so from whom will we seek information about their condition?"[67] From this vacant terrain, the poet proceeds to compose his lament about the loss of place and culture. In filling the absence with images of Cordova's mosque, the palace at Madīnat az-Zāhira, and the flourishing Umayyad caliphate, the poet recalls and transforms the past and gives it new shape in the present. Ibn Shuhayd posits the obscure, which is represented by the trace of the abandoned encampment, as that which generates a twofold creation, a lyric poem and a transformed image of the past in the present.

The *via negativa* was invoked in many kinds of medieval discourses, although in none so evident as the Christian philosophy and theology that associated the divine with undefined shapes, since God initially resided in absence, before the creation of forms. The fifth-century philosopher Pseudo-Dionysius the Areopogite and his medieval commentators believed that the most deformed, negative shapes paradoxically best revealed the transcendent, since higher forms of understanding could be reached only through an embrace of both the misshapen and the symmetrical.[68]

Between the twelfth and fourteenth centuries, writers such as Thomas Gallus and Alan of Lille lauded the role of the deformed, claiming that the most horrible images truly and ironically revealed the divine through their negation of its beauty.[69] Monsters best represented the abject and deformed for much of the medieval period, which is demonstrated by their ubiquitous presence on Romanesque church capitals, in Romanesque cloisters, and in the marginal drawings of medieval manuscripts. They also adorned the borders of medieval maps, as shown by the sciapodes with large feet that they lifted above their heads as umbrellas for shade. Unlike the traditional belief in their marginalized, exiled status, monsters on the borders of medieval maps were not necessarily disempowered. Rather, they were most intimately connected to the divine on the outer limits of the universe, since God resided in negation, outside the world of forms.[70]

The auspicious role of the monstrous and deformed confounds the marginal and disposable value that scholars and students of the medieval period usually give them. In fact, monsters on the liminal boundaries of Romanesque architecture and manuscripts serve a crucial purpose in delimiting the space of the sacred and profane. However, scholars such as Michael Camille suggest that they are not meant to create hierarchies of worth between sacred and secular realms. Instead, monsters show that the medieval representation of the profane is crucial for the instantiation of each realm: "The centre is . . . dependent upon the margins for its continued existence."[71] Both the positive and the negative had favorable, contrastive value in the medieval period, which Juan Ruiz also demonstrates in the *Libro de buen amor*, since one had to know profane love in order to know sacred love.

The negative was paradoxical, since it was simultaneously base and auspicious in its abjection. Monsters best demonstrated this paradox because they were at once perceptible and unreal, and present and absent just like the divine. They most resembled and revealed the transcendent because both were based in paradox, and medieval supporters of the negative way believed that the divine could be reached only by obscure or paradoxical means. Thus, monsters were thought to reside closest to God in the marginal space outside the realm of forms because they best exhibited paradox and deformity. Medieval artists often expressed these precepts in allegory, a figurative mechanism that complicated rather than simplified meaning because it simultaneously revealed and concealed. This is evident in medieval riddles and fables, where allegory offers both a surface plane of meaning and a second, extended level of signification that is created through the like relation of analogy. Allegory is founded on the paradoxical, meshed relation of obscurity and darkness on the one hand, and the affirmative connection of analogy on the other.[72]

Medieval writers and artists employed allegory and negative principles not only to reach the transcendent, but also to demonstrate the complexity of being and thought. For example, writers in the Arabic tradition believed that allegorical representation conveyed information about their intricate subjectivity and identity, and they often used allegorical dreams and visions to legitimize and affirm social and financial status. Samaw'al al-Maghrībī (d. 1174) considered dreams the motivating force behind his conversion from Judaism to Islam, since through their obscured, blurred vision he saw the truth about the veracity of Islam.[73] This clouded, negative path to knowledge and being permeated medieval discourse.

Augustine was one of the earliest Christian writers to incorporate and endorse the negative in his assertion that all mortal and rational beings, no matter how deviant from the human model, comprised part of God's divine plan.[74] In the *City of God*, he speculated about how monstrous races fit into God's order as he described people with only one eye in the middle of their foreheads, the dog-headed cynocephali, and bigendered groups who alternated in their sexual practice between "begetting and conceiving."[75] He explained the logic of God's plan in the following way:

> God is the creator of all, and he himself knows where and when any creature should be created or should have been created. He has the wisdom to weave the beauty of the whole design out of the constituent parts, in their likeness and diversity. The observer who cannot view the whole is offended by what seems the deformity of a part, since he does not know how it fits in, or how it is related to the rest.[76]

According to Augustine, the whole was always composed of diverse parts, and even the enigmatic, but mortal and rational, fragments adhered to the divine plan in their deviance from the human norm. He suggests that the negative was required to achieve coherence.

This effort to account for divergence in a calibrated rendering of the world, as opposed to the attempt to banish it, is apparent throughout medieval discourse and representation. The integration of the negative in schemes of thought and artistic practice indicates the high medieval regard for the symmetry of contrasting qualities and things. The equilibrium of contrasts was a fundamental aesthetic ideal, as Umberto Eco and Doris Behrens-Abouseif indicate in their studies of the medieval concept of beauty. They show that Arab and Christian artists and writers aimed for the balance of dissimilar qualities, which largely informed medieval aesthetics and concepts of beauty.[77] Catherine Brown further demonstrates that contrasts and the negative were crucial to the pedagogical objectives of medieval logicians and rhetoricians. Medieval scholars such as the twelfth-century Parisian theologian Peter Abelard embraced contrast and contradiction. Abelard held to the complex formula of "yes and no" (*sic et non*), in which truth was not composed of the affirmative or the negative alone, but of both at the same time.[78] For Abelard, truth was arrived at provisionally, with the knowledge that it would be "further deepened and transformed by additional debate and inquiry," and by continued questioning and dissent.[79] David Williams reinforces the interdependent relation of the positive and negative when he asserts that the *via negativa* was not opposed to the *via affirmativa* in the Middle Ages. Rather, the two modes offered "complementary understandings of the same reality."[80] The positive and negative were not necessarily separate and divided, but they coexisted equally in the same domain.

Medieval artists and scholars often emphasized the correspondence of different things, but contrasting positive and negative qualities were not always clearly delimited. The lack of distinction between them complicates medieval concepts of alterity and shows that making difference was complex and varied. Juan Ruiz illustrates this in the *Lba* with the frequently indistinguishable and mutable realms of carnal and sacred love, and thus verifies the confounding and intricate connection between negative and affirmative modes. Mystical writing further evidences the complex relation of divergent elements, such as the works of Ibn ʿArabī and Ramon Llull, which suggest a constant yearning for and movement toward another, an object of desire that defies stable categorization and is at once erotic and divine. Whereas mystical thought became increasingly marginalized through the sixteenth century, its medieval Iberian legitimacy is reinforced by communities of Jewish scholars of the Kabbala in Gerona and other Iberian regions, and by mystical strains of theology in Christian and Islamic thought. Mystical thought was highly esteemed in al-Andalus, particularly prior to the fundamentalist Almoravid consolidation of power in 1090.[81]

Ramon Llull demonstrates the intricacies of meaning and identity in mystical discourse when he describes the ambiguous relation between the desiring self and the other in the *Llibre d'amic et amat* (*The Book of the Lover and the Beloved*):

Ajustaren-se molts amadors a amar un Amat qui els abundava tots d'amors; e casú havia per cabal son Amat e sos pensaments agradables, per los quals sentien plaents tribulacions.

[Many lovers come together to love One alone, their Beloved, who made them all abound in love. And each one had the Beloved as his precious possession, and his thoughts of him were very pleasant, making him suffer a pain which brought delight.][82]

Mystical writing corroborates the integrative relation of contrasts, while further complicating the simplistic distinction between unlike things. Llull's passage obscures the limits of the positive and negative, since suffering and delight both originate in the same desired source. The negative suffering is auspicious because it engenders its affirmative contrast, delight. Llull complicates the easy differentiation between the negative and positive and destabilizes the worth of suffering and pleasure.

This elaborate relation is crucial to medieval Iberian alterity and is further evidenced in the work of the Murcian and Sevillan Ibn ʿArabī (1165–1240 C.E. / A.H. 560–638), who rejected the absolute separation of opposites, such as subject and object or self and other. Menocal significantly dubs him "perhaps the most influential Spanish Muslim."[83] Like much Sufi writing, his poetry obscures and melds contrasts, and it suggests a reconciliation or correspondence between erotic and spiritual love.[84] Michael A. Sells likens Ibn ʿArabī's poetry to a kaleidoscope in which each lyric overture turns toward or away from the prior and subsequent descriptions or concepts: "As in a turning kaleidoscope, the configuration changes before we can adequately take it in."[85] In refusing to limit the desiring self and its other, or to distinguish profane from sacred love, mystical writers such as Ibn ʿArabī and Llull present identity as constantly mutable.[86]

Scholars of medieval Iberia struggle to categorize Ibn ʿArabī and Llull as either wholly Muslim or Christian, and in Llull's case, they often fail to note Sufism as an influence in his writings.[87] Just as modern readers find the medieval balance of contrasts difficult to grasp,[88] so are critics often challenged by the intricate variety of Llull's and Ibn ʿArabī's thought. Scholars have recast their multifaceted lives and works to adhere to more monolithic and coherent religious, historical, literary, and ideological notions. Despite scholars' manipulation, many aspects of Llull's and Ibn ʿArabī's works, such as their articulation of the relation between subject and object, are not anomalous or idiosyncratic in medieval Iberia. Instead, their writings attest to the diverse medieval role of the negative, which was not solely contrastive or complementary, but also frequently indistinguishable from the affirmative, and thus convergent.

Although Llull's and Ibn ʿArabī's writings demonstrate the significance of mutable qualities, the cultural value of this medieval meshing was in decline. Menocal points to its deterioration by noting that Llull was stoned to death in Tunis in 1316 for espousing an ideology and a way to knowledge "that no one could understand anymore," that of conversion and the union and reunion of contrary characteristics.[89] The waning of these complex relations is borne out in the church's antagonistic response to his writings. Likewise the many years that Ibn ʿArabī spent in exile away from al-Andalus in the latter part of his life, dying in Damascus in 1240, suggest that his ideology and writings challenged the contemporary Almohad and Almoravid orthodoxy.

However, at the same time that the paradoxical blending of contrasts was in decline, Juan Ruiz's fourteenth- and fifteenth-century *Lba* resembles Ibn ʿArabī's and Ramon Llull's mystical efforts at self-fashioning. Like them, Ruiz highlights the lack of distinction between sacred and profane love, since the *Lba*'s narrator suggests that *buen amor* could be both carnal and divine.[90] The archpriest even refers to his unstable book as good love itself in strophe 933, a compliment that he ironically attributes not to God, but to the *vieja* (old woman), probably his go-between, Trotaconventos. Ruiz's work resembles the writings of Llull and Ibn ʿArabī in the interweaving of diverse elements, and in the formation of identity as a perpetual process of desire and becoming, rather than as an innate quality or state.

During the same period that the *Lba* was circulated and read, the principles that reinforced it began to give way to more rigid notions of subject formation and to the rejection of the negative. By the fourteenth century, affirmative modes of deduction and speculation often avoided the negative way instead of incorporating it into calibrated schemes, or allowing its mutability and convergence.[91] Following the lead of Thomas Aquinas and the rise of Aristotelian logic, late medieval scholars increasingly relied on the separation of the negative and affirmative, as well as on the empirical, positive apprehension of being and thought. The late medieval, early modern focus on affirmative modes of reasoning and deduction indicates a shift in beliefs about signification and the making of meaning, from the medieval confidence in *assimilatio*, the absolute unity of diverse, fragmentary parts, to the early modern rupture in this belief. Medieval cognition was viewed holistically as the "aggregate" of "fragmentary" instants of understanding,[92] although more selective models of discernment that emphasized the affirmative apprehension of knowledge and being exceeded this principle in later periods.

The move toward the affirmative is further evident in artistic creation as analogy surpassed medieval allegory to become the dominant mode of representation in the early modern period. Whereas medieval allegory went hand in hand with the *via negativa* because it underlined the simultaneity of the positive and negative, early modern analogy established "the adequacy of affirmation" in the understanding of the real. Medieval allegory demonstrated that the affirmative was intertwined with the negative, a principle that changed with the early modern emphasis on the separation of unlike things. Early modern Iberian discourse largely centered on the positive likeness of analogy, rather than on the complex relations of allegory: being was rendered solely "present and intelligible," and not simultaneously obscure and distant.[93] Early modern deduction and thought generally stressed the affirmative intelligibility of knowledge and being, leading to the eighteenth-century creation of discrete particulars, which Mary Poovey calls the rise of "the modern fact."[94]

The value of contrasts and the negative eroded throughout the later Middle Ages, as did the complementary worth of the *via negativa* and the *via affirmativa* and the mutability of contrasting qualities. These shifts had repercussions in artistic modes of representation from medieval allegory to early modern analogy, but they also coincided with momentous historical events. The loss in value of contrasts and the negative, the expulsion and conversion of Muslims and Jews, and the forging of the early modern nation-state demonstrated profound changes in cultural values, which necessitated static, categorical hierarchies of value between subjects and things.

Early Modern Alterity and the Castilian Nation-State

The medieval embrace of variation and the negative was incompatible with the categorical ideals of the Castilian nation-state, whose proponents created gaps between denigrated groups of others and supposedly faultless, dignified subjects, such as untainted Old Christians. Many late medieval and early modern discourses demonstrate this divide, including didactic sermons that condemned women and Jews, and conduct manuals that delimited social roles for women and men. Most writers no longer showed the kaleidoscopic oscillation of difference as in the poetry of Ibn ʿArabī, or the complementary worth of the positive and negative. Instead, they increasingly separated negative and affirmative behaviors, subjects, and realms of value.

Textual production began to center on the gaps in variation as the negative and diverse came to be seen as isolated from the positive, and not dependent on it. The negative no longer was considered paradoxically favorable in its contrast to the affirmative, but was a threat to be extinguished. Division became a mechanism to create deprecatory knowledge about the everyday world, and principles of separation, absolute classification, and homogeneity surpassed the former tenets of medieval alterity. These shifts in the worth of difference were perceptible not only in textual discourses, but also in political and governmental efforts to determine a more stratified social order. Worsening relations between Christians and Jews resulted in heightened violence against Jewish communities, starting in the late fourteenth century, and hierarchies among the educated and the working classes became increasingly pronounced through professionalizing efforts in the fifteenth and sixteenth centuries.[95]

Many of these sociopolitical conditions and events were not unprecedented but represented the exacerbation of medieval social relations. It would be erroneous to argue that medieval Iberia was transformed in a short time from a placid, idyllic realm of absolute tolerance to a region suddenly beset by dangerous confrontation and hatred. Change did not take place in this manner, which is evidenced by the vicissitudes that occurred in ritualized violence against Iberian Jews. David Nirenberg shows that in the medieval period the contained, ritualized stoning of Jews by children during Holy Week had a stabilizing social effect that allowed for the existence of Jews in Christian culture.[96] However, mass violence against Muslims and Jews in the fourteenth century suggests an alteration of the previously conventional disturbances. The rise in violence is complex because it shows the simultaneous continuity and discontinuity of two different modes of discord, one that had a pacifying effect and another that resulted in increased harm.[97] Nirenberg contends that more severe violence against Jews in the fourteenth century both follows and diverges from previously ritualized medieval disorder, which makes the idea of progressive injury against them difficult to sustain. Because ritual violence was enmeshed in the fabric of medieval Iberian society, Nirenberg thinks it misleading to describe the fourteenth-century shifts as incremental, from the supposedly placid, harmonious Iberian territory of *convivencia* to one of pure aggression and injurious dominance.[98] Instead, the transition was more complex and is difficult to characterize in definitive terms. This example shows that derogatory attitudes toward late medieval, early modern others were not wholly novel, since Jews constituted at times a target of medieval violence. However, disparaging sentiment became more heightened and widespread in the fifteenth century.

The other always inhabited medieval Iberia because people clearly viewed one another as different. Yet the other as a person pejoratively different from more esteemed individuals, as we understand it today, was an early modern creation that accompanied the replacement of the medieval tenets of alterity with homogeneous subject formation and rigid classification. These new principles coincided with the ideals of the Catholic Kings and were bolstered by fifteenth- and sixteenth-century literatures and institutions that collaborated in the effort to unify the peninsula politically and culturally. This imagined community was engendered through material and ideological means that partially focused on static concepts of identity and difference. As evidenced by the statutes of purity of blood (*limpieza de sangre*) and the establishment of the Inquisition in Castile in 1478 by the Catholic Kings, Fernando and Isabel, individual identity increasingly was defined by absolute categories of religion and ethnic origin.

These homogenizing efforts never were complete in the early modern period, since the creation of the nation-state did not eradicate diversity from its realms. In fact, modern circumstances today, such as the Basque separatist movement, the regional polemics in Catalonia and Valencia, and Ceuta and Melilla's Spanish national status continue to demonstrate that throughout its history Spain's imagined community has enveloped cultural, regional, administrative, and linguistic difference. However, the everyday reality of cultural heterogeneity within the ideal of the homogeneous nation-state does not undermine the cultural and historical force and significance of a unified polity. The theoretical homogeneity of the nation-state is crucial to its very existence, even when uniformity is not borne out in the everyday world. Polities may deal in varying ways with complex heterogeneity so as not to threaten the ideal of the unwavering nation. Authorities may not absolutely reject oppressed identities and minority groups within the polity because such groups can serve the integrity of the nation-state, national identity, and nationalism. For instance, marginalized groups are at times assimilated into the collective national memory in order to connect the present with a dignified past.[99] This relation might be based on the past struggles of certain peoples, which come to characterize in the present the resilience of dominant groups and the nation. Xavier Rubert de Ventos further demonstrates that minority identities often become compatible with national integrity because they fulfill roles and necessities that are publicly ignored:

En buena medida, la "función" de las minorías en una sociedad es precisamente ésta: salvar los principios. Las minorías se encargan de satisfacer deseos o necesidades que la sociedad establecida no quiere hacer explícitas ni reconocer como tales.[100]

[In good measure, the "function" of minorities in a society is precisely this: to save principles. Minorities are charged with satisfying desires or necessities that the established society does not want to make explicit or recognize as such.]

Unsavory others are at times compatible with the nation-state because in their impropriety they reveal the principles on which the polity is forged.[101] This may be one reason why Spanish society today deals ambivalently with immigrant groups, who often are exalted in news media for their high birth rates in the face of declining childbirth among Spaniards.[102] This favorable portrayal exists alongside other powerful cultural anxieties about immigrants in Spain, such as Moroccans and Latin Americans, who frequently are perceived as poor and uneducated. Their positive reproductive role suggests that immigrants supply Spain with future workers and citizens, pillars of the nation-state that native Spaniards are unwilling to provide. The media's esteem of immigrants' supposed fecundity usually does not include an examination of any verifiable, long-term danger of declining birth rates in Spain. Instead it reveals a series of cultural insecurities about the potential weakening of nuclear families, heterosexual relations, and citizens' loyalty to the nation, all of which constitute foundations of the modern Spanish polity. Thus cultural diversity does not invalidate the power and significance of the simultaneously real and imagined polity, since variation may be absorbed into cultural memory and paradigms of governance.

Although the early modern conditions of nation building by the Catholic Kings and successive monarchs were different from today's modern practices of "nation maintenance," both time periods show that institutions use a variety of strategies to deal with diversity and the other. As much as early modern authorities tried to expel unwanted groups from their midst, others were significant to the Castilian polity, which relied on them in order to identify dignified subjects, such as Old Christians and chaste women and men. Yet, authorities did not acknowledge the implicit contrastive value of the early modern other, nor did they interweave cultural diversity with the social fabric. Instead, they declared that the diverse had to conform to cultural and religious norms or be expelled. The sixteenth-century assimilation of converts was not an effort to integrate diversity in society, but to eradicate it. Muslims were forced to convert from 1500 to 1525, but never successfully integrated into Christian society as *moriscos*. When these Muslim converts failed to follow laws entreating them to speak Castilian and forego traditional Muslim dress, acculturation efforts reached a disastrous peak with their final expulsion in 1609.[103] The identification of the other, the conversion of Jews and Muslims, and territorial sovereignty distinguish the Castilian nation-state from less vindictive medieval polities, such as the caliphate.[104]

The demand to conform to cultural and religious practices in the early modern period grew increasingly repressive during the Counter-Reformation after the Council of Trent and crystallized in the Inquisition's measures to encourage Christian conventions and morality. The Inquisition's activities verify the collusion of the church and monarchy, since the kingship bolstered the Holy Office from the reign of Carlos V to Felipe V in the eighteenth century. In return, the church pursued enemies of the crown, such as *moriscos* and Aragonese rebels in the 1590s, and thus collaborated with the monarchy in the establishment of a unified apparatus of control to bolster the polity.[105] The church's participation in this effort combined further areas of civic command, since 90 percent of the church's inquisitors belonged not to the religious but to the secular clergy. The majority of the inquisitors were trained lawyers, which leads J. N. Hillgarth to emphasize their secular, administrative role as bureaucrats rather than as religious authorities.[106] The composition of the Inquisition exemplifies the remarkable partnership of the monarchic, religious, and legal apparatuses in the construction of the nation-state.

The effort to organize and consolidate society under the dominant aegis of the polity had significant effects in the early modern period. It promoted and necessitated the establishment of cultural principles that continue to predominate in the present day about identity, cultural difference, and the hierarchical organization of society. It also abetted the institutionalization of corrective, disciplinary measures, such as incarceration and confession.[107] The tasks of the nation-state and the cultural ideals it reinforced diverged sharply from medieval Iberian cultural values and the social composition.

Early modern textual discourses demonstrate this shift. Poets, physicians, literary writers, artists, and cartographers illustrate the changes in cultural beliefs about difference and alterity, which they generally represent on the body. Although these disciplines initially may appear unrelated, they constitute areas of cultural production that were pillars of the newly created, early modern nation-state. The poetry, medical treatises, and discourse on the monster that are discussed in the following chapters upheld the tenets of alterity in the Middle Ages and were converted into early modern modes of circulation, which Benedict Anderson identifies as transmitters of the ideology of the imagined, modern polity. These early modern texts conveyed to readers the values of the nation in the same way that the mass media, the education system, and administrative regulations promulgate national ideology nowadays.[108] These discourses often bolstered the increasingly homogeneous ordering of early Spanish society, while the rise of printing in the fifteenth and sixteenth centuries facilitated the alliance of national, institutional ideals with artistic and cultural production.

Early modern poets, physicians, and other writers and artists often belonged to noble classes, which began to direct government and education in the fifteenth century.[109] According to José Antonio Maravall, the administrative nobility of the late fifteenth century complied with the tenets of the Catholic Kings:

Todo el país, entendiendo entonces por tal los grupos minoritarios que dirigen el gobierno y la vida social en todos sus puntos—con predominio de funcionarios reales y altos mercaderes—. . . se siente atraído por la ilusión de superar la historia inmediata y acepta el programa de nuevos ideales que parece emanar de la corte de los mismos Reyes Católicos.[110]

[The entire nation, that is, the elite groups that direct the government and social life in all their aspects—with the predominance of royal bureaucrats and
high-ranking merchants—. . . is attracted by the illusion of surpassing imme-
diate history, and it accepts the program of new ideals that seems to emanate
from the court of the Catholic Kings themselves.]

Noble poets supported the nation-state because they were frequently aligned with
the principles and ideology of early modern governance, as Maravall observes. They
became purveyors of the mores of the crown of Fernando and Isabel and later monarchs, in contrast to medieval writers who were not always affiliated with "national,"
courtly projects. Early modern poets often enacted and reinforced the newly predominant tenets of early modern alterity, and they encouraged the recreation and diversion that characterized the principles of the leisure classes, including the sixteenth-
and seventeenth-century noblemen or *hidalgos*. They helped to disseminate the newly
static, ennobling ideology of love, and they aided in the forging of discrete subjects,
such as the noble male lover and the heretical *converso*.

The humanist diffusion on the peninsula of revised, classical poetic meters by
such writers as the Marquis of Santillana, Íñigo López de Mendoza, attests to the
fifteenth- and sixteenth-century cultural revamping that accompanied the early modern political shift. Maravall and Menocal attribute this cultural move in part to the
desire to avoid the plural Iberian Middle Ages through the imitation of classical writers. In this way, early modern Iberian society strove to verify its own renovation and
to show that it had overcome the "dark," multicultural Islamic and Jewish past in
order to be reborn in the era of the "renaissance."[111] Early modern poetry contests in
Valencia and Castile also reinforced the objectives of the nation-state in their effort to
determine the best composition in praise of the Virgin. As part of the *gaya ciencia*
(Gay Science), the norms of writing poetry, these poems demonstrated a newly created Catholic moral order in which Mary and female saints are contrasted with earthly
women in order to highlight the latter's human weakness, sin, and fault.[112] Early modern lyric stylized Mary more than medieval verse, which presented her as a holy figure accessible to all and willing to aid everyone in distress, as shown by Alfonso X's
thirteenth-century songs about the Virgin, *Cantigas de Santa María*. Early modern
poets usually portrayed the Virgin as an abstract female icon to worship at a distance,
rather than as a figure to invoke for her tangible intervention.

Early modern medical writers constituted another foundation of the Castilian
polity, since they often complied with its exclusive and homogenizing principles. The
late fifteenth- and sixteenth-century professionalization of medicine sought to elevate medicine as the most capable form of healing and to dignify male physicians as

the most efficacious healers. Newly professionalized male doctors attempted to ap-
propiate the cultural influence and authority that healers wielded over the body and
social relations. The professionalizing efforts included exclusionary tactics whereby
physicians were required to fulfill university medical training and obtain licenses.
These restrictions explicitly and implicitly marginalized women and male Muslim
and Jewish healers from traditional medical practice. Starting in the late fifteenth
century, municipalities created authoritative boards for the licensing of physicians,
as did the Catholic Kings with the establishment of the Real Protomedicato. These
councils represented the institutionalization of a newly categorical social order that
privileged Christian male physicians over Muslims, Jews, and women. The professionalization of medicine thus complied with the ideals of the ruling classes to regulate and homogenize civic life through hierarchical divisions of professionals and
nonprofessionals, Christians and non-Christians, and men and women.[113]

Early modern medical writers demonstrated this cultural emphasis on hierarchy
and division in their description of the human body. They made certain male bodies
worthy for their use value to the early modern nation-state or republic, while they
often reduced women to sexual objects who were serviceable in procreation. Conventional medieval medical discussions of women's health were largely substituted
in the early modern period by conduct manuals that prescribed that women be
confined to the home as wives and mothers. Hence, early modern writers who were
complicit with the ideals of the Castilian nation-state devised societal well-being not
only according to individual health, but also in relation to gender-specific social
roles and categories.

Literary authors constituted another pillar of the early modern polity, since they
participated in the revision of the tenets of medieval alterity. This is nowhere more
evident than in the early modern changes to the cultural worth of the monster. With
the consolidation of the monster's pejorative value, writers such as Fernando de Rojas
in La Celestina (1499) began to cast Castilian social groups as threatening, monstrous
others. The disposable worth of the negative and deformed in the late Middle Ages
and early modern period caused artists and civil authorities to identify people, such
as women, prostitutes, thieves, Jews, and the poor, as palpable monsters. These "deformed," monstrous groups had to be expelled or corrected in order to preserve the
integrity of the social order. The monstrous and abject no longer represented a legitimate way to reach union with the transcendent, but they constituted a path to moral,
physical, and social decomposition.

The investigation of medieval and early modern alterity culminates in the study of
the monster because shifts in its worth were wide ranging in many kinds of disciplines and discourses, such as entertaining literature, cartography, and theological

and philosophical theories of being, cognition, and the divine. A variety of late medieval and early modern artists and scholars attributed a pejorative value to the deformed, which attests to a broad change in the cultural worth of the negative. The
monster's extensive denigration reinforced the solidified Castilian polity because it
contributed to a social system whose governing institutions strove for clear divisions between acceptable subjects and unacceptable others. The monster's change
in worth had its most serious repercussions in the church's locating of the deformed
in tangible, societal others, and in unacceptable religious discourse and practice.
The church gained institutional cohesion during the fifteenth and sixteenth centuries
through a series of measures that were directly linked to the debased, early modern
value of the deformed, including the search for heretics by the Inquisition and the
marginalizing of mystical discourse. Thus early modern theologians and philosophers
often bolstered the nation-state, along with poets, physicians, and literary writers,
especially during the Counter-Reformation. They complied with its efforts to situate
the negative in everyday others, such as "heretics," converts, and women, and to marginalize rather than integrate them. The early modern change in value of the monstrous and deformed demonstrates the reinforced institutional alignment of church
and state and further points to far-reaching ontological shifts in the esteem and denigration of certain bodies, as evidenced by political policy against societal others.

Chapter 2 investigates how lyric poetry manifested the changes in medieval and
early modern alterity. It shows that Andalusi verse such as the *muwashshah* and *zajal*
enacted and reinforced the tenets of medieval Iberian alterity through its formal
features and its depiction of the body. Andalusi lyric largely confirmed the pliable
formation of gendered and sexual subjects and the complex interdependence of contrasts and the negative. Its malleable subjectivity, equivocal characteristics, and variation distinguished it from early modern poetry, such as the lyric of the Aragonese
gaya ciencia and the fifteenth- and sixteenth-century *cancionero* poems of courtly love.
Late medieval, early modern poetry demonstrated more rigid cultural values since it
often cast the identities of noble lovers and their women beloveds as absolute and unyielding. Early modern courtly poets frequently created inflexible hierarchies that
marked a shift from the work of Andalusi composers and performers.

CHAPTER TWO

The Lyric Body

Writers in al-Andalus composed a vast, diverse corpus of secular and sacred poetry in Arabic and Hebrew, and one strophe, the *jarcha,* in Andalusi Romance. Poetry was highly regarded in Andalusi culture and in all medieval Arab realms, since it constituted "the supreme, most widespread, and most discussed art of the medieval Arab world."[1] Verses were written conventionally on paper, and they were imprinted on common objects, such as women's garments, shoes, head-gear, handkerchiefs, fans, jewelry, furniture, cushions, curtains, and carpets.[2] Andalusi lyric was esteemed in many ways, including as popular oral and musical entertainment, and as an exemplary device to highlight arguments in treatises such as Ibn Hazm's eleventh-century work on love, *Tawq al-hamāma* (*The Dove's Neckring*).

Poetry was performed in a variety of venues, such as public, urban spaces and the palaces of nobles.[3] Courtly patrons or benefactors, including al-Muʿtamid of Seville, supported professional poets such as Ibn al-Labbāna of Denia (d. 1113), who entertained nobles and patrons in the urban centers of Cordova, Seville, and Granada.[4] Up to the fall of the caliphate at Cordova in 1031, some official court poets were "state functionaries whose duty it was to issue bulletins of foreign policy," a bureaucratic, austere kind of writing that James T. Monroe called "uninspiring."[5] Other kinds of poets included the ambulatory Jewish writers, who traveled from place to place in search of economic subsistence.[6]

Andalusi poetry's cultural role was not limited to writers in Arabic, since Andalusi-Jewish intellectuals such as Solomon Ibn Gabirol, Moses Ibn Ezra, and Yehudah Halevi composed a variety of verses in Hebrew as well as Arabic. Jewish writers may have employed Arabic on account of its scholarly and intellectual prestige, but more likely they knew the language because al-Andalus was a multilingual society. In contrast to the scholarly belief that Jewish writers imitated and altered the literary and textual conventions of Andalusi-Arab writers, Ross Brann contends that Andalusi-Jews crafted their verse like their Muslim neighbors because they were fully integrated in a multifaceted Andalusi society: "Rather than viewing the Jews' Arabization as a sign of external 'influence,' perhaps we can take it as evidence of their circumscribed cultural convergence within the multiethnic, multireligious configuration of Andalusi society."[7] Thus it is probable that the correspondences between Andalusi-Jewish and Arabic writings attest to the cultural meshwork of al-Andalus, and not to cultural and linguistic divisions.

Andalusi men and women of all social classes composed poetry on a variety of topics, such as panegyrics to patrons, religious poems, and celebrations of warfare or the hunt.[8] Andalusi-Arab women poets were relatively prolific, although few writings remain by Andalusi-Jewish women.[9] Andalusi women wrote about topics similar to those of their male counterparts, including panegyrics to important figures, eulogies upon the death of a relative, religious verse, satires, and poems about women's vocations and social roles. Andalusi men and women wrote abundantly about love, and they created an immense body of lyrical verse that Michael Sells calls "love talk" or *ghazal*.[10] *Ghazal*'s renown continues in today's Arab world, along with the music and song that fully comprises and defines it. Modern-day composing "in the Andalusian style" often refers to creation in the *muwashshah* and *zajal* traditions, that is, the performative, strophic forms that originated and developed in al-Andalus.[11]

Ghazal comprises various kinds of strophes, and a number of them reveal the two tenets of medieval Iberian alterity. The *muwashshah* and *zajal* are notable, however, because they were invented in al-Andalus, and they clearly embody the region's heterogeneity. The *muwashshah* was composed in classical Arabic, starting in the ninth century, and Jewish poets later began to generate them in Hebrew in al-Andalus and in other Jewish regions.[12] When they were initially written in the eleventh century, the *muwashshah*s started as secular love lyrics and later gained popularity as panegyrics to patrons and royalty. The *zajal* greatly resembled the *muwashshah*, although it was composed in vernacular Arabic and maintained occasional structural differences.[13] Because the first literary examples of the *zajal* date from the twelfth century, about one hundred years after those of the *muwashshah*, it was believed that the vernacular *zajal* derived from its classical predecessor. However, it is likely that they coexisted since the *zajal* frequently was called a *muwashshah* in dialect.[14]

The formal features of the *muwashshah* and *zajal* tended to vary and did not always conform to generic expectations.[15] For instance, the *muwashshah* generally consisted of five stanzas, although it often exceeded that number. Both strophes incorporated a final, short stanza called the *jarcha* (exit), which was written either in the vernacular Andalusi Romance or in a mixture of colloquial and classical Arabic. The composition of the *muwashshah* was based on a *jarcha* that was chosen by a poet, according to the twelfth-century treatise by the Egyptian Ibn Sanāʿ al-Mulk, who suggested that the *jarcha* simultaneously constituted the poem's beginning and end because it brought the *muwashshah* to a close and served as its initial foundation.[16] Men or anonymous poets wrote most of the *muwashshah*s and *zajal*s, and many of the erotic, love-related ones were directed to both women and men as the receivers of the poets' affections.

Men's voices usually narrated the *muwashshah*, while the *jarcha*'s speaker was plucked from a variety of possible narrators, identified as "'he,' 'she,' or 'I'; a dove or a gazelle; or, more rarely, a group of people, a town, or an allegorical figure."[17] Human narrators frequently were highly ambiguous, although critics have traditionally insisted on their expression by women, since the *jarcha*s often painfully lamented the absence of a male lover. Presumably, homophobic taboos have prevented scholars from attributing that sorrow to men. Medievalists have further insisted on the woman narrator of the *jarcha* in order to characterize the strophe as the first example of traditional, popular Romance lyric.[18] By ascribing a woman's voice to the *jarcha* and a man's voice to the *muwashshah* and *zajal*, critics have devised hypothetical generic demands that determine the languages and voices of the three strophes.[19] Yet, the *jarcha* was linguistically inconstant, since it was composed in classical Arabic or the vernacular and often had an unidentified speaker. The narrator's gender ambiguity is evident in an eleventh-century panegyric by the Andalusi-Jewish poet Yosef al-Katib, "the scribe," which ends with the following *jarcha:*

¡Tanto amar, tanto amar, / amigo, tanto amar! / ¡Enfermaron unos ojos brillantes / y duelen tan mal![20]

[So much loving, so much loving, friend, / so much loving! / Some bright eyes became ill / and they hurt so badly!]

The editor, Josep María Solá-Solé, believes that the speaker is the poet and concludes that the *jarcha* praises the receivers of the panegyric, Abu Ibrahim Samuel (probably the famous Samuel Ibn Nagrila) and his brother Ishaq: "[The *jarcha*] está puesta en labios del propio poeta quien, con términos amorosos, proclama su profunda admiración por el elogiado" [(The *jarcha*) comes from the lips of the poet himself, who, in loving terms, proclaims his profound admiration for the one he praises].[21] Thus, Solá-Solé indicates that women were not the only intended speakers of the *jarcha*s, while other recent critics such as Anthony P. Espósito question the fixity of identity in the *jarcha*, and emphasize instead its complex narration.

Just as narrators varied and sometimes were unknown in the *jarcha*, so was subject identity in the *muwashshah* vague and ambiguous, as evidenced by a gender conflict in the Spanish translations of a *muwashshah* by Ibn Arfā' Rā'suh (1043–1075). Emilio García Gómez translated the *muwashshah*'s beloved as a woman, while Solá-Solé interpreted him as a man, thus revealing the doubt about the homo- or heteroerotic relation between the narrator and his beloved. García Gómez opted for a heteroerotic relation between them, while Solá Solé chose a homoerotic one. This discrepancy illustrates that, like the *jarcha*, the *muwashshah* resists facile categorization and does not conform to philological expectations about what Espósito calls "canonical desire," that is, the gender and sexual identity of individuals in different strophes.[22] The *muwashshah*'s vacillating character is reinforced by the fact that poets frequently directed love to both male and female figures in the same poem, such as in an eleventh-century composition by Yahyà al-Gazzar, who names the male beloved *mi asesino, el deseado*, and *el bien amado* (my assassin, the desired one, and the very beloved) in strophes one, four, and five, and the female beloved, the *pequeña gacela* (little gazelle) in strophes two and four.[23] The *muwashshah* also revealed considerable variation in its combining of secular and sacred subject matter. For instance, a twelfth-century *muwashshah* by Al-A'mà al-Tutili, "the blind man from Tudela," connects the sacred Islamic pilgrimage to Ka'ba to an amorous journey toward the beloved. This integration of the sacred and profane was not an isolated instance, nor was it obscure in Andalusi verse; rather, it characterized a variety of writings, such as the mystical Sufi poetry of Ibn 'Arabī (1165–1240) and Ibn al-Sabbagh (d. 1266). Tova Rosen notes that Ibn al-Sabbagh's *muwashshah*s became very popular in the Middle Ages.[24]

The *zajal* also demonstrates much of this Andalusi heterogeneity, although it is linguistically more constant than the *muwashshah*. The *zajal* has largely been considered a popular strophic form composed for illiterate audiences, in contrast to the classical *muwashshah*, which was supposedly written by erudite poets for an educated public. Yet, poets such as Ibn Quzmān (d. 1160) crossed the boundary between them and composed both types, suggesting that they were not inevitably divided between learned poets, who wrote only *muwashshah*s in classical Arabic and Hebrew, and less educated writers, who were forced to write *zajal*s in the vernacular. Nor did these strophes necessarily belong to different social classes, as shown by Ibn Quzmān, who wrote many of his pedestrian *zajal*s for wealthy patrons and not for the common people. Thus, *muwashshah*s and *zajal*s were not by definition poems of "high" or "low" culture.[25] While it is evident that the *muwashshah* and *zajal* differed from one another, their resistance to facile categorization indicates one way in which they manifest the idiosyncrasy and variety of Andalusi culture and society.

The *muwashshah* especially embodies Andalusi heterogeneity in the ambiguous identities of its speakers and their beloveds, as well as in the contrasts of different strophic forms, languages, objects of desire, sexualities, genders, and subject matter. Jewish and Muslim writers alike composed these bitextual hybrids, which juxtaposed classical Arabic or Hebrew and the vernacular, men's and women's voices, and distinct forms of desire. Rosen shows that the *muwashshah* paralleled Andalusi society because it was whole in its contradictions and diversity:

> Thus, the muwashshah exemplifies a pluralistic cultural politics that allowed for difference and plurality, clashes and juxtapositions. It admits non-Arabic and nonlearned cultures, recognizes the female voice, and expresses both secular sentiments and religious yearnings. If the muwashshah continues to fascinate us today, it is precisely because of the cultural hybridness that it embodies. It is appropriate to reiterate this fact because of those who would reduce the muwashshah to a product of a "pure" and prescriptive poetics.[26]

Instead of representing a constant, absolute strophic form, the *muwashshah* manifested the prevalent ideal of variety in al-Andalus.[27]

Variable Subject Formation in the *Muwashshah* and *Zajal*

*Muwashshah*s and *zajal*s demonstrate and reinforce the multifaceted subject formation that characterizes medieval Iberian alterity, since poets often depict lyrical subjects according to their gender, sexual, and erotic variance. The poems juxtapose different voices, social registers, genders, languages, and modes of expression in order to present a diverse range of poetic subjects. Subjectivity in the poems is complex and variable rather than rigid and fixed, which is shown in the relations between the different narrators and in their ambiguous connections to their intended receivers of the poems. Instead of establishing absolute divisions between subjects, the counterpositioning of contrary strophes and voices demonstrates their compatibility and ironic correspondence. This is evidenced by a wide variety of writers, including Ibn Quzmān, Ibn Shuhayd, and Abū Nuwās, whose works often contrast women and men, and hetero- and homoerotic desire.[28]

The prominence of diverse subject formation in these poems is illustrated by a twelfth-century *zajal* by Ibn Quzmān, in which the poet-narrator declares two forms of desire toward his benefactor Abu al-Hasan 'Ali al-Baiyani. The male narrator of the *zajal* first implores al-Baiyani to provide things for his house because the holidays are approaching, and he exhibits a second form of desire in his erotic longing for his patron. At the end of the *zajal*, the poet's yearning turns into a lament in which he evidently seeks assistance:

Dame a aquél cuyo poder es aceptado / y reúneme con él: / rubio, hermoso, por él pasan mis cuidados.[29]

[Give me over to him whose power is accepted, / and unite me with him: / fair, handsome, because of him I am so tormented.]

Ibn Quzmān's poem melds the panegyric and the topic of love, which is a highly common practice in the *zajal* and *muwashshah*. The erotic mourning complements the poet's petition to his benefactor, as homoeroticism blends easily with the request for the patron's monetary protection.

Finally, in a third depiction of desire, a woman narrator relates her yearning for a man in the concluding *jarcha*. The poet's transition leading into the *jarcha* suggests a harmonious agreement between the young woman's song and the poet's own mournful appeal:

Movióme a que hiciera versos / en este ritmo, / una muchacha bonita, dulce, que cantaba / un canto bello.[30]

[A young girl, pretty and sweet, who was singing / a lovely song, / moved me to write verses / in this rhythm.]

The poem then ends with the young woman's *jarcha*:

"Locamente enamorada estoy, ay madre, yo de este vecino mío / Alí, el morenazo."[31]

[Crazy in love, o Mother, am I with my neighbor, / Ali, the big brown man.]

While this change in the narrator's gender may be viewed as a purely rhetorical device dependent on the differing conventions of the *zajal* and *jarcha*, its repercussions are not merely rhetorical and aesthetic but have broader implications for Andalusi gender definition. The poem stresses affinity rather than antagonism between the male and female speakers, since the narrating poet declares that the young woman's lament induced him to compose his own mournful poem. This claim emphasizes the relation between the strophes and their speakers rather than the differences between them. Thus, the woman's anguished, desiring voice in the *jarcha* prompts the man in the *zajal* to comment on or imitate it. The change in gender and genre from the *zajal* to the *jarcha* constitutes a move between different social codes that are simultaneously inseparable and mutually compatible, from male to female and from colloquial Arabic to Andalusi Romance.

A twelfth-century Andalusi-Hebrew *muwashshah* by Abraham Ibn Ezra (c. 1089–1167) further demonstrates the paradoxical affinity between different genders and strophes. Ibn Ezra describes the beauty of the male beloved throughout the *muwashshah*, such as in the following stanza where he equates him with a deer:[32]

> Huerto de amor, y ciervo
> en el que se juntan gracia y belleza.
> ¡Sea mi alma su liberación y rescate![33]
>
> [Orchard of love and deer
> where grace and beauty meet.
> Let my soul be his liberation and rescue!]

Toward the beginning of the poem, the narrator bemoans the absence of the graceful deer, his friend:

> Amigos míos, por favor cogedme de la mano,
> que quema como el fuego de mis visceras
> por la ausencia del corzo gracioso, mi amigo.[34]
>
> [My friends, please take me by the hand,
> which burns like the fire of my entrails
> for the absence of the graceful brown deer, my friend.]

Finally, the poem ends with a *jarcha* from the mouth of a young woman who, like the voice in the *muwashshah*, laments the absence of her male beloved:

> Dime ¿qué he de hacer? ¿(cómo viviré)? A este amigo espero, por él moriré.[35]
>
> [Tell me, what am I to do? (How shall I live?) I await this friend; for him I will die.]

Like Ibn Quzmān in the *zajal,* Ibn Ezra fashions the poetic voice of the *muwashshah* as one that identifies with the young woman's suffering:

> Lloro en mi alma por una doncella
> que gime con voz amarga como cierva
> por su amado que marchó al destierro.[36]

> [I cry in my soul for a maiden
> who moans with a bitter voice like a doe,
> for her (male) lover who left for exile.]

Hence, the man's lament resembles the woman's, as Ibn Ezra emphasizes their likeness rather than their contrast.

These poems demonstrate that gender definition depends on the interrelation between the male and female and not on their divisions, a pervasive principle in many *muwashshah*s and *zajal*s. Ibn Quzmān and Ibn Ezra show that even poems that follow the ostensible conventions of male narrators in the *muwashshah* and *zajal* and of female speakers in the *jarcha* create fluid identities and pliable forms of erotic desire. The divergent genders, languages, and voices are intimately parallel and not utterly anomalous, since the male narrator does not distance himself from the female voice of the *jarcha,* but embraces and identifies with it as mirroring his desire in a different way. It is not that male poets sought to become women, or that they all engaged in homoerotic or homosexual practice in their daily lives. Instead, some of their poems indicate that they considered gender and sexual contrasts more parallel than divergent.

The analogous, contrasting *muwashshah, zajal,* and *jarcha* create a lyric continuum of sexual and gender identity in which the borders between the male and female and between the hetero- and homosexual and -erotic are porous and fluid. Male poets identify with women's lament, and their financial petition to their patrons becomes conflated with homoerotic desire. The elasticity of identity in the *muwashshah* and *zajal* is entirely consistent with other kinds of Arabic poetry, as shown by the variable subject formation of Ibn 'Arabī's mystical verse, where the union between a lover and the divine takes place through a process that erodes the limits between them. Just as the desiring voices of the *muwashshah* and *zajal* evidence an open affinity to other genders, the mystical lover must maintain "an open heart" for self-acceptance in mutable forms and for reception of the beloved/divine in changing shapes.[37] In agreement with Andalusi lyric, these mystical tenets suggest an embrace of fluctuating subjects rather than a need to forge unyielding identities. Mystical and poetic writings were intertwined because they mutually influenced one another in the Middle Ages.[38]

As we have seen, permeable subjects in the *muwashshah* and *zajal* reinforce and demonstrate important cultural values about individual identity and diverse social relations. Yet, fluid subjectivities are problematic because they ironically demand absolute subjects prior to permeable ones. Ibn Ezra and Ibn Quzmān's poems suggest that elastic identities are impossible without their comparison to momentarily stable male and female subjectivities. The *muwashshah*'s lyric continuum encompasses all possible gender and sexual subjects, which include stable and fluid ones that are always incongruously in flux. Fixed identity is ironic in the poems because it is simultaneously permanent and impermanent, and because its rupture permits individuals to enter into varying relations of power and subservience that are crucial to the poems' subject formation. While at first they might seem antithetical to permeable subjectivity, domination and subordination play important roles in the varying connections between the poet and patron of the *muwashshah* and *zajal,* as well as between the lyric voices of the *muwashshah, zajal,* and *jarcha.*

Relations of power and subservience occur within two models, which are common in Arabic poetry: those of courtly love and sexual domination and submission. These paradigms constitute the frameworks within which synthetic subjects are created in Ibn Ezra's *muwashshah* and Ibn Quzmān's *zajal.* While not all *muwashshahs* and *zajals* invoke these models, they were prevalent in many poems, such as a *muwashshah* by al-Qasim al-Maniši, one by Ibn Baqi, and another by Yehuda Halevi that confounds gender identification when the male lover who was abandoned in the *muwashshah* sings like a young girl in the *jarcha.*[39]

The courtly love paradigm casts the lyric figures of the poet and patron in the *muwashshah* and *zajal* as parallel to the courtly lover and beloved. Mary Jane Kelley believes that poets identify with female desire in the *jarcha* as a strategy of subordination that "flatters [the poet's] patron and disposes him to offer a reward."[40] Thus, the poet subjugates himself in the *muwashshah* and *zajal* by identifying with a woman in the *jarcha* in order to celebrate and receive compensation from the male patron, who occupies what would become in medieval troubadour poetry the courtly position of the forceful woman beloved. The poet's subservience is complex, because at the same time that he occupies the male singer's inferior position, his submission has an aspect of weakness that is often equated with the female gender; hence his affiliation with the woman's voice of the *jarcha.* The poet's subjugation is further complicated by the fact that it is a strategy for his own eventual empowerment, since the position of power in relation to the male patron is reversed when the poet receives the patron's favor. According to conventional gender divisions, the poet is at once a subjugated female and, eventually, an empowered male in his role as petitioner in the courtly love model. Yet his complex identity ironically depends upon the initial establishment of his male subjectivity and on the contrast of different genders and forms of desire.

The patron's gender identity is equally complex because he assumes what would become in troubadour poetry the elevated position of the powerful woman beloved, but then gives his command over to the poet when he grants the latter's petition. Thus, the relation between the benefactor and the male poet blurs gender, sexual, and erotic categories: the poet is a man who identifies with a woman; the poet occupies the female-coded position of a subordinate courtly singer; and the poet praises a male patron often in both erotic and amicable terms. Courtly love in Andalusi poetry creates multifaceted subjects and does not reinforce gender inequities like much of the later troubadour poetry of southern France and Catalonia. In the later medieval Occitan lyric, the ideology of courtly love exposed women's supposed threat to men and justified misogyny;[41] courtly love in the *muwashshah* and *zajal* has a very different effect.

The *muwashshah* and *zajal* also correspond to the second model of the forceful penetrator and the servile penetrated, a paradigm that figures the lowly, inferior penetrated as boys, women, and "pathic" males.[42] Unlike today's gender distinctions between men and women and the sexual divide of the homo- and heterosexual, this model constituted the main sexual division in Andalusi and Arab society. The way it is invoked in Andalusi lyric suggests that men poets occupy women's deferential position in order to take part in a sexual paradigm of domination and subordination in which they metaphorically become the servile penetrated for sexual arousal, and in order to receive the patron's favor.[43] The models of courtly flattery and of sexual dominance and subservience indicate that men poets enervate themselves discursively in order to identify with the hypothetically weaker female gender and achieve their own financial or sexual gain. Identification with the weak or anguished female gender paradoxically allows men to profit from the patron's flattery or gift (whether sexual or monetary) and from the eroticism of the model of sexual dominance. Male poets subvert the usual positions of power with respect to their patrons, since the inferior position of women and submissive men results in the poet's advantage.

The variable positioning and meaning of men's and women's voices in these two models contrasts with their separation in Kelley's assessment that the more powerful male poet and voice controls and subsumes the female one: "As male creations employed metaphorically in male literary discourse, the female voices in the *kharjas* do not reflect any absolute truth about women in the world outside the poems. Instead, the female voice is subjected to masculine control."[44] However, rather than appropriate the weak, disparaged female gender in order to dominate it, poems such as Ibn

Ezra's and Ibn Quzmān's demonstrate that men ally with women's voices and laments. While it is evident that the *jarcha*s do not "reflect any absolute truth about women" or men in the ordinary world, *muwashshah*s and *zajal*s transmit values about subject formation that both illustrate and reinforce Andalusi ideals. While control and subjugation are evident in the courtly love and sexual models that frame the poems, they are means to effect elastic subjectivity rather than methods to create stable identities.

Fixed categories of identity yield to permeable subjects in the *muwashshah* and *zajal,* and stable subjects are not the end result of the framing models of courtly love and of sexual domination. Whereas power and subordination in Andalusi lyric partially resemble the roles of dominance and subjection in modern theories of subjectivity posited by Michel Foucault and Judith Butler, the use and effect of power in the formation of the subject ultimately differ in the discourses. Although Butler's and Foucault's theories have no direct relation to subjectivity in the *muwashshah* and *zajal,* their broad ideas about power and the subject are useful as points of comparison with subject formation in the medieval lyric. Foucault shows that power is mobile among institutions and individuals, but that it is always required in the construction of the subject.[45] He indicates that subject formation occurs through the subject's internalizing of power, while Butler believes that the subject constitutes, in part, an effect of power.[46] Andalusi lyric suggests a similar scheme. After the rupture of his stable identity, the male poet crosses the bounds of gender and sexuality by participating in mutable and inconstant relations of power in the courtly love and sexual models. This act of subject crossing is evidenced by the variable roles of the dominant and subservient when the poet receives recompense from his benefactor.

However, unlike Butler and Foucault, who propose the creation of the subject through power, the *muwashshah* and *zajal* stress the role of power in the erosion of the delimited subject. Ultimately Andalusi lyric emphasizes the synthetic rather than absolute quality of subjectivity, which is achieved through three paradoxical, contrasting acts: first, the rupture of the lyric speaker's subjectivity; second, the speaker's participation in relations of power and submission; and, third, the speaker's decisive act of affiliation when, for instance, he identifies with a woman's lament. The balance between stable identity, its breakup, and the affinity with others stands out in Andalusi lyric and contributes to the creation of a kaleidoscopic, poetic space in which circumscribed identities constantly give way to other possible identifications.[47] The lyric subject enters into the power relations of courtly love and sexual control, where the limits between domination and subjection are constantly in flux.

The *muwashshah* and *zajal* forge a lyric continuum that contains both mutable gender and sexual identities and rigid subjectivities that yield to these identities. Fixed categories of the male and female make synthetic subjectivity possible, since momentary establishments of stable subjects constantly cede to permeable ones within the courtly love and sexual models. Yet in the end fluid and stable subjectivities are not at odds with each other because they constitute diverse parts of a porous, lyric whole. At an undetermined point along the lyric continuum, the momentary fixity of gender and sexuality in the poetic voices gives way to varying gender and to mutable positions of power and weakness that are demonstrated in the courtly love and sexual models. The permeability of gender relies on the integrity of the poet's male subjectivity prior to lowering himself to the denigrated female position.

Andalusi lyric demonstrates complex, mutable relations of power and subjectivity that obscure the limits between categories of identity. The paradigms of courtly love and of sexual control show the constant permeability of gender and human expression and their ever changing relation to domination. But they also demonstrate the difficulty of determining where subjectivity and power begin and end, since men's identification with supposedly abject women in the *jarcha* ultimately empowers them and expedites their gain in relation to their patron. Men's identification with women blurs gender limits and gender's relation to power, creating not a circumscribed, androgynous subject, but a fused one that obfuscates categorical differences between women and men. Delimited subjects are difficult to pinpoint in the *muwashshah* and *zajal*, but they are required in order to fracture the subject and arrive at more variable identities through relations of power and of affiliation with other subjects.

The *muwashshah* and *zajal* embrace complex subjectivities and ultimately emphasize the seamlessness of identity, rather than the breaches and gaps between subjects. This principle is reinforced by the definition of the *muwashshah* itself, which derives from the Arabic *wishāh*, a word that designates a girdle composed of varying colors that encircles the body.[48] The *muwashshah* is thus a kind of ring that achieves coherence in the circular composition of its different strophes, voices, languages, genders, and erotic expressions. The circle is the most perfect shape because it has no breaks, that is, no beginning, middle, or end. The theorist Ibn Sanā' al-Mulk emphasized this ideal of lyric oneness in his belief that the *jarcha* constitutes both the poem's start and finish, calling it the foundation and the tail to place the head:

> The *jarcha* is the pepper of the *muwaššah;* it is its salt, its sugar, its musk, its amber. Since it is its final outcome, it must be commendable; and to be the final seal, it must be the beginning, even though it is placed at the end. I say that it must be the beginning because it must be the first thing that comes to the mind of the poet, that which the poet composes before everything else and before deciding on a meter or rhyme. Being free, unencumbered, unconstrained and in the mood, when the poet thinks of rhythmic measurements and light

words, which are pleasant to the ear, naturally suited to the soul, and sweet to
the taste, he welcomes them, receiving them, working on them, and making the
muwaššah out of them; for then the poet has found his ground and seized the
tail where he is to place the head.[49]

The *muwashshah* begins with the *jarcha,* since the poet chose it as the base for building his *muwashshah,* and it also constitutes the poem's tail because of its location at
its end. The *jarcha* was at once an entrance into the *muwashshah* and an exit from it,
demonstrating that the poem began and ended in the same place. Thus, like a girdle
or circle, the entire poem formed a perfect, contained shape, unbroken by a start or
finish. The *muwashshah* ring was cast as a continuous orb that was simultaneously
seamless and diverse, since it comprised elements of mutable, varying worth. The
movement from the *muwashshah* to the *jarcha* marked a dislocation that took place as
the *muwashshah* reached its end, entered into the *jarcha,* which was ironically start
and finish, and completed the seamless orb.[50] The poem's complex rhyming patterns,
which María Rosa Menocal calls an "encircling device," further contributed to its
spherical character.[51]

These formal principles of the *muwashshah* extend to the realms of gender and
sexuality, where the perfection of identity depends upon the seamless circularity of
diverse genders, sexualities, and acts of dominance. Just as the *muwashshah* begins
and ends with the *jarcha,* so does the male voice of the *muwashshah* begin and end
with the often female-coded voice of the *jarcha.* And in the same way that these diverse lyric parts form a unified ring without a standard start or finish, so does the
poetic understanding of gender and sexuality imply an unbroken sphere that does
not seek to delimit gendered and erotic voices in a rigid way.[52] The poem's start and
finish are difficult to distinguish because the poem begins and ends in the same ambivalent place. Similarly, the beginnings and ends of gender and sexuality often are
indeterminate because they start and finish in the same location of the variable, multifaceted subject.

Contrasts in Andalusi Lyric

Many kinds of lyric and other discourses in al-Andalus evidenced
fluid corporeal identity, which often was based on the interdependence and mutability of contraries. They did not always characterize Andalusi subjects by absolute
categories, but often by the compatibility of contrasting classifications. The cultural regard for coexisting contrasts is illustrated in the work of an eleventh-century Hebrew

writer from Cordova, Yishaq Ibn Jalfun, who composed love poems to both women and men. The selections below are from two poems that do not employ the verse forms of the *muwashshah* and *zajal*. The passage from the first poem is directed to a man:

> Con falaz cortesía, boca halagadora y hablar tierno
>> engañarme quieres y aplacarme;
> mi corazón robar pretendes con lisonjas,
>> te finges hermoso y no lo eres.

> [With fallacious courtesy, a flattering mouth, and tender words
>> you want to deceive and placate me;
> my heart with flattery you attempt to rob,
>> you [male beloved] pretend to be handsome and you are not.]

The second poem reveals desire for a woman:

> Me despierta el amor y brinco,
>> cual ciervo, para mirar los ojos de mi amada.[53]

> [Love wakes me and I leap
>> like a deer to look at my [woman] lover's eyes.]

Ibn Jalfun's Spanish editors attribute his complaint about a male beloved to generic conventions, indicating that it does not relate to the ordinary world.[54] While it need not demonstrate Ibn Jalfun's everyday experience, the easeful juxtaposition of these two forms of desire belongs to a constellation of Andalusi cultural values that authorized and compelled diversity.

Contrasts such as this from the hand of one poet destabilize presumptions about rigid medieval categories of desire. An example from the Andalusi woman poet, Hamda Banāt Ziyād de Guadix, illustrates the same point. A possibly homoerotic encounter between two women takes place in the poem identified as "Poema, que compuso Hamda cuando fue al río con una joven. Y cuando ésta se desnudó completamente dijo . . ." [A poem that Hamda composed when she went to the river with a young woman. And when that woman was completely naked, Hamda said]:

> Las lágrimas revelan mis secretos en un río
>> donde hay tantas señales de belleza:
>> es un río que rodea jardines,

y jardines que bordean al río;
entre las gacelas hay una humana
que posee mi alma y tiene mi corazón;
cuando entorna los ojos por alguna razón,
esa razón me impide a mí dormir;
cuando suelta sus bucles sobre el rostro,
parece la luna en las tinieblas de la noche;
es como si a la aurora se le hubiese muerto un hermano
y de tristeza se hubiese vestido de luto.[55]

[Tears reveal my secrets in a river
where there are so many signs of beauty:
it is a river that surrounds gardens,
and there are gardens that border the river;
among the gazelles there is a woman
who possesses my soul and holds my heart;
when she half closes her eyes for some reason,
that reason impedes my sleep;
when she loosens her curls over her face,
she looks like the moon in the night's darkness;
it is as if the aurora's brother had died,
and, from sadness, she had dressed in mourning.]

Significantly, Banāt Ziyād does not clearly identify the narrator as either female or male, but instead depicts an ambiguous voice that expresses a form of desire that is not easily classified. In her informative anthology of Andalusi women's poetry, María Jesús Rubiera Mata denies a homoerotic interpretation of this poem when she assumes that Banāt Ziyād adopts male "expression" and a masculine "point of view" according to the conventions of poetic composition. Rubiera Mata describes this practice in Hamda's and her sister Zaynab's works:

[S]u expresión es idéntica a la de los poetas varones, usan el punto de vista masculino, incluso dedicando poemas a otras mujeres. No creemos que se trate de lesbianismo sino de la asimilación total de los esteriotipos de la poesía árabe culta.[56]

[Their expression (the sisters') is the same as that of male poets. They use the masculine point of view, even dedicating poems to other women. We do not

believe that this involves lesbianism but, rather, the total assimilation of the
stereotypes of high Arabic poetry.]

Rubiera Mata indicates that the sisters simply adopt male strategies and rhetorical devices in order to imitate the poetic norms of men poets. It may be that these women
poets merely wanted to imitate men's lyrical conventions, but Hamda's ambiguous
speaker also resembles the frequently uncertain speakers of the *muwashshah* and *zajal*,
suggesting that Banāt Ziyād's indefinable narrator requires further interpretation.
Rubiera Mata does not take into account the esteem Andalusi culture had for poetic
ambiguity.

Rubiera Mata is not alone in relying on poetic convention to explain gender and
sexual indeterminacy or blending in poetry. Dan Pagis uses it to account for male-
to-male desire in Andalusi verse when he claims that male homoerotic desire does
not "directly reflect reality" in Andalusi-Hebrew poems.[57] Pagis examines the distribution of Hebrew poetry in al-Andalus and Christian Iberia, as well as in fourteenth-
and fifteenth-century Italy, where such homoeroticism did not appear. He argues
that Hebrew poets adopted generic conventions from Arabic verse, and when they
were no longer culturally relevant in late medieval Italy, poets employed new styles
and imagery. Pagis claims that if illicit forms of desire truly represented the sexual
experience of Hebrew writers, the renowned poets writing between 1100 and 1300,
such as Ibn Gabirol, Moses Ibn Ezra, and Judah Halevi, would have to be designated
"homosexual" or "bisexual," while subsequent poets in Italy would not.[58]

Pagis also attempts to make a distinction between works about "real" homosexual
encounters and discursive expressions of homoerotic desire. He contends that poetry and other writings that "intended to present actual homosexual instances" had
a connection to ordinary life, but they were strongly condemned.[59] Hence, he sepa-
rates "true" homosexual encounters in poetry from "false" expressions of desire, which
he isolates from everyday experience because they imitate literary convention. Pagis
fails to explain how to arrive at a distinction between the two.

While homo- and heteroerotic Andalusi love verse or *ghazal* does not necessarily
represent the sexual and erotic behavior of every poet, it need not be categorized by
sterile literary convention as these critics have suggested. For, even as a supposed
rhetorical convention, Andalusi *ghazal* enacts and reinforces important cultural
ideals about multivalent eroticism, sexuality, and gender. It is evident that modern
categories of "gay," "straight," and "bisexual" are anachronistic when applied to Andalusi poets, and that homo- and heteroerotic expression does not necessarily correspond to poets' sexual practice. Instead, Andalusi culture seems to sanction multifaceted, ambiguous erotic desire in verse, despite the denunciation of certain sexual

and erotic practice in some religious and legal forums. In contrast to Pagis and Rubiera Mata, Raymond P. Scheindlin argues that homoerotic desire certainly formed part of the poetic and cultural life of al-Andalus. Instead of rejecting the "reality" of homoeroticism in verse, Scheindlin incorporates it into his interpretive scheme. He emphasizes the innovative "spiritualization of love" in Andalusi-Hebrew poetry, whereby hetero- and homoerotic sensual pleasure leads upward rather than down toward the base and mundane.[60]

Pagis also imposes modern concepts about poetry and poetic composition on the medieval past in positing a biographical correlation between poet and poem. In contrast to this view, the frequent fluidity of medieval lyric may be due to its lack of fixity in an originating person, place, or source, and not to its requisite association with an individual poet. This is evident in the many anonymous poems from medieval Iberia, as well as the nameless, unspecified origins of *jarcha*s and their circulation among lyric singers. In his study of the lyric subject of the Middle Ages and "renaissance," Gregory B. Stone argues that the early modern period brings about the "death of the troubadour" and "the birth of a way of thinking that locates the origin, source, or foundation of song in the lived experience of a specific, named individual." According to Stone, the medieval troubadour was "no one in particular," since his or her song usually was not grounded in historical specifics. He proposes that lyric was the originator of the subject in the medieval period, but that in the early modern era the subject became the creator of lyric, thus allying poetic creation to the life of a single composer.[61] Conversely, Pagis seems to view lyric in accordance with the early modern change, as representing a person's lived experience.

Stone's concept of the lyric song as the generator of the subject is evident in Andalusi poetry, where the juxtaposition and harmony of sexual, linguistic, and gender variation within the same poem or within the works of one poet constitute a basic precept of Andalusi thought and cultural practice. The eleventh-century poet Ibn 'Ubada al-Qazzaz ("the poet from Malaga") further demonstrates this principle of contrasts in a *muwashshah* that consists of a panegyric to a king who goes unnamed, with a *jarcha* from the mouth of War about someone who is afflicted:[62]

Cuántas veces le cantó la guerra, / cuya victoria es penosa, / el canto de quien está afligido.[63]

[How many times did War, / whose victory is arduous, sing him the song about the one who is afflicted.]

War's song about someone who suffers follows in the *jarcha:*

"La muerte es mi estado, / porque mi estado (es) desesperado. / ¿Qué haré, oh madre mía? / El que me mima va a marcharse."[64]

[Death is my station / because my station is desperate. / What will I do, o Mother? / He who pampers me is headed off to war.]

Despite the fact that a young girl is never directly named in this *jarcha,* the poem's editor and translator, Solá-Solé, believes that War's song is based on that of a despairing girl: "La *jarcha,* al final de la quinta estrofa, es entonada por la guerra, a base de una canción de una muchacha desesperada" [The *jarcha* at the end of the fifth strophe is sung by War and is based on a song by a desperate girl].[65] However, rather than reflecting the specific lament of a girl in the everyday world, it is more likely that the association of the *jarcha* with War's "female" voice is a standard relation that makes possible the poet's self-imposed subservience and consequent flattery of his patron.

The male poet links himself to someone who is afflicted by the loss of her lover, thereby assuming the pain and identity of a traditionally female voice. The possible erotic meaning of the verb *mimar* (to fondle or to pamper) is also significant and expected in the *jarcha* lament, indicating both sexual submission and servility based on the paradigm of courtly love. The ease with which poets connect themselves to both the male and female gender suggests a fluid rendering of gender and sexuality not according to fixed, bodily states, but in keeping with linguistic and cultural codes. Al-Qazzaz's *muwashshah* shows the ironic harmony of contrasting genders and voices, rather than an absolute divide.

*Muwashshah*s and *zajal*s such as al-Qazzaz's demonstrate that contrasts were not viewed as separable in al-Andalus, but as interdependent in their juxtaposition. This principle was not limited to poetic creation, since a gamut of Arab and Andalusi disciplines and discourses upheld the balance and interdependence of dissimilar attributes. For instance, Arab aesthetics held that beauty was achieved in the equilibrium of contrasting qualities.[66] This concept is evidenced by the ninth-century writer al-Jāhiz, who launched a literary genre that dealt with contrasts and polarities.[67] In *Risālat al-qiyān* (*The Epistle on Singing-Girls*), he maintained that physical beauty resulted from the proportionate arrangement of positive and negative features, such as a tiny-eyed man with a big nose, or a small-chinned man with a large head.[68]

The interdependence of contrasting things that marks Arabic culture extended to Islam's most revered written text, the Qur'ān, for which the "validation or confirmation of its divine provenance" depended on its relation to poetry as one of "text to antitext" and "scripture to antiscripture."[69] As Suzanne Pinckney Stetkevych recounts, Muhammad's only proof of the Qur'ān's divinity was that the poets and orators who challenged him failed to produce any written work like it. This was assumed to be proof of the miraculous nature of the text, and the contrast of poetry and the Qur'ān came to form the tenets of the Qur'ān's inimitability.[70] The contrastive dependence of the Qur'ān and secular poetry, of text and antitext, demonstrates another way in which the mutual relation of different properties pervades Arab and Andalusi life and thought.

Andalusi-Jewish intellectuals and poets shared the Arabic proclivity for describing subjects and things according to a balance of opposing characteristics.[71] Hebrew secular verse constantly demonstrated the importance of the juxtaposition of contraries, such as this wine song by the eleventh-century poet Samuel Ibn Nagrila Ha-Nagid from Cordova:

> Take from a fawn the crystal filled with blood
>   Of grapes, as bright as hailstones filled with fire.
> Her lips are a scarlet thread; her kisses, wine;
>   Her mouth and body wear the same perfume.
> Her hands are crystal wands with ruby tips—
>   She tints her fingers with her victim's blood.[72]

Ibn Nagrila juxtaposes opposite qualities intrinsic to wine, that is, that it is cold but warms the body and that it is red but is served in clear crystal. Hence the poem shows that wine is "a paradoxical combination of fire and ice."[73] Descriptive wine poems centered on visual juxtapositions such as this one, and meditative wine poems frequently evoked "contrary sensations of joy and sorrow."[74]

The juxtaposition of opposites constituted a strategy of rhythmic balancing that was crucial to poetic composition in al-Andalus. In his treatise *Kitāb al-Muhādara wal-Mudākara* (Book of Conversation and Deliberation), the Andalusi-Jewish intellectual Moses Ibn Ezra (c. 1055–1138) emphasized rhyme and prosody for the attainment of poetic symmetry: "Como saben poetas y entendidos en prosodia, la equidad de las rimas y su composición [se consiguen] con el arte de la prosodia, que es la balanza de la poesía" [As poets and experts in prosody know, the equity of rhyme and its composition are achieved through the art of prosody, which is the balance of poetry.][75] Rhythmic balance in verse was achieved through contraries and correspondences, such as wine's opposing qualities in Ibn Nagrila's poem, and the poetic strategy of using a word and its homophone.[76] Ibn Ezra further deals with the significance of the balance of opposites in chapters on parallelism and antithesis, where he demonstrates the pervasiveness of these techniques in sacred Hebrew texts and in Arabic writings.[77]

The interrelation of contrasts is also evident in the long tradition of Arabic letters of using sacred language to speak of profane love. This custom suggests that Arab and Andalusi groups regarded ambiguous expression as normative and unexceptional. One example of this tendency is the ambiguity of earthly and divine delights found in Sufism, which frequently associates divine and sensual love. The Qur'ān itself presents the notion of ambiguity in a sura that states that divine revelation consists of both "'firm' or univocal" verses and of "ambiguous" ones.[78]

The conventional value of the equivocal is further shown in the blending and interdependence of female and male principles throughout the history of Islam. For instance, the Sufist Ibn 'Arabī believed that the feminine was linked to, and not separated from, the masculine, an idea that exerted great influence from about the twelfth century on.[79] Ibn 'Arabī further believed that God was more perfectly contemplated in women because, since they were created from men, they embodied two forms of human material rather than only one.[80] Annemarie Schimmel relates that even religious men assumed a female identity in order to approximate more closely the divine: "[P]ious dervishes sometimes dressed up as women in order to acquire the additional outward appearance of being 'God's handmaid.'"[81] These concepts attest to the inextricable relation of female and male elements in Islam, rather than to their inevitable division.

Further examples from secular literature demonstrated the legitimate value of the equivocal, such as the figure of the *ghulamiyat* in Ibn Shuhayd's eleventh-century poetry. Ibn Shuhayd lauded the attractiveness of the *ghulamiyat,* the women slaves who dressed as boys, sang to and entertained men, and ostensibly competed with boys for men's attention.[82] The blending of genders in the transvestite *ghulamiyat* created a third gender, which shows the complexity of gender and sexual desire in al-Andalus, since the desire for the transvestite was not simply categorized by the division of binary opposites of the female and male. Ibn Shuhayd seems to have considered erotic desire and, potentially, sexuality as indefinite, that is, as belonging to neither facile category of the homo- or heterosexual.

Sexual contraries were not always formally delimited in Andalusi poetry and, perhaps, in artists' lives, as shown by the complex forms of sexuality among Andalusi-Arabic women poets. For instance, scholars have long alluded to the bisexuality of one of the most renowned women poets of al-Andalus, an eleventh-century princess from Cordova, Wallāda bint al-Mustakfi, or, as she is commonly known today, Wallāda la Omeya. Judging from her amorous and satirical poetry to the well-known male poet Ibn Zaydūn, some critics have concluded that the two were intimately involved, but that their relationship ended when Zaydūn took up with one of Wallāda's woman slaves. In her scathing, satirical poems Wallāda accused Zaydūn of being a fornicator, a male prostitute, and a "fag": "[P]ues eres marica, puto y fornicador / cornudo, cabrón y ladrón" [You are a fag, a whore, and a fornicator, a cuckold, a jerk, and a thief].[83] But scholars have also pointed to Wallāda's amorous relationship with another woman poet, Muhŷah, the daughter of a fig vendor in Cordova whom Wallāda educated and introduced to court society. Asad AbuKhalil claims that most of Wallāda's poetry to Muhŷah has been lost because of prejudices against their explicitly sexual language.[84] Whether verifiable or not, the speculations about Wallāda's bisexuality are validated by the bitextual traditions of the *muwashshah* and *zajal* and by Arabic epistemological models that recognized the reciprocity of contrasting pairs.

Homoerotic relations between women did indeed exist in medieval Arabic society. One twelfth-century male writer, Sharif al-Idrisi, confirmed erotic relationships between women, whom he called "more intelligent" than other women, while claiming that they could be found in social circles that included "educated and elegant women, . . . scribes, Koran readers, and female scholars."[85] Yet even this account of homoerotic relations between women in medieval Arabic society is insufficient in explaining the bitextual and bisexual qualities of Andalusi poetry, which, from the *muwashshah* and *zajal* to Hamda Banāt Ziyād's ambiguous erotic poem to a nude woman by a river, to Wallāda's verse, to Ibn Shuhayd's ode to a transvestite, suggests a parallel relation between gender and sexual categories that surpasses the contrast of simple binaries. It is not that contemporary critics may easily render these poets and their poetry as either "gay," "straight," or "bisexual," but that the textual and sexual variations that seemingly confound these facile divisions indeed reflect important cultural values about the compatibility and interdependence of contrasts in al-Andalus.

Thus a variety of Arab and Andalusi disciplines required and reinforced the juxtaposition and confluence of contraries in the making of meaning, suggesting the mutual dependence of opposite qualities and things instead of their necessary separation. As we have seen, this cultural principle is particularly reflected in the formation of lyric subjectivity in the *muwashshah* and *zajal*, where contrasting erotic, sexual, and gender depictions show the interdependence of opposites rather than their divide. The poem by Hamda Banāt Ziyād de Guadix further demonstrates ambiguous gender identification in its narrator, thereby allowing for an indeterminate expression of desire for another woman that was culturally codified and ratified. The doubtful gender of Banāt Ziyād's speaker shows an uncertainty about gender that also pervades the *muwashshah* and *zajal*.

Andalusi gender and sexuality in literature and life were not always viewed as inflexibly divided, but as conjoined or intermingling. This refutes Kelley's suggestion that the "domination" of female speech by male poets in the *muwashshah* and *zajal* was by definition an affront to mundane women, since it is more likely that bodily juxtapositions were crucial to the resilient way in which subjectivity, gender, and sexuality were formed in al-Andalus. It may be that modern readers today see in the *jarcha* a long, derisive tradition of linking the female gender to woe and vulnerability, which nowadays has come to constitute an insulting feature of women's gender. Yet poets may have sometimes connected women's gender and suffering in the *jarcha* not to delimit rigidly these mundane women, but to function within a cultural paradigm of subjectivity and gender that required the convergence of dissimilar terms rather than their mutual exclusion.

Andalusi poetry establishes an analogous relation between the textual, sexual, and corporeal through contrasts and the principle of correspondence. The contrasting codes contained in the *muwashshah* and *zajal* represent more than the diverse linguistic production of cultures in contact, the Christian, Jewish, and Islamic. They also demonstrate the compatibility of two opposing erotic codes, the hetero- and the homoerotic, and the elasticity of gender categories of the female and male. Many examples from Andalusi poetry approach gender and sexuality in ways familiar to the postmodern reader because gender, sexual, and linguistic difference is not conceived as a gap that divides their variation, but as an agreement between them. The compatibility of difference within the same subject and in poems by the same writer suggests a rendering of gender, eroticism, and sexuality that is based on the coexistence of contrasts, rather than on their incongruity.

Changes in Late Medieval and Early Modern Lyric

As Andalusi territory and power diminished through the thirteenth century, so did the impact of its poetry wane on the Iberian peninsula. Andalusi poetry remained popular in the kingdom of Granada, as well as in other Arab regions, and it likely affected lyric outside al-Andalus, such as Galician-Portuguese *cantigas,* Occitan verse, and *cancionero* lyric. But as Muslim control and Andalusi poetic influence abated, Romance poetry began to dominate the Iberian peninsula from approximately the thirteenth century on. While an analysis of Iberian lyric's trajectory from al-Andalus to the era of the Catholic Kings is beyond the scope of this chapter, a comparison of the *muwashshah* and late medieval, early modern court lyric shows the extent to which the changed precepts of alterity in poetry paralleled shifts in broader cultural values. Although the poetry of both periods manifested these precepts through corporeal representation, the dominant court poetry in the Christian kingdoms of the late fourteenth, fifteenth, and sixteenth centuries generally no longer reinforced multifaceted subjects and interrelated contrasts and instead strengthened more categorical approaches to people, knowledge, and things.

Many late medieval and early modern noble court poets depicted polarized bodies, as poets themselves became purveyors of the hierarchical values of difference that accompanied the consolidation of social and political power by the Catholic Kings and their successors. The shift in bodily depictions from fluid Andalusi lyric to more delimited, later poetry manifested new cultural ideals about gender and corporeal variation, which are most apparent in two kinds of lyric production: poems to the Virgin in the poetry contests of the *gaya ciencia* and the courtly love poetry in the *cancioneros*, or songbooks, of the fifteenth and sixteenth centuries. While *gaya ciencia* generally refers to Catalan poetry collections and the *cancioneros* denote Castilian poetic anthologies of the fourteenth through sixteenth centuries, they point to similar efforts in Aragon, Castile, and Valencia to employ poetry as a means to promulgate cultural values of the noble or leisure classes.[86]

The area of study and performance known as the *gaya ciencia* started in the fourteenth century in the kingdom of Aragon when nobles and royalty began to institutionalize and promote the poetics of the Provençal troubadours. Authorities established a royal poetry academy where they carried out the formal study of rhythm and meter, and they instituted festivals and poetry contests to determine the best poem in praise of the Virgin.[87] Many of these Marian compositions show how the Virgin changed from a medieval figure who physically aided sinners in times of need to a late medieval icon far removed from ordinary people. The Virgin was omnipresent and accessible in the Middle Ages, but increasingly became a symbol to worship from afar in late medieval and early modern cultural production. This change had important consequences for her role as a paradigm for ordinary women, since she constituted an important model for their gender and behavior in premodern periods.[88] Medieval women were intimately connected to the Virgin because they were supposed to imitate her goodness and beneficent ministrations, which many carried out in their vocations as healers.[89] But in the fifteenth and sixteenth centuries ordinary women no longer resembled Mary, because they were cast as more similar to sinful Eve.

The divide between the Virgin and earthly women shifted the focus of women's emulation from the Virgin's compassionate medieval interventions to her early modern chastity, an ideal that epitomized Mary's now favorable distance, immobility, and inactivity. Her motionlessness is evident in the Marian verses that were compiled in works such as *Les trobes en lahors de la Verge Maria*, a Catalan collection published in Valencia in 1474 as part of the Gay Science. One of its renowned poets, Bernat Fenollar, composed the following verses of praise:

Mare de deu/dels angels alegria
Font de saber/dels apostols maestra
Pilar de fe/dels martres sants deiusa
Flor odorant/deles vergens bandera . . .[90]

[Mother of God/happiness of angels
Fountain of knowledge/teacher of the apostles
Pillar of faith/goddess of the sainted martyrs
Fragrant flower/standard of virgins . . .]

Fenollar's exaltation demonstrates the Virgin's renovated status as a stylized icon to be worshiped and admired rather than a female force to rely on for physical intervention in moments of distress. Instead of portraying her as rescuing believers from dangerous situations, as she did in Alfonso X's *Cantigas de Santa María* or Gonzalo de Berceo's *Milagros de Nuestra Señora,* Fenollar converts the Virgin into a static object, such as a fountain, pillar, and flag or emblem. He makes her worthy for her exemplary, inert attributes rather than her charitable and salutary ministrations.

Fenollar and other poets of the Gay Science dignified the Virgin in an effort to undermine her traditional, medieval likeness to ordinary women and create a gap between them. This coincided with other misogynist strategies by men writers to assail earthly women, such as women's association with sinful Eve by the Valencian physician Jaume Roig. In his antifeminist book in verse, *Spill, o Llibre de les dones* (c. 1460), Roig created separate genealogies for earthly men and women, in which he repeatedly cast women as "the daughters of Eve" ("filles d'Eva") and aligned men with the Virgin through the singular birth of her son, linking them to Mary's positive qualities.[91] He thus created an unbridgeable gap between mundane women and the Virgin. Roig further connected women to sin and sexuality in heightened ways through their bond with Eve, original sin, and childbirth.[92]

Like Fenollar, Roig composed a poem of adoration to the Virgin in *Les trobes en lahors de la Verge Maria* that further reinforced the Virgin's distance from ordinary women. He elevated her and linked her favorably to her son, Jesus Christ, claiming that she reigned with him, seated on his right side ("Ab deu son fill / regnant seu ala dret" [With her son God / reigning on his right]).[93] Roig did not align the Virgin and Jesus in order to demonstrate the affinities between men and women, but to emphasize earthly women's implicit distance from men and sacred women. He suggested that the Virgin was the only female figure worthy of being close to God because she was unique and superior to ordinary women. He thus linked male and female genders for very different reasons than the *muwashshah* and *zajal* poets, who represented ordinary women's voices in nondenigrating ways in the *jarcha* and often connected their song to men's. By the late fourteenth and fifteenth centuries, not only were earthly women linked to Eve more completely than in the past, but the Virgin's connection to God was meant to show her inimitability and distinctiveness. The only role that ordinary women played in the poetry of the Gay Science was that of contrast and deprecation.

In dignifying the Virgin and her son the poets of the Gay Science disseminated cultural values about subjectivity that greatly differed from those of Andalusi lyric. Their devotional poetry contributed to the breach between earthly women and the Virgin, as well as to the gender divide between women and men. The Virgin resided far above earthly women next to God, while mundane women were hostile threats to men in their connection to Eve. The Virgin's poetic elevation had repercussions in earthly women's increased debasement and in their reduced status and roles in late medieval and early modern society. It also was consistent with men's dignification and affirmative, emblematic status as ideal citizens and workers, since they were associated with the Virgin through her son.[94] The denigration of ordinary women and the elevation of the Virgin and men were key components of an early modern gender system that was reinforced by sixteenth-century conduct manuals, such as Juan Luis Vives's *Formación de la mujer cristiana* (translated into Spanish from Latin in 1528). Vives prescribed distinct social roles for men and women in showing that men were active social participants outside the home, while women were to be Christian wives and mothers with hardly a public role. Unlike the complementary alignment of different genders and subjects in the *muwashshah* and *zajal,* early modern poets and other writers often demonstrated and supported more static and hierarchical ideals of gender by casting men and women as unmistakably opposed.

Fifteenth- and sixteenth-century *cancionero* poets in the courtly love tradition also revealed bodily gaps between subjects rather than affinities between them, thus revealing serious changes to the fluid rendering of corporeality in Andalusi lyric. The role of courtly love in *cancionero* poetry marks the culmination of its long medieval presence, from al-Andalus to the poetry of southern France and Catalonia, which critics variously refer to as the poetry of the troubadours and trobairitz, as well as Provençal, Occitan, or langue d'oc poetry. Scholars such as Ramón Menéndez Pidal, María Rosa Menocal, and Roger Boase affirm a lineage of medieval courtly love lyric in different regional and political contexts. Menocal proposes the concept of a medieval "love system" that would incorporate Romance and Arabic love poetry and study them collectively for their general similarities and discrete differences, instead of separating them according to linguistic variation or modern national and regional boundaries.[95] These critics further postulate close links between Andalusi and Romance courtly love verse.[96] For instance, Boase adheres to his thesis of 1977, in which he defined courtly love as "a comprehensive cultural phenomenon . . . which arose in an aristocratic Christian environment exposed to Hispano-Arabic influences."[97] Menocal reinforces this claim in her belief that Andalusi literature and performance were part of the cultural background of medieval troubadour poets such as Guilhem IX, and she views the overlap of Andalusi and Provençal lyric as inevitable, since both were performed orally to music.[98] In her discussion of the close links between Andalusi women's poetry and the lyric production of the trobairitz, Susan Boynton describes the similarities of the eleventh-century exchanges between the Cordovan princess Wallāda and her male lover Ibn Zaydūn and the debate poems, or *tensos*, of Occitan lyric. She believes that the Andalusi poems may have inspired the Occitan debates about a century later.[99] Thus the field of courtly love lyric extends beyond the traditional critical confines of "troubadour" poetry from southern France into an expansive, interconnected medieval network of love poetry.[100]

These scholars highlight the close relation of Arabic and Romance love lyric, and they acknowledge the evident permutations of courtly love poetry through the Middle Ages. Menocal's idea of a medieval love system could be broadened to include the *cancionero* love lyric of the fifteenth and sixteenth centuries, since many *cancionero* poems retain the courtly model of the elevated female beloved and the submissive male troubadour. The use of this paradigm by *cancionero* poets demonstrates a genealogy of sorts in the development of courtly love lyric from al-Andalus to the early modern period, while its changes during different time periods reflect ideological shifts and vicissitudes in prevailing cultural values. Andalusi poetry depicted the relation between the dominating male patron and the subjugated male poet, while *cancionero* verse, like the troubadour poetry before it, replaced the male Andalusi patron with the female beloved. The homoerotic or homosocial relation between two men in Andalusi poetry became in the *cancionero* lyric a heteroerotic relation between lovers. The opening lines of a poem by Lope de Stúñiga (c. 1414–1480) demonstrate this shift in gender:

Señora, grand sinrazón
me fezistes, en buena fe,
condenarme sin porqué.[101]

[My lady, a grave injustice
you committed, in good faith,
by condemning me without reason.]

Following the conventions of courtly lyric, Lope de Stúñiga submits himself to a more powerful woman beloved who harmed him through her captivating love. Despite the evident plurality of topics and depictions in *cancionero* verse, such as the grotesque imagery found in the *Cancionero de obras de burlas,* poets like Lope de Stúñiga, who employed the model of courtly love, usually homogenized their poems according to a heterosexual paradigm and often created clearly delimited subjects.

These poets continued the standard depictions of male Occitan poets, who showed women as objects of desire and men as desiring subjects. While Occitan poetry was mainly formulaic, it also revealed nuances that made representation more complex, such as the fact that clothing sometimes altered women's usual portrayal and rendered them desiring subjects.[102] Many amatory *cancionero* poems did not manifest this variation, as poets largely followed courtly norms of praise in exalting their beloved, such as in this example by an anonymous poet of the *Cancionero general* of 1511:

> Y tras vos, yo, sospirando,
> iva cual nunca os halléis,
> aquella tierra adorando
> do poníades los pies.
> Iva con mucha tristura,
> puestos mis ojos en vos,
> quexando por mi ventura
> del valer y hermosura
> que vos quiso poner Dios.[103]

> [And behind you went I, sighing,
> though you will never know,
> adoring that ground
> where you put your feet.
> I went with great sadness,
> my eyes fixed on you,
> lamenting my fate
> of the worthiness and beauty
> that God granted you.]

This poet follows the norms of courtly love and elevates his beloved, while occupying the subjugated position of his Occitan and Andalusi counterparts as the suffering follower of his lady.

The objectives and significance of *cancionero* courtly love greatly changed with its more narrow parameters, especially in contrast to fluid Andalusi verse. Male *cancionero* poets exalted cherished women according to the heterosexual conventions of the nobility, while Andalusi composers often created the *muwashshah* and *zajal* as petitions for money or other recompense from their patrons. *Cancionero* poets requested compensation as well, but they hoped to receive the woman's love or acceptance, or to suffer or die because of her. Despite the exalting of another person in both the *muwashshah* and the courtly lyric of the *cancionero*, the gender variation of the patron and beloved contributed to the poems' differing cultural worth. Andalusi lyric frequently combined homoeroticism or sexuality with the wish to elicit financial or material gain from a patron. The standard same-sex relation between poet and patron responded to complex relations of cultural power and sexuality in a society that permitted and embraced a variety of sexual and erotic portrayals. In contrast, *cancionero* poetry of courtly love corresponded to more delimited and homogeneous cultural conditions and expectations.

Like the earlier troubadour poetry, the heterosexual bond in *cancioneros* addressed cultural anxieties about gender relations and women's potential dominance over men. Courtly love became a tool that male poets often used to show that women presented a threat and to demonstrate the need for men to regain control over them.[104] Women often dominated in *cancionero* poetry to the extent that their superior beauty, clothing, and behavior caused male narrators to wish to die. This desire may have been part of courtly love's ennobling ideology, but it also fashioned women as so powerful that they could indirectly kill men, even through dreams. This is evidenced in the last lines of a poem by Carvajal or Carvajales, the most prolific poet of the mid-fifteenth-century *Cancionero de Stúñiga*:

> En su fabla, vestir e ser
> non mostrava ser de mandra;
> queriendo su nombre saber,
> respondióme que Casandra;
> yo, con tal nombre oír,
> muy alegre desperté
> e tan solo me fallé,
> que, por Dios, pensé morir.[105]

> [In her speech, dress, and appearance
> she showed she was not from the hills;
> when I wanted to know her name,

she responded to me, Cassandra;
I, upon hearing that name,
very happily awoke
and found myself so alone
that, by God, I wanted to die.]

After praising the woman's beauty and richness of her dress earlier in the poem, Carvajal turns to her lethal effect on the male narrator at the end when he awakes from his dream. The narrator's solitude seems to constitute the final step in his wish to die, but it is indeed because of dreaming of Cassandra that his isolation proves so unpleasant.

Cancionero poets such as Carvajal likely demonstrated women's dominance and the male poet-narrator's subjugation to reveal women's threat and perhaps effect a change in gender relations, from women's perceived command to men's control. Andalusi lyric also sought a shift in power, in which receipt of the patron's gift (whether sexual, financial, or both) would empower the poet and alter the superiority of his patron. Hence, the models of dominance and submission in Andalusi and *cancionero* lyric were alike because they portrayed the strength and command of the patron or beloved while also exposing and subverting them. Yet, despite this similarity, the genders of the patron and beloved responded to different concerns about relations between women and men. Andalusi lyric included women's voices in the *jarcha* and emphasized the similarities of men's and women's song and distress, while courtly love in the *cancioneros* largely enshrined women without giving them a voice, or it often tried to undermine their perceived power.

Thus subjectivity and the body continued to play significant roles in *cancionero* lyric, as they had in Andalusi poetry, but with very different objectives and effects. Fifteenth- and sixteenth-century poets stylized ordinary women as threats to men and in this way contributed to other misogynist tactics of the period, such as women's link to Eve and separation from the Virgin. Rendering women as dangerous, commanding agents bolsters Boase's claim that fifteenth-century court lyric was more abstract than before, since it characterized sacred and secular women by ideals rather than by everyday qualities.[106] In the same way that male writers idealized the Virgin as an icon to be worshiped instead of an aide to be petitioned in emergencies, so did *cancionero* poets glorify earthly women in order to undermine their supposed supremacy.

The abstract language and sterile descriptions in *cancionero* lyric and in Marian poems of the Gay Science not only demonstrated and reinforced prevailing values about gender and relations between women and men, but they also illustrated the progressive change in poetry's social role from oral entertainment to written diversion with the fifteenth-century invention of the printing press. Unlike the oral performance of the *muwashshah* and *zajal* in Andalusi courts, many of the *cancionero* verses were destined for written transmission. Keith Whinnom and Jane Whetnall have shown that the frequent artificiality and complexity of *cancionero* verse likely made it as difficult to understand for fifteenth- and sixteenth-century readers as it can be for modern audiences today.[107] Austere, written poetry lent itself better than oral song to the late medieval and early modern forging of categorical approaches to meaning and knowledge because texts more readily codified descriptions, information, and social values.[108] In general, late medieval and early modern lyric contributed to the making of a noble, courtly lifestyle and ideology, which aided in the efforts toward political, religious, and linguistic consolidation in the sixteenth and seventeenth centuries. Poetic developments during this period further include the introduction from Italy in the fourteenth and fifteenth centuries of genres that were compiled in *cancioneros,* such as the sonnet and the *dolce stil nuovo.* With these genres, nobles such as Íñigo López de Mendoza, the marquis of Santillana, sought to infuse Iberian realms with written poetic models that harkened back to antiquity, in an effort to create a classical "renaissance" on the peninsula that would move beyond medieval oral traditions. Thus, the "rebirth" of such genres in *cancioneros* evidenced the nobility's influence in the institutionalization of poetry as a written, rather than oral, activity, and as a tool for new forms of classification and division about gender and the relations between women and men.

At the same time that the Iberian realms of the Catholic Kings became increasingly dependent upon written textual production, so did courtly love bolster the values of the early modern nation-state, a link that Georges Duby points out in his discussion of medieval French poetry:

> Courtly love proved an extremely effective means of strengthening the State.
> In fact, it was so influential that no study of the progressive rationalization of
> power can afford to ignore it, although at this period it is only documented in
> literary works, often centered on the theme of "fine amours," or refined love.[109]

Although he refers to a different time period and place, Duby's observation about courtly love's role in "the rationalization of power" affirms what would become the complicity of fifteenth- and sixteenth-century poets of courtly love with the values and ideology of the Castilian nation-state. Such rationalization, values, and ideology are clearly articulated in the representation of subjects who ascribe to rigid categories of gender, eroticism, and sexuality. Corporeal difference took on heightened importance as the wide gap between women and men demonstrated women's threat and men's need to control them. In contrast to the early modern courtly model, in which the heterosexual paradigm of the poet and his beloved fortified cultural anxieties about women and their gender, the same-sex courtly model of the dominating patron and the submissive poet from al-Andalus blended homosexuality and eroticism in its rhetorical game. *Cancionero* lyric of courtly love characterized subjects not by their overlap, but by the chasm between them.

Late medieval, early modern courtly love lyric transmitted a new set of cultural ideals about corporeal difference, which was made manifest in the changes to medieval precepts of alterity. A rigid concept of subjectivity extinguished the medieval tenet of heterogeneous subject formation, since men and women were contrasted to stress the separation between them, and not their congruity. With increasing attempts in late medieval and early modern poetry to depict the body as more abstract, gender and sexuality prevailed as categories of corporeal differentiation, and not as porous fields of bodily constitution. This was evident in the *cancioneros*, where ordinary women's nominal superiority was implicitly based on their eroticism, sexuality, and gender, as well as on their tacit link to Eve and contrast to the Virgin. Late medieval, early modern Spanish lyric enacted and reinforced a change in the medieval embrace of contrasts and the negative, since it contributed to the portrayal of women as societal others in need of management and control. It indicated that contrasting subjects and things were not considered crucial for the making of meaning, but were dangerous to the social order.

The changes to the medieval tenets of alterity will become increasingly evident in chapter 3, where the early modern shifts in the medieval *cartas de tijera* (cutting poems) demonstrate prominent cultural values that differed from those of the medieval period. Cutting poems changed from a medieval genre of love, aesthetics, and occasional satire to poems that were employed against *conversos*. Allusions to scissors and other sharp, cutting implements also became ludic motifs in the recreational poetry of early modern nobles.

CHAPTER THREE

The Divided Body

In an anonymous poem from the *Cancionero de Hernando del Castillo* (1483–1511), a Jewish *converso,* a cloth shearer (*tondidor*), is favorably described as a devout Christian who prays and regularly attends mass:

Soys de agarenos [Muhammad]   gran perseguidor
pariente y amigo   delos defensores
de ayunos muy buenos   soys gran causador
soys gran enemigo   de blasfemadores
De forma de juda [Judas]   cerrays vuestra puerta
servis de verdad   a Dios y alos reyes
enla trenidad   teneys fe muy perfecta
poneys mucha dubda   enlas falsas leyes[1]

[Of Muhammad you are   a great persecutor
relative and friend   of the defenders
of very good fasts   you are a great cause
you are a great enemy   of blasphemers
On the way of Judas   you shut your door
you serve in truth   [to] God and the kings
in the trinity   you have most perfect faith
you put much doubt   in false laws]

The last stanza provides the reader with instructions to cut physically the poem in half with scissors between its two hemistichs after reading the poem. The cutting divides formerly whole lines into separate columns, which, when each column is individually read from top to bottom, give an opposite interpretation of the formerly devout convert, who is now transformed into a despicable man, who cannot be trusted to follow the Catholic faith. The directions at the poem's end tell the reader that the truth will be revealed in the middle of the poem ("quenel medio esta la celada / delo cierto" [as the trap is in the middle / of the truth]), or in the cut, wherein lies the truth, that the convert is a man marked by false appearances and a duplicitous interior.

This denigrating Castilian cutting poem, or *carta de tijera*, written at the intersection of the medieval and early modern periods, belongs to a long line of earlier medieval Arabic and Jewish writings that allude to composing with scissors. Medieval scissors writing, whether purely metaphorical or actual, was accomplished by cutting out letters of words in order to create a lacelike, yet legible, effect on a paper or parchment.[2] In an allusion to this decorative result, scholars have referred to Arabic cutting poems as a kind of calligraphy.[3] But the medieval Arabic and Jewish poems were intended for very different purposes than the early modern *cancionero* poem about the cloth cutter, since they dealt with diverse themes such as love and aesthetics.[4] The *cancionero* poem greatly contrasts with its antecedents because, through the cut, it seeks to denigrate the *converso* and show the incompatibility of his two sides.

Medieval cutting poems were integrative; for instance, they praised the paradox that was established in the beauty or meaning of a literally empty page. They reveled in the contrast between the empty space where letters should be and the paper itself. Medieval cutting poems were harmonious in their balance of two varying materials or qualities, such as paper and empty space, or nothingness and meaning. Rather than rejecting difference, which is the unstated goal of the later *cancionero* poem, medieval cutting poems sought the equilibrium of two opposing qualities. Modern scholars have struggled to explain and analyze the significance of these poems, and critical commentary on them has been largely at a standstill since the 1950s and 1960s.[5] Yet, the interdependence of contrasting qualities in the medieval poems suggests that Andalusi alterity was based on the synthesis of variation in a system of cultural values.

The difference between medieval and early modern cutting poems demonstrates and plays out in part the momentous transformations in medieval Iberian society from the multicultural Iberian Middle Ages to the increasing early modern efforts to homogenize the peninsula in the fifteenth century, especially after 1492.[6] More specifically, the distinction between the *cancionero* poem and its medieval antecedents illustrates the change that took place in the forging of medieval alterity with the early modern effort to divide instead of to synthesize contrasting things. The *cancionero* poet ridicules and exposes the convert rather than showing the balance between his two opposing characters. Furthermore, the poet implicitly devises a contrast between the supposedly heretical convert and a model that was so valuable in the early modern period, that of an Old Christian whose identity was constant. This insidious contrast of the normative Christian model and the convert is the basis of the latter's denigration, and of his creation by the poet as "other."

Medieval alterity and cutting poems were strikingly different from early modern otherness and the *cancionero* poem. Medieval Arabic cutting poems, for instance, possessed high aesthetic value, which is not surprising, because poetry was a primary aesthetic mode in Arabic culture, and thus in al-Andalus. 'Abd Allāh al Ansārī al-Qurtubī praised cutting poems for their undeniable beauty:

> Es un calígrafo que adorna a maravilla el papel,
> pues no lo hace con tinta ni con pluma,
> sino con una tijera, que lo deja tan bello
> como el jardín regado por generosa lluvia.
> Recortándolas, da existencia a letras inexistentes:
> maravíllate de una cosa cuyo ser es el no ser.[7]

> [He is a calligrapher who marvelously adorns paper
> because he does it with neither ink nor pen,
> but with scissors, which makes it as lovely
> as a garden watered by generous rain.
> Cutting them out gives existence to nonexistent letters:
> marvel at a thing whose existence does not exist.]

Beauty for this poet is constituted by the paradox that, aesthetically, emptiness, or the nonexistent, is most pleasing. The vacuum created by the missing letters is ironically associated with a beautiful, fertile garden.

The mid-fourteenth-century Andalusi poet Ibn Játima de Almería pinpointed the cutting poems' aesthetic merit in the "nothingness" of their ability to make meaning:

> 1. Ahí te va esta página llena de las quejas de un enamorado
>
>   · · · · · · · · · · · · · · · · ·
>
>   No las ha escrito con aire en vano.
> 2. Pasea tus ojos por mi trazado, y verás
>   una escritura donde la tinta es aire.

3. . . . si quiero escribir un secreto,
   he de hacerlo en la página del aire.[8]

[1. Here, for you, a page full of a sad lover's complaints

   .   .   .   .

   He has not written them in air in vain.
2. Cast your eyes on my design, and you will see
   a composition where ink is air.
3. . . . if I want to write a secret,
   I have to do it on the page of air.]

Ibn Játima suggests that the cutting poem's worth lies in its ability to establish meaning from and with nothing, which he names air. In calling the ink and paper "air," he emphasizes the contrast between the conventional making of meaning with paper, ink, and pen, and the unusual making of meaning with air and scissors.

The aesthetic value of cutting poems that these writers allude to is closely related to the significance of beauty in medieval Muslim culture. Beauty was not intended solely for its own sake, but also for more profound reasons, such as its link to the divine. A popular medieval phrase, still repeated often in contemporary Islamic culture, attests to this powerful connection: "God is beautiful and loves all beauty." Beauty and divinity are crucial elements of textual revelation in the Qur'ān, as it invites readers to contemplate the beauty of the universe "in order to recognize the signs of God's majesty."[9] Beautiful writings and things revealed God in medieval Muslim culture.[10]

Adornment and decoration were important attributes of beauty. In the Qur'ān, adornment is associated with God's embellishment of the universe through his acts of creation, and Muslims rendered God as an artist who created a beautiful universe and a book of sweet and pleasing language.[11] The significance of ornamentation was carried over into secular realms of aesthetic production such as poetry, which was figured as a technical skill, like weaving or the making of necklaces. Writers such as Ibn Hazm de Córdoba in his eleventh-century *Tawq al-hamāma* (*The Dove's Neckring*) often equated the stringing together of words in poems and the threading of beads in necklaces.[12]

The similarity between composing poetry and other skills such as embroidery, weaving, or jewelry making was founded not only on the aesthetic worth that these items produced, but also on the qualities of proportion and harmony that were implicit in their composition and beauty. Medieval writers in Arabic generally considered beauty a subjective proportion that was arrived at through the skillful arrangement of contrasting positive and negative qualities. In his treatise *Risālat al-qiyān*

(*The Epistle on Singing-Girls*), the ninth-century writer al-Jāhiz stated that beauty was constituted by completeness and moderation, and that moderation consisted of the equilibrium of a thing. The idea of balance was crucial to aesthetic value and could result, for instance, as al-Jāhiz mentions, when a man with a small snub nose also possessed a large eye.[13] The twelfth-century writer al-Ghazali thought that the beauty and perfection of written works were found in the harmony and correct organization of words.[14]

Medieval cutting poems were beautiful to Arabic writers because they corresponded to popular ideas about aesthetic value. The harmonious proportion achieved in the juxtaposition of opposites, paper and air, coincides with contemporaneous theories of beauty that elevated positioning and balance over universals of beauty. The eleventh-century literary theorist 'Abd al-Qāhir al-Jurjānī believed that beauty was achieved through contrast, which he called "the affinity of contraries" ("shiddat i'tilāf fī shiddat ikhtilāf").[15] Al-Jāhiz initiated a literary debate genre on contrasts in which he elucidated the attributes and shortcomings of a thing.[16] This genre was further based on the confluence of qualities and their mutability within the same object.[17] Al-Jāhiz and other Arab writers believed that favorable and unfavorable qualities in people and things were variable and changing.

The medieval belief in the proportionality and balance of opposite qualities is a main criterion of beauty, and it further supports the contentions of poets of cutting poems in Arabic who laud the aesthetic value of these works. Paper and air are not competitive in cutting poems, but instead they complement one another to form a unity of opposites. In contrast, the early modern *cancionero* poem demonstrates a change in the relationship of proportions, since its author does not attempt to integrate the convert's two parts, but rather tries to inform the reader about his true, deceptive nature. The *cancionero* poem contrasts with another poem from the *Cancionero general de Hernando del Castillo,* written by the count of Paredes, in which he attacks a *converso* writer, Juan Poeta (Juan of Valladolid), for having three names:

De como vos llamaran
dexares fama y renombre
no seyendo mas dun ombre
cada qual de ellas su nombre
juan simuel [Samuel] y reduan [an Arabic name]
Moro por no ser muerto
[cr]istiano por mas valer
pero judio es lo cierto
a lo que puedo saber[18]

[Depending on what they call you
you would leave fame and renown
not being more than one man
each one of these is your name:
John, Samuel, and Reduan
a Moor for not being dead
a Christian for being more worthy
but a Jew is the most certain
as far as I can know]

Unlike the anonymous poet of the cutting poem, Paredes acknowledges the existence of Juan Poeta's three simultaneous identities, although his tone is derogatory.[19] The cutting poem's author, on the other hand, seeks to separate the cloth shearer's identities textually and physically with scissors. Dividing the cutting poem in this way is concomitant to the disjuncture between the cloth shearer's false and true bodies, one that is loyal and the other disloyal to the Christian faith. Instead of trying to show the proportional composition of the cloth shearer's good and bad qualities, the cutting poem casts even his positive aspects as duplicitous and ultimately harmful in their deceit.

Medieval Muslim thought and writing also taught that beauty could be deceptive, suggesting that its harmonious organization of contrasting qualities was at times believed to be false.[20] But, in general, Muslim thought diverged from the dismissive rhetoric that permeates the later *cancionero* poem because it was more integrative than exclusive. This focus on integration is evident in medieval Arabic cutting poems, which further differ from the succeeding early modern *cancionero* poems because they illustrate and embody connection. Some of them emphasize the poem's ability to link individuals who are held apart, such as the poet and his lover. For example, when Ibn Játima de Almería found himself pained and saddened by separation from his lover, he wrote him poems that he composed with scissors:

Cuando mi deseo me llenó de tristeza, escribí
el secreto de mi amor bordándolo con la tijera,
pues, si hubiera querido escribirlo de otro modo,
el cálamo habría ardido entre mis manos.[21]

[When my desire filled me with sadness, I wrote
the secret of my love, embroidering it with the scissors,

because if I had wanted to write it another way,
the pen would have burned in my hands.]

The excess of his sadness and desire is such that conventional writing would have burned his pen. Writing with metal scissors is Ibn Játima's only solution to stem his emotions, and the excesses of the body stand in paradoxical contrast to the cutting away or absence of letters in the cutting poem. When Ibn Játima calls the ink and paper "air" in the examples given earlier, he suggests that the void or negative space caused by the physical separation from his lover is akin to "the secret of his love" and to the poem's empty page. The cutting poem evidently links Ibn Játima and his lover in ways that an everyday poem does not.

The significance of cutting poems is always dependent upon their implicit contrast to ordinary poems and poetic composition, although they may have been considered more similar than different. For the Arabic noun for poetry, *qarīd*, which excludes the meter *rajaz*, whose lines are not bipartite, belongs to the same lexical family as the verb "to cut," *qarada*.[22] This same verb is used to mean "to write poetry" or "to make verses" in the phrase *qarada al-shi'ra*. The lexical root *qrd* suggests that bipartite Arabic poetry lends itself to cutting, because its twofold structure invites separation. The shared derivation and meanings of *qarīd* and *qarada* explain the prevalent relation in medieval Arabic writing of poetry and cutting, which is so clearly imitated in the division of the *cancionero* poem's two hemistichs. The Arabic for scissors, *maqārīd*, also comes from the same family root, *qrd*, which further indicates that ordinary writing in poetry and scissors writing through cutting constitute two sides of the same coin, because they both transmit messages based on language, one by removing words and the other by creating them. As makers of meaning, writing and cutting are homologous activities, but in their sameness they are also clearly different. Medieval cutting writers hold this paradox as true in the Middle Ages, while the early modern *cancionero* poem evidences contempt for it. The *cancionero* poem demonstrates the early modern change in the relationship of proportions, whereby two contrasting qualities must stand at odds instead of being perceived as compatible. It also marks the transformation of medieval alterity, showing that differences within things, such as the *converso*'s "split personality," as Ernest Grey calls it, are no longer compatible, but are instead injurious and hypocritical.

This is a far cry from medieval Arabic cutting poems and from their medieval Jewish counterparts. For Jewish examples of cutting poems also demonstrate the contingency of difference, that is, the dependence of different things not for the expulsion of one element, but for their mutual existence. The fourteenth-century writer

Sem Tob de Carrión wrote two satirical cutting works that clearly demonstrate, even in their ironic intent, that the paradoxical absence of words produces meaning. Sem Tob was less consistent than Muslim writers in their unequivocal exhorting of the cutting genre, since he used it in an ironic way. For instance, in the *Proverbios morales,* he adopted the cutting poem to make fun of an acquaintance, an *astroso* (perhaps an irritating objector in debates), whom he scorned.[23] Sem Tob sent this know-it-all a cutting poem indicating that he should have been able to understand the empty page if he was, indeed, as intelligent as he thought himself to be.[24] Sem Tob's little joke tries to deride the *astroso*'s supposed cleverness through the nonexistence of signs, that is, the letters of words. Ironically, however, the letters transmit a great deal of information to their receiver even in their absence, either because their outline can be read, or because the lack of letters would have made Sem Tob's ridicule evident to the fourteenth-century reader.

Despite his satiric intent, in another work Sem Tob shows that scissors constitute the perfect paradox, since they can be whole and fragmented with their two blades held together and apart. He comments on their ironic unity in his Hebrew *maqāmā* debate between a pen and scissors, the *Milhemet ha-'Et ve-ha-Mispāraim* (*Debate between the Pen and the Scissors*), calling the scissors superior to the pen because they embody separation and unity in their very makeup: "The scissors desire greatly to stand united, and nothing that divides them shall be between them. / In order to make their two one, they divide in two any one that comes between them."[25] Cutting poems are analogous to the ironic identity of scissors, since they are both complete and divided in and of themselves. Meaning does not derive from words, but from the cut, or, in other words, from the negative absence of words.

Cutting poems are like scissors because they are paradoxically harmonious and divided. In his eleventh-century treatise on rhetoric, Mose Ibn Ezra alludes to the curious character of poems in general when he quotes al-Husrī's linking of poems and letters:

> Dijo otro [al-Husrī]: "El poema ha de ser como una carta cuyos extremos son armoniosos, pero si te guardas de esto o cosa semejante, concordarán los primeros y segundos hemistiquios de tu poema y enlazarán sus metáforas con los fines (propuestos)."[26]

> [Al-Husrī said: "The poem has to be like a letter whose extremes are harmonious. But if you keep this or a similar thing in mind, the first and second hemistichs of your poem will agree, and will link their metaphors with the objectives."]

In the same way that letters joined two extremes, that is, the sender and recipient, so could a poem link its metaphors to its objectives, and its hemistichs to one another. The scissors embody the simultaneous conjoining and dividing of two distinct parts.

The early modern *cancionero* poem about the cloth shearer is also emblematic of Sem Tob's claims about the nature of scissors in his *maqāmā*, for the *cancionero* poem shows that the convert is a whole man, who consists of two parts like the scissors. In that poem, the scissors enact on the page the very violence or incompatibility that the convert represents. As the scissors become unified, they divide that which lies in their path, revealing the "truth" about the convert. Unlike the scissors, once the page has been separated, it can never be whole again, in the same way that the convert cannot be read as a devout Catholic after his "true" *converso* identity has been revealed.

But, unlike the early modern poet who wishes to maintain the convert's two parts divided, the fourteenth-century writer Sem Tob concurs with Ibn Ezra and al-Husrī about the integral and interdependent nature of poetic composition. He often demonstrates in his writings that contrasting qualities are mutable and reversible, and that they ironically constitute wholeness. Scholars such as Jacques Joset, T. A. Perry, Clark Colahan, and Alfred Rodríguez show the extent to which Sem Tob's ideas in the *Proverbios morales* are based on mutability, reversibility, opposition, and balance. Like his Arab and Andalusi counterparts and predecessors, Sem Tob believed that all things consisted of a constant balancing and rebalancing of contrasting qualities. He thought that things were different in and of themselves because they were never the same. Sem Tob further maintained that all things were formed by opposites, such as good and bad, and ugly and pretty, which were frequently reversible. Since every thing was mutable, no thing was of an absolute nature.[27] Perry believes that Sem Tob imagined a universe in which difference was largely constituted by distinctions between the sacred and earthly realms. He thought that the ordinary world was other when it was contrasted with the divine sphere of absolutes: "For Santob the radical Other is not God but *mundo*."[28] Although the ordinary world constituted the manifestation of the divine order, it was never perfect and always infinitely changing.

One of Sem Tob's most compelling tenets entails the reversing of values, whereby things have opposite, changing worth such as good and bad, or ugly and beautiful.[29] Scissors and cutting writing fully represent this duality, since scissors are one when their blades stand together and two when the blades are separated. The early modern *cancionero* poem illustrates this belief as well, since the *converso* seems to be both a Christian and a heretic. The reversing of value in Sem Tob's work, and the way in which the later *cancionero* poet enacts it in his poem, suggest a connection to or knowledge of a technical device used by al-Harizi in a *maqama* called "La carta de doble lectura." In that work, al-Harizi provides a proverb that highly praises a prince.

But in reading the passage backwards, its meaning is reversed, and the proverb's message becomes one of harsh vilification:

> O príncipe, contigo está la honradez
> > y no hay en ti doblez;
> la benevolencia está contigo.
> > Instrucción sin impiedad puso Dios en ti,
> porque tú, en verdad, eres encanto sin oprobio.[30]

> [O Prince, honesty is with you
> > and there is not duplicity in you;
> benevolence is with you.
> > Instruction without impiety God put in you,
> because you, in truth, are enchantment without opprobrium.]

When read backward, these verses relate an opposing view of this righteous man:

> En ti se encuentra la vileza,
> > toda maldad en ti habita;
> no hay en ti honradez, príncipe.
> > Oprobio sin encanto,
> porque la impiedad sin instrucción puso en ti Dios.[31]

> [In you vileness is found,
> > all evil lives in you;
> honesty is not in you, Prince.
> > Opprobrium without enchantment,
> because impiety without instruction God put in you.]

The striking device of opposites is used very differently in this *maqāmā* and the *cancionero* poem. For al-Harizi suggests that the man's identity consists of the two contrasting parts, while the *cancionero* poet tries to persuade the reader that the convert has a truly heretical identity. Al-Harizi's method accepts the double, reverse way in which the prince may be interpreted, but the *cancionero* poet tries to dissociate the cloth shearer from a favorable, Christian identity.

The *cancionero*'s early modern approach to individual identity differs from that of medieval writers. Indeed, for Sem Tob, subjectivity is formed through an attempt to integrate and balance inevitable dualities within oneself. According to Jacques Joset, scissors perfectly represent this fashioning of identity: "Cette quête de l'identité et de l'adéquation à soi-même et au monde est admirablement symbolisée par les ciseaux" [This quest for identity and for the harmony of oneself and the world is admirably symbolized by scissors].[32] Sem Tob corroborates Joset's observation in a tribute to scissors in the *Proverbios morales,* where he claims that scissors are the ideal example of brotherhood:

> [P]arten al que las parte, e non por se vengan,
> sinon con gran talante que an de se legar (juntar).[33]

> [They divide what divides them, and not to take revenge,
> but with great desire to unite].

In making their two parts whole, the scissors inevitably divide whatever comes between their blades and continue the unwavering course of unification and division that characterizes all things.

Sem Tob makes manifest this back-and-forth reversing of value in both the *Proverbios morales* and the *maqāmā* debate between the pen and scissors. The pen and scissors argue about which object would make for a better, more eloquent intercessor between a writer and a page or parchment. The scissors are accused of violent division in the pulling apart of their blades, and in the destruction of the page through their cuts, while the pen proposes that its activity is whole and generative. At one point the scissors retort to the quill pen that it forgets that it, too, is divided, apparently referring to its separated point where it extracts ink from the inkwell:

> Unless this
> is done [the splitting of the point] you cannot write
> a word. Not until you have
> been divided, and then your form is comparable to ours
> [the scissors'].
> In the pride of your heart you forget on whom you
> rely,
> and so you speak in error and find fault with a
> writing
> of perfect beauty.[34]

The pen relies on the same principle that characterizes the scissors, that of division. Despite the fact that the pen ultimately wins the debate and is deemed the superior writing instrument, Sem Tob curiously states that he completes the entire treatise using the cutting method.[35] While this declaration is certainly meant to be entertaining and funny, it also bears a more serious level of meaning with regard to textuality and writing practice. The supposedly definitive excellence of the quill is called into question in the satiric debate by Sem Tob's announcement, and the reader is left to ponder the reliability of the pen's hypothetical predominance. Sem Tob's use of pen and scissors writing depends on the context of their use. Arab and Andalusi poets of the cutting genre such as Ibn Játima de Almería demonstrated the same belief. Ibn Játima declared that his pen would have burned had he used it to write a conventional letter, so he opts for metal scissors instead.[36]

John Zemke believes that Sem Tob's debate is "a satire of the theme of appointed times and places."[37] However, the debate is not merely ironic and entertaining, since it invokes constantly opposing arguments for and against the same thing, which provide the work with an important continuity. Through his satire, Sem Tob demonstrates his own ingenuity and skill at manipulating arguments, altering them according to their context within the debate.[38]

Furthermore, Sem Tob's rendering of the value of scissors writing is not as derisive as it may appear, for he indicates throughout the debate that pen and scissors are a contrasting pair that carry out the same tasks. They both alter the paper or parchment, which he figures as the customary tilling of a valley.[39] Also, they each create harmony by making two things one. The pen joins two activities by simultaneously reading the writer's thoughts and transcribing them, while the scissors are better than the pen because they embody separation and unity.[40] Although Sem Tob's declaration in the debate is probably tongue-in-cheek, like his homage to scissors in the *Proverbios morales,* it also addresses the interdependence of likeness and difference that characterizes medieval alterity. Sem Tob acknowledges this necessary association in the contrasting pair of pen and scissors.

Nowhere is this link between likeness and difference more evident than in the Hebrew etymologies of the verb "to write" (*safar*) and the noun "scissors" (*mispāraim*), which both derive from the same root, *spr.*[41] This remarkable connection dissolves the hypothetically rigid separation between scissors and pen composition and demonstrates that scissors and pen writing are not unconnected activities, but are profoundly interrelated. Ordinary and cutting writing are different and the same. Like conventional poems, cutting poems can be beautiful and pleasing. They also can be emblematic of the division of lovers, who figuratively become whole through the cutting poem.

The early modern cutting poem in the *cancionero* brings with it a change in medieval alterity, whereby once something is viewed as duplicitous it can never be whole again. The cutting poems, along with the attempt to establish hierarchies among subjects in late medieval, early modern Iberia demonstrate that writing and art interrelate with society, for cutting poems both play out and encourage prevailing cultural values about difference. Cutting poems show that texts may simultaneously generate ideas about variation and confirm popular ones. The *cancionero* poem about the convert illustrates the fact that the cutting poem becomes a tool of marginalization for describing people pejoratively as heretics or as racial and religious inferiors. The poem's presumably Christian or *converso* author appropriates the medieval Arab and Andalusi tradition of scissors writing and transforms it into a mechanism of vilification against Jewish converts to Christianity.

Divergence and Diversion

In addition to contributing to the denigration of others, cutting poems conform to the shape of early modern society in another way. They divert from their medieval predecessors, since sixteenth- and seventeenth-century poets use the imagery related to cutting in jocular riddles and enigmas of diversion that aim to entertain noble and aristocratic audiences. These poems often connect sharp instruments, including pens, scissors, knives, or swords, to human communication, such as writing or speech. For instance, in the following riddle, the physician and poet Cristóbal Pérez de Herrera (b. 1558) plays with the triple meaning of *hoja* as a leaf, a page in a book, and the blade of a sword:

De árbol, de libro, de espada
te sirvo con eminencia;
hago de árbol tu morada;
de libro te enseño ciencia,
y esotra es defensa honrada.[42]

[With a tree, a book, a sword
I serve you with eminence;
I make from the tree your dwelling;
from the book I teach you science,
and the other one is an honored defense.]

Pérez de Herrera goes on to explain the exact connection between the three meanings, claiming that in their differences they serve human beings well: leaves and branches are used to build huts in the country, books indoctrinate and teach readers, and the sword always defends one's honor.[43] Hence the diversity of meaning is reduced to a singular merit, that of the *hoja*'s tripartite benefit to humankind, and the three meanings further underscore significant values of the upper classes, which are unfettered country life, learning, and honor. Pérez de Herrera's poem demonstrates two ways in which early modern riddles changed the value of medieval cutting poems. First, riddles and enigmas largely seem intended to be read as capricious diversions by erudite audiences, and, second, instead of allowing contrary meanings to exist as such, his enigmatic poem controls diversion by rendering it singular in its value to human beings.

The early modern riddles and enigmas emphasize the antithesis of contraries over their complementarity, such as in an enigma about scissors by Pérez de Herrera:

> Juntas vi presas estar
> dos hermanas vizcaínas
> que de agudas y ladinas
> se acostumbran maltratar
> como suelen las vecinas.[44]

> [Together I saw captured
> two Vizcayan sisters
> who by sharpness and cunning
> are used to maltreating one another
> as neighbors are in the habit of doing.]

Difference in the scissors is the two shears that are figured in the poem as two women neighbors who only come together to argue and fight. The contrary women or blades do not complement one another, but, instead, they stand in divided counterposition and unite with one another in an antagonistic way.

These early modern riddles and enigmas alter the medieval significance of diversion and literary pleasure, since, unlike medieval cutting poems, they create indivisible oppositions between contrary things, and they demonstrate that early modern diversion often became valued for its own sake. In contrast to this understanding of early modern amusement, medieval diversion and recreation always had a salutary function to improve the reader's well-being. Medieval literature could improve one's frame of mind, or put a reader or listener in a good mood because *ludus* (play), *delectatio* (pleasure), and *recreatio* (recreation) had important corporeal effects. Significantly, medieval theories of amusement and recreation stressed entertainment's ethical component, asserting that recreation was propitious in moderation. They held that entertainment enlivened the spirit and "re-created" the body so that an individual could dutifully continue to carry out everyday work and tasks.[45]

However, by the sixteenth and seventeenth centuries, literature often lost its salutary, medieval value. Authors largely composed funny or clever riddles and witty word games to reinforce the intellectual superiority of their creator, and early modern riddles and enigmas chiefly became instruments of amusement and diversion for the leisure classes. At the crossroads of the differing values of medieval and early modern recreational literature, Glending Olson shows, late medieval, fourteenth-century entertainment needed to justify itself, and thereby exposed the cultural discomfort of that transition in values:

> Recreational and hygienic ideas reveal both a tolerance of the purely entertaining, one based on the conviction that pleasure promotes well-being, and at the same time a feeling that such experience cannot stand by itself, that without constant reassertion of its acknowledged values and limits vacation becomes too much like truancy.[46]

Olson demonstrates that the incongruity between enjoyment and the need to justify enjoyment became most apparent in the later fourteenth century, mainly due to an increasingly secularized society. Eventually, pleasure in early modern fiction was deemed worthy without the need to defend its recreational value.[47] Olson shows that the three different stages of recreational literature in the medieval and early modern periods evidenced varying cultural and historical worth. Early modern entertaining fiction lost the medieval requirement to "re-create" or rejuvenate a reader or listener, and amusement came to be esteemed for its own sake. Early modern literature became hermetic in its value, unlike the medieval works that affected readers in a salutary and ethical way.

This alteration in the cultural significance of cutting poems indicates a profound change in the merit of literature. The medieval examples demonstrate the interdependence of contrasts, a value embedded in medieval alterity, whereas sixteenth- and seventeenth-century riddles and enigmas highlight the wittiness of composition and the cleverness of their composer, revealing the cultural values that underlie early modern recreation. Riddles show in general the allegorical approach to matter and meaning that so characterized the medieval period, since "the dark speech of the riddle veils, even as it describes precisely, a familiar object."[48] In the medieval period, the riddle's allegorical capacity to simultaneously reveal and conceal instantiated the legitimate, complementary worth of the *via negativa* and the *via affirmativa*.

By the seventeenth century this cultural value changed as riddles became appreciated for their entertainment value as indicators of a noble's wit.

The formerly legitimate epistemological and ontological worth of the negative was reduced in part in early modern society to its ludic appeal. The change from the medieval restorative function of *recreatio* to the aggrandizement of the singular, early modern literary work and author coincided with the changing organization of Iberian society. The rise of the nobility, extended bourgeois leisure time, progressive unemployment, and increased early modern literary production brought about fundamental shifts in the relations between author, text, and reader.[49] Cristóbal Pérez de Herrera exemplified these developments, since he was a member of the noble elite that set policy and determined the social order. He was directly involved in the establishment of medical and social administration, as evidenced by his service as a *proto-médico* for the military wards of the Armada.[50] He participated in many naval battles in that capacity, served as a doctor to Felipe III (1598–1621), and wrote extensively on medical matters.

Pérez de Herrera also concerned himself with the social issues of his time in founding the first shelter for the poor (*casa de albergues*) in Madrid. He wrote treatises on societal conditions, such as *Discurso de la forma y traza cómo se pudieron remediar algunos pecados y desórdenes* (Discourse on the form and design of how some sins and disorders could be remedied) (Madrid, 1598), and *Remedios para el bien de la salud del cuerpo de la república* (Remedies for the good of the health of the body of the republic) (Madrid, 1598). He actively participated in the organization of society, as demonstrated by the connection these two treatises make between church, state, and the social order. The first treatise links sin and disorder, and the second connects the republic with health, and human anatomy, suggesting an intimate relation between medicine and social well-being. Treatises such as these on the state, social disorder, and the poor reflect the interests of the ruling classes in the establishment of social control and in the creation of an ordered society. Pérez de Herrera was an important member of a ruling class for whom recreational literature also played a significant role as part of a set of class-bound values that signaled the author's wit and intelligence. Early modern riddles and enigmas lacked the instructive or ethical quality that so significantly characterized the salutary effects of medieval amusement and recreation.

It is not that the social conditions of medieval cutting poems were utterly contrary to those of a writer such as Pérez de Herrera. In fact, Arab and Andalusi poets often were affiliated with courts that highly regarded entertaining and recreational composition, and frequently they were connected to patrons who possessed sufficient leisure time to delight in poetic recital. Even the rebellious twelfth-century poet al-Rusāfī (d. 1177), who disdained the decadence of courtly life, earned a partial living as a poet for wealthy patrons.[51] Moreover, enigmas and riddles were included in the compositions of Andalusi and Arab writers such as Ibn Játima, suggesting the prominence of the same amusing, ludic quality in medieval verse and in early modern riddles.[52]

Despite these similarities, the sixteenth- and seventeenth-century riddles about cutting differed from many medieval examples because they lacked the two elements that characterized the older poems: the complementary nature of contraries and the salutary, ethical feature of recreational literature. Early modern riddles and enigmas lost the versatility of medieval cutting poems, as they focused on pleasurable, entertaining literature that was esteemed, in effect, for its failure to connect to the ordinary world. Gone was the intimate relation between text and body that so significantly characterized medieval cutting poems and that enacted and made palpable the medieval worth of contingency and variation.

Cutting poems changed from a medieval verse that lauded beauty, linked lovers, and satirically commented on the nature of writing to an early modern one that sought to denigrate new Christians and dignify the wit of noble poets. These vicissitudes further demonstrate the transformation of cutting poems' ontological ramifications, that is, the transformation of cultural beliefs related to corporeal and textual alterity. Pérez de Herrera's riddles and enigmas represent an effort to disconnect early modern cutting poems from the contingent relations between body and text that were so apparent in the previous medieval examples. Unlike many medieval cutting poems, Pérez de Herrera creates a stylized cutting model with little connection to the everyday realm.

The early modern *cancionero* poem about the cloth shearer realizes more tangible links between text and body because the convert's deceptive identity constitutes both an ontological and a textual warning about the meaning and value of Iberian subjects. But it clearly marks a change from the medieval period in the ontological value attributed to certain kinds of bodies. For the *cancionero* poem implies that undesirable bodies should be marginalized and eliminated, and it suggests that the existence of others is no longer necessary in order to measure social norms.

In contrast, medieval Muslim and Jewish writers demonstrated the need for the existence of a variety of characteristics, subjects, and things in order to comprehend and make meaning in the world. The early modern cutting poem about the cloth shearer bolsters the predominant political and social climate in late-fifteenth- and sixteenth-century Iberia, which increasingly called for the elimination of people who did not correspond to prescribed social models. Modern alterity progressively became based on the separation of things rather than on their mutual dependence.

This modification in the principles of medieval alterity becomes evident in the exploration of medical concepts of the body in chapter 4. Medieval medical writers often did not depict human bodies with regard to the divisions between them, but according to their relative similarities. However, sixteenth-century medical treatises reveal a change in this corporeal principle, as physicians began to stress the gaps between certain kinds of bodies, such as men's and women's, rather than their likeness.

CHAPTER FOUR

The Medical Body

Iberian physicians and healers composed an array of medical literature throughout the Middle Ages. Arabic medicine, in particular, was renowned for its sophisticated concepts about well-being and the body, as evidenced by the medical encyclopedists ar-Rāzī (Rhazes; d. 925) and Ibn Sīnā (Avicenna; d. 1037), the compendium on surgery by Abu l-Qāsim Halaf b. 'Abbas az-Zahrāwī (Abulcasis; d. after 1009), and the medical works of Ibn Rusd (Averroes; d. 1198).[1] These theorists and practitioners disseminated, explicated, and enhanced the ancient medical ideas of Aristotle, Hippocrates, and Galen. Translation projects throughout Europe in the eleventh, twelfth, and thirteenth centuries in cities such as Monte Cassino, Salerno, and Toledo made Latin and vernacular translations and commentaries available to medieval Christian regions. Ancient and Arabic ideas and commentaries were fundamental to the development of medieval medicine and often were transmitted to physicians in the West with the rise of university medical faculties in the thirteenth century.[2]

The broad dissemination of ancient and Arabic medical traditions in the late medieval period made available to many regions a wide range of information about the human body, including concepts on gender and sexuality. Late medieval Iberian treatises reveal a significant interest in these topics, because gender and sexuality were intimately connected to well-being. Physicians believed that coitus constituted one of the most efficacious means for expelling excess seed, which when retained in the body could cause a number of illnesses and conditions that were dangerous to peoples' well-being. In order to avoid them, medical writers related information about a variety of topics on sexuality and gender, which included men's and women's sexual desire, coital positions, and menstruation. Sex and gender continued to be important salutary concerns in the sixteenth and seventeenth centuries, although early modern physicians often theorized about and described them differently than their medieval predecessors. A number of medieval treatises supported the tenets of medieval alterity in their depictions of gender and sexuality, while early modern treatises often evidenced their demise.

Medieval treatises often demonstrated more pliable depictions of sex and gender because medieval writers sometimes viewed the body as more fluid than did early modern physicians. Both medieval and early modern medicine were generally based on malleable ideas of corporeal well-being according to complexion and humoral theories. These concepts went hand in hand with permeable sex and gender, although early modern medical writers demonstrated increasingly rigid corporeal ideas, as well as shifts in concepts of well-being.

Medieval well-being was constituted by ideals of corporeal balance that were developed most notably by Galen in the second century C.E. and elaborated extensively in the Middle Ages. Physicians used these concepts to diagnose and treat ailing patients, since they believed that illness was generally caused by a bodily imbalance of the contrasting qualities of wet and dry, and heat and cold. The physician's main task was to equalize this disproportion, which was achieved through the efficacious emission of bodily substances known as the four humors: cholera (red or yellow bile), phlegm, black bile, and blood.[3] Ancient and medieval gynecological tracts also pointed to the menses as a further kind of corporeal elimination that seriously affected women's health.[4] Corporeal evacuation was one of the most important processes among the nonnaturals, that is, the six categories of elements external to the body that could reestablish its balance: air, exercise and rest, sleep and wake, food and drink, repletion and excretion, and passions and emotions.[5] Physicians and healers often prescribed remedies from the nonnaturals in order to restore a client's health.

Medieval medical writers believed that individuals normally tended toward a distinct composition of the four qualities hot, cold, moist, and dry, which coincided with a system of four humors (red or yellow bile, phlegm, black bile, blood), four elements (fire, earth, water, air), and four temperaments (choleric, melancholic, phlegmatic, sanguine). A person's predominant complexion and humor indicated the preponderance of certain elements and temperaments. Thus, if yellow bile prevailed in the body, it brought about a choleric disposition because of its relation to fire, which was hot and dry. Black bile caused a melancholy disposition due to its connection to earth, which was dry and cold. Water dominated in phlegm and was cold and moist, thereby producing a phlegmatic temperament. And, finally, air dominated in blood, which caused a sanguine temperament because it was moist and warm.[6] Physicians believed that an unbalanced composition created bodily illness, which was diagnosed and treated according to the equilibrium of qualities and humors.

Complexion and humoral theories thus provided medieval medicine and society with a system for determining character and personality traits and individual disposition. They also reinforced general stereotypes about diverse groups, which were found in medical literature and other disciplines. For instance, Galen's discussion of the differing complexions of Ethiopians and Scythians mirrored Ptolemy's explanation of the effects of geographical variance in his works on astrology.[7] Medieval complexion theory also offered specific ways to differentiate the female and male genders, claiming that they varied according to qualities. Women's cold and moist constitution often associated them with phlegm, the cold and damp humor, and at least two Latin treatises, the *Liber minor de coitu* and the *De curis mulierum,* identified women with phlegmatic men, who were unusually cold and damp.[8] In contrast, men generally were hot and dry, and the heat in their bodies allowed them to produce more semen or seed than women, a distinction that linked men to activity and women to idleness.[9]

Genitalia and anatomy accompanied complexion theory as sites of gender differentiation in the Middle Ages, although medical writers disagreed about the meaning of men and women's variation. The uterus, or *matrix,* was women's determining organ, and the penis or *virga (verga)* constituted men's. Medical authors concurred that men's genitalia were external and women's internal; although some believed this demonstrated gender opposition, others claimed it showed the genders were virtually equivalent and only differently organized. These two interpretations coexisted in the medieval period.[10] Medical treatises also pointed to facial hair as a marker of gender differentiation and associated its production with men's hotter temperament. Beards were a direct result of the emission of corporeal superfluities through the pores, excesses that women discharged in menstruation. When women did not menstruate properly they were known to grow small beards, as evidenced by facial hair on elderly women. Thus the development of hair on the body depended upon corporeal heat, the principal component of gender differentiation in the medieval period.[11] Treatises on physiognomy rounded out the criteria used in gender variation and held that physical characteristics transmitted information about individual disposition and personality traits.[12]

Discussions about gender in medieval medical treatises often evidence a variety of bodily configurations beyond the simple binary of male and female. For instance, medical writers discuss masculine females, feminine males, and hermaphrodites.

The elasticity of complexion theory permitted such vicissitude, since its principles were founded less on absolutes than on varying individual conditions and circumstances. For example, the passage of time altered corporeal complexion during life cycles that included adolescence, adulthood, and old age. And while most theorists agreed on men and women's bodily tendencies, they also widely acknowledged individual variation; some women and men were hotter or colder than members of their opposite genders.[13] Despite the flexibility of complexion theory and the middle terms of gender that were recognized by many medical writers, gendered bodies commonly were codified in medieval discourse according to the normative binary of the female and male. Joan Cadden believes that authors from disciplines within and beyond medicine and natural philosophy "extended and abstracted" the two-term model, suggesting that they intensified the connection between feminine and masculine disposition and comportment, and physiology and anatomy. Instead of reinforcing an expansive order of multiple terms of gender, writers often used the dual model to delimit so-called womanly men and manly women within the narrow range of the female and male. Yet, at the same time, Cadden shows that the two terms exposed the extent to which a plethora of bodies did not fit into the binary system.[14]

The varied concepts of gender that medical treatises conveyed overlapped with discussions of human sexuality. The norm of masculine and feminine carried over to the preponderance of normative heterosexuality in medieval discourse. It is well known that medieval people did not divide sexual behavior and identity into discrete categories of the hetero- and homosexual, although medical writers were vocal about a range of topics concerning sex and sexuality.[15] Cadden demonstrates the noted teleological link between heterosexual coitus, reproduction, family, and familial ties.[16] Yet, at the same time that medieval physicians reinforced the connection between coitus and human production, they also recognized the necessary, salutary benefits of sex for the maintaining of well-being. Sex constituted one of the nonnaturals, since many medical writers considered it crucial to the elimination of dangerous excess seed. As prescribed by Galen in works such as *On the Affected Parts*, moderate heterosexual coitus could aid the body in avoiding illness caused by seed retention. Immoderate use of the nonnaturals, however, had detrimental corporeal effects.[17]

Men and women's pleasure was often taken into account in discussions of coitus and sexuality, particularly as it related to reproduction. Medical writers generally agreed that men's pleasure was connected to the emission of seed, which formed part of the generative process and served a salutary purpose. However, they were less unanimous about the role of women's pleasure in reproduction, since some physicians relied on Aristotelian reservations about the effect of their enjoyment and seed.[18] Yet, women's pleasure retained a "teleological status" because delight frequently was considered crucial to the continued desire for coitus, and thus to humanity's perpetuation.[19]

These varied medical concepts about gender and sexuality generally reinforced the medieval principles of alterity because deviations from sex and gender norms were seemingly ordinary rather than egregious. While hermaphrodites challenged the simple gender dichotomy of the female and male, the presence of masculine women or feminine men was explained by natural causes in the predominance of male or female sperm in the right or left sides of the uterus. Normally, if the male and female sperms landed in the right section of the uterus, the child was born male, while female babies were thought to originate in the left sector. But feminine men, masculine women, and hermaphrodites demonstrated a more intricate relation between the sperm and uterine development. Women and men could exhibit each other's traits, and subjects such as hermaphrodites were not easily categorized. As stated above, the *Liber minor de coitu* and the *De curis mulierum* identified women with phlegmatic men, which suggested men's and women's correspondence rather than their unquestionable division.[20] Indeed, medical and scientific acknowledgment of sex and gender variation led some writers to fashion sexual differentiation along a continuum of possibility rather than according to fixed bodily states.[21]

Medieval medical literature often reinforced the tenet of heterogeneous subject formation because it affirmed divergent bodies and explained them through natural processes. Complexion theory bolstered the sanctioned role of contraries and the negative in its positing of the balance of qualities, humors, and elements. None of these contrasting elements and qualities possessed an intrinsically positive or negative value, but each varied in worth according to a subject's general temperament as choleric, melancholic, phlegmatic, or sanguine. The effects of their excess or deficiency depended upon a subject's general composition. Heat may be viewed as an exception to this claim, since it was associated with men and considered auspicious because of its power to activate, expel, and induce fluids. But humors, qualities, and elements operated differently in distinct bodies, and, as Cadden shows, corporeal concepts in the Middle Ages cannot be reduced to any one principle, such as the primary importance of heat. Medical writers relied on a wide variety of theories and models to explain gender difference and sexuality, which occasioned a "multifaceted, multilayered, nonreductive way of working."[22]

The frequent lack of a hierarchical, moral tone in medieval medical writing also permitted a more heterogeneous corporeal order than that of other kinds of texts, such as religious tracts. Cadden avers that legal and religious authorities largely reviled nonnormative bodies and considered physical ambiguity aberrant rather than correct and sanctioned. Although some physicians condemned the body, Cadden stresses that medical and scientific tracts frequently lacked value-laden discussions of corporeal diversity.[23] Unlike the punitive way in which religious discourse often presented discussions about sex and gender, medical principles and theories did not emphasize their link to morality. Although men were routinely considered stronger than women, medical and scientific treatises did not depict men as more virtuous because of their gender.[24] Furthermore, in the realm of human reproduction, medieval medical scholars in the thirteenth and fourteenth centuries debated and elaborated on the Aristotelian and Galenic ideas about the role of female and male sperm in reproductive processes. They did not automatically privilege the superiority of male sperm, but often attributed like cause to each one.[25] With regard to nonnormative or illegitimate sexual acts, such as "sodomy" (not necessarily associated with anal sex, but signifying the male's placement of semen in an inappropriate receptacle), medical and scientific writing largely commented on them only insofar as they affected health and well-being. Again, Cadden believes that condemnation was reserved for doctrines and canons on Christian orthodoxy:

> Furthermore, although medical writers were frequently concerned with sexual conduct in the context of particular health problems such as sterility, they did not (with certain notable exceptions) express views about the morality or propriety of sexual states or habits unless they had a bearing upon health. And they did not often represent either anatomical variations like hermaphroditism or behavioral variations like anal intercourse as essentially unhealthy. It is largely beyond science and medicine that the strongest rhetoric for the enforcement of sex definitions as gender constructs occurs.[26]

Hence, the classification of sex acts and gender definition into dignified and denigrated divisions largely did not take place in medical and scientific discourse, but in religious and legal writings. This is particularly evident in the later Middle Ages with increased ecclesiastical reform and the condemnation of heresies.[27]

This general pattern also characterized medieval Iberia, since religious discourse reviled corporeality and sexuality more often than did medical literature. The antagonistic stance toward the body assumed a more strident tenor in Iberia during the late fifteenth and sixteenth centuries, when the church increasingly became an arbiter of a more categorical social order of approving and disparaging human bodies. Before that time, medieval Iberian medical treatises often contained relatively favorable discussions about men's and women's bodies and coition, and they largely corresponded to the general concepts about the body that have been discussed thus far.

Medieval Iberian Gender and Coition

Many medieval Iberian medical treatises shaped variable concepts of gender and sexuality because they provided readers with models of salutary sexual behavior. These models attest to a long tradition of medical writing on coitus by Andalusi-Arabic authors, Andalusi-Jewish physicians, and non-Iberian Muslim writers. Many Iberian authors adopted the idea that moderate coitus formed part of healthy living, which originated with the Hippocratic tradition, was extended by Galen, and became a tenet of Arabic medicine. Non-Islamic, Western audiences largely received the Arabic and ancient ideas on coition through the translation of Arabic texts at Salerno and Toledo in the twelfth and thirteenth centuries.[28] As a result of the availability of new medical information, the late medieval period witnessed the dissemination of general practical health guides in the vernacular, such as two from the fourteenth century, Arnau de Vilanova's *Regiment de sanitat* (Regimen on health) and Jacme d'Agramont's *Regiment de preservació de pestilència* (Regimen against the plague), written in 1348 in response to the plague known as the Black Death.[29] Bernard of Gordon's fifteenth-century *Lilio de medicina* (Iris of medicine) was published as a manual for inexperienced practitioners to find diagnoses and cures for common illnesses.[30] Much of this medical literature in the vernacular was intended as practical health manuals for the general public.[31]

The late medieval demand for these manuals manifests in a vernacular text on sexual well-being, the anonymous, fifteenth-century Catalan work *Speculum al foderi* (*Mirror of Coitus.*)[32] The *Speculum*'s author specifically names only two Galenic treatises as preceding medical guides on coition, although historians have identified two other tracts that serve as medical paradigms, the eleventh-century work *De coitu* by the monk Constantine the African and the anonymous, thirteenth-century Latin treatise, *Liber minor de coitu.*[33] The *Speculum* presents a variety of practical issues concerning coitus, such as the benefits of moderate sex, the dangers of excessive coitus, methods of foreplay, what a man should do when a woman rejects his overtures, possible coital positions, and the best time of day to engage in sex.

Ideas about coition were further contained in longer works and compendia on general well-being, such as a book by the fourteenth-century Granadan writer Ibn al-Jaṭīb, *Libro del cuidado de la salud durante las estaciones del año, o "Libro de higiene"* (Book on health care during the seasons of the year, or "Book on hygiene"), and three treatises from the fifteenth century, Bernard of Gordon's *Lilio de medicina* (Iris of medicine), Juan de Aviñón's *Sevillana medicina* (Medicine of Seville), and the anonymous *Tratado de patología general (Tratado médico)* (Treatise on medical pathology [Medical treatise]), all of which followed Galen's mandates about sex and good health.[34] They encouraged women and men to participate in moderate heterosexual coitus in order to eliminate excess seed, and they indicated that love, sex, and eroticism were important for their corporeal, pleasurable benefits and salutary worth.

Late medieval medical writers often believed that moderate coitus aided people in a number of ways, since it caused them to eat healthier foods, to sleep and digest better, and to feel happier in general. In the *Libro del cuidado*, Ibn al-Jatīb delineated its salutary benefits:

> El coito reduce la plétora, da vitalidad al espíritu—lo mismo que el campesino se alegra cuando introduce la semilla en la tierra húmeda—calma la cólera, restablece el pensamiento alterado . . . y sosiega la pasión oculta. . . . Otros efectos son aligerar la pesadez de cabeza, clarificar las sensaciones enturbiadas y cooperar con los órganos en la nutrición.[35]

> [Coitus reduces plethora (a pathological condition caused by an excess of blood), invigorates the spirit—as a farmer is happy when he puts the seed into the moist ground—calms cholera, restores disturbed thought, and quiets hidden passion. Other effects are alleviating heaviness in the head, clarifying confused feelings, and cooperating with organs in nutrition.]

According to Ibn al-Jatīb, coitus induced physical and psychological benefits, such as emotional stability and the alleviating of headaches. He also used the image of planting seed as a metaphor for sex, in order to illustrate the happiness derived from the expulsion of seed through coitus. The twelfth-century medical writer from Seville Abū l-Alā' Zuhr (d. 1130) also discussed topics related to coitus in his treatise on remedies for illness, *Kitāb al-Muyarrabāt* (Book on medical experiences). He addressed the enhancement of sexual performance in two passages on aphrodisiacs, and in another section he prescribed opopanax to allay the shaking that could occur after sex.[36] These descriptions of coition did not abet the social and moral order like the later, early modern models, since they gave sex and sexual conduct nonmoralizing, legitimate roles in medieval society, beyond the merely procreative.

Unlike the sharp focus on a number of topics related to coitus in manuals such as the *Speculum al foderi*, general treatises on health usually embedded information about sex in larger discussions of genital disorders. For instance, in the *Lilio de medicina* Bernard of Gordon discussed coitus in several short sections such as one on lovesickness, and then devoted many chapters of the treatise's final book 7 to genital disorders. In their discussions on coitus, medical writers often followed a pattern that started with the biblical command and justification on coitus to "be fruitful and multiply."[37] Later, they usually emphasized the benefits of coitus, which were based on the belief that all people needed to expel excess semen or seed in order to maintain well-being. As propounded by Galen, they feared that a lack of coitus caused the body to retain seed, leading to ill effects that included headaches, fever, loss of appetite, paralysis, nausea, insanity, and eventual death.[38] Because seed was believed to originate in the brain, physicians such as the fifteenth-century Johannes of Ketham in his *Compendio de la humana salud* (Compendium of human health) cited the report by the Muslim physician Avicenna that it could turn to poison when retained there.[39] Superfluous seed could cause suffocation of the womb in women, a disease from which widows often suffered because presumably they were sexually inactive without a husband.[40] But medical theorists agreed that excessive sexual activity also had injurious effects, such as loss of eyesight, spasms, nausea, and kidney and liver problems.[41] Hence, moderate coitus was prescribed, and doctors provided detailed information about the best time of day to engage in it, usually at night and long after the body had time to digest its food.[42]

These medieval medical models of sexuality carried little or no moral weight, although Bernard of Gordon failed to include some of Avicenna's explanations about coitus because they were improper:

Avicena cuenta muchas cosas que no son honestas del coytu e cuenta las a fin delo estoruar, pero, por quanto el ayre se ensuzia de las tales cosas, porende dexolas de contar.[43]

[Avicenna recounts many things that are indecent about coitus, and he recounts them in order to impede it (coitus). But since such things foul the air, I will desist from recounting them.]

He also stipulated that coitus could be practiced only by those who had permission, suggesting its illicit practice by religious personnel:

Pues aquel coytu es templado que alegra & escalienta & faze buena digestion bien conuiene a los que lo tienen permisso: quiere dezir a los que tienen licencia para lo fazer: en tal manera que lo fagan templadamente.[44]

[Coitus is moderate when it enlivens, warms up, and creates good digestion for those who are permitted to engage in it, that is, those who have license to do it, provided they do so in moderation.]

Going beyond Bernard of Gordon's limits on those who could engage in coitus, Juan de Aviñón declared that virgins could not conceive without being "corrupted" by men, which tacitly gave coitus a pejorative connotation. Yet, Aviñón seemed to aim for providing information about sex rather than for passing moral judgment on women's virginal or nonvirginal status.[45]

These features of late medieval Iberian coition agree with the general medical description of medieval sexuality that was discussed in the first part of this chapter. They demonstrate that medieval Iberian medical treatises provided physicians and their clients with authoritative information that dictated and sanctioned moderate sexual activity for the maintenance of general well-being. This information had significant consequences for the domestic and social orders because it helped to shape and reinforce largely positive intimate relations between women and men. It demonstrated the legitimate and often propitious role that women played in coition and human regeneration, even though medical writers showed at times definite hierarchies of value regarding men and women's sexual capacities. Physicians sometimes esteemed men over women in discussions of their sexual enjoyment, such as when they argued that men delighted in coitus more than women because they were warmer complected.[46] Doctors reinforced from time to time the idea of men's active, superior role in coition by claiming that women took a double pleasure in coitus through their own expulsion of seed and through their enjoyment in receiving the semen of their male partners. Bernard of Gordon further maintained that men's superior strength allowed them to tolerate excess seed better than women, since women were weaker and less active in their role as guardian of the house.[47]

Some medical writers evinced prejudicial beliefs about gender value, such as Johannes of Ketham in the *Compendio de la humana salud*, where he stated that nature always opted for the conceiving of males because females were said to be imperfect and monstrous males.[48] Thus it is clear that medical attitudes toward women were not always "feminist" or entirely approving, yet, at the same time, physicians also showed a serious interest in women's general and sexual well-being. In his twelfth-century book on treatments, Abū l-Alā' Zuhr provided information on menstrual ailments, such as amenorrhea (the failure to menstruate), excessive menstruation, and menstrual problems after abortion, and he included a passage on sterility in women.[49] In the later medieval period, Ketham devoted the entire treatise 4 of his compendium to women's illnesses, which he entitled "De las dolencias de las mujeres" (On the illnesses of women). In a question-and-answer format, he addressed many issues concerning childbirth, hermaphrodites, menstruation, seed, and coition. In his fifteenth-century treatise *Menor daño de la medicina* (Medicine's least harm), the physician Alfonso Chirino also devoted a chapter to women's health, which he

called "De los males de las mugeres" (On the illnesses of women). Chirino enumer-
ated a series of remedies for ailments especially related to menstruation.[50] Salutary
information for women was included in the lengthy chapter 22 of the fifteenth-
century treatise *Tratado de patología general,* which was entitled "Las dolençias de la
madre de la muger" (Disorders of women's uterus).[51]

In the *Lilio de medicina,* Bernard of Gordon dedicated twenty chapters of book 7
to genital disorders, many of which entailed explanations of women's illnesses and of
their role in coitus.[52] These chapters demonstrate Gordon's concern about women's
well-being and sexual health, which other late medieval physicians shared. For instance, Gordon addressed the potential danger to women who failed to eliminate
seed or sperm:

> Quarto es de notar que el retenimiento de la esperma contra lo acostumbrado
> mas daña a las mugeres que a los varones: que peores acidentes trahe: assy
> commo suffocacion de la madre & semejantes.[53]

> [Fourth, it is worth noting that the unaccustomed retention of sperm harms
> women more than men; it brings worse irregularities, such as suffocation of
> the womb and other similar ills.]

Gordon cited Galen in attributing the dangerous effects of retained seed in women
to their inactivity as keepers of the house, and he declared retention of the sperm
(seed) more dangerous than a failure to expel the menses. Yet, both conditions concerned him, since he focused on menstrual retention in chapter 8 of book 7, which
he entitled "De las passiones de las mugeres: & primeramente del retenimiento de
las mestruas" (On women's illnesses, and primarily on the retention of the menses).
Women's inability to menstruate could lead to the harmful and prevalent ailment of
suffocation of the womb, which physicians often remedied by prescribing coitus
and eventual motherhood.[54] However, Gordon opted for remedies that included
baths, herbal drinks, and phlebotomy to cure it. In medieval Iberian discourse, uterine diseases had a variety of names, such as *mal de la madre, prefocacion de la madre, suf-
focacion de la madre,* and *afogamiento de la madre.* These pathologies and their symptoms stemmed from the ancient belief that the womb could wander inside the body
and cause women great aching and discomfort. It probably refers to what we call today
premenstrual pain, which would explain the prevalence of menstrual ailments in medieval discourse, as well as why it was believed to be common to all women. Physicians thought that the womb's movement produced symptoms such as "shortness of
breath, aphonia, pain, paralysis, choking and suffocation as well as a violent seizure

of the senses."[55] Juan de Aviñón addressed suffocation of the womb in the *Sevillana medicina* and called it *afogamiento de la madre*. But he cited its cause not as the failure to menstruate, but as the retention of seed:

> Assi como alas mugeres que se amortecen por una dolencia que llaman afogamiento dela madre: quando reyna en ella mucho de aquella materia (la simiente).[56]

> [For instance, women who become faint because of an illness they call suffocation of the womb, when much of that material (seed) predominates in the womb.]

Gordon's and Aviñón's accounts attest to the frequent ambiguity about whether or not women's menses and seed were different or the same, since medieval writers often were unclear about the definitions of women's fluids.[57] Indeed, in the *Compendio de la humana salud*, Ketham conflated seed and menstruation in responding to why women had red seed, a quality that he attributed to its location in the liver.[58]

Despite their ambiguity, Gordon's, Aviñón's, and Ketham's accounts illustrate the late medieval physician's often broad and encompassing medical interest in women's well-being, including uterine ailments, women's need to expel seed or menses in order to avoid illness, women's role in coitus, and childbirth. While Ketham's treatise evidenced occasional misogynist beliefs about women, other medical literature portrayed them in more varied ways. This is shown by the correspondent roles that women and men played in coition: physicians believed that both genders possessed seed that had to be expelled, both women and men greatly enjoyed coitus, and each gender played a significant role in fetal development. For instance, Juan de Aviñón noted that women's and men's seed labored together to produce a child; women's seed was converted into the child's body, while the male seed thickened and formed it. Aviñón further noted that both men and women took pleasure in coitus.[59] Although it may seem that women's favorable portrayal was due to a medical concern with salutary human reproduction, this was not always the only motivation. Reproduction and women's well-being often coalesced in these treatises, which makes it difficult to separate in all cases a genuine interest in women's welfare from a singular concentration on childbirth and humanity's perpetuation. This is evident when physicians instructed men on the importance of foreplay in augmenting women's desire; although their advice clearly recognized women's sexuality, perhaps it was only in the service of human reproduction. Aviñón addressed foreplay when he developed a sequential logic to show that it was indispensable to human reproduction.

He believed that, since desire for sex was crucial to the evacuation of seed, and since women's expulsion of seed was obligatory for conception, foreplay was essential to the heightening of women's desire for coitus.[60] This example demonstrates the frequently dual value of women's depictions in medical treatises: women served the ultimate goal of human reproduction, but at the same time they required medical attention to their general and sexual well-being.

Women's and men's similar roles in coition and reproduction probably were due to the more or less permeable late medieval medical ideology about the body that was discussed earlier in this chapter. These malleable corporeal concepts also are demonstrated by men's and women's occasional gender correspondence in Iberian medical treatises. These descriptions attest to Cadden's remarks about the elasticity of medieval gender traits in a number of medical tracts.[61] For example, in the *Libro del cuidado,* Ibn al-Jatīb portrayed some women as masculine and proposed that certain kinds of men should engage in sex with them. If in the winter men with a balanced complexion should have a "violent" desire for coitus, they were to practice coitus with warm young women who resembled adolescent males:

> Si el deseo es violento, se cohabitará con mujeres de complexión cálida, parecidas a muchachos, no entradas en años y en edades próximas a la pubertad.[62]

> [If the desire is violent, he will cohabit with women of a hot complexion who resemble young men, are not too old, and are of an age near puberty.]

A similar prescription also applied to sanguine men who sought coitus in the winter; they should have sex with thin, young women with well-formed breasts, but who appeared to be young men. Choleric men with a predominance of yellow bile should also practice coitus in the winter with masculine young women ("muchachas hombrunas").[63] Thus physicians recognized the flexibility of gender traits and body types under certain conditions, such as during the winter. According to Ibn al-Jatīb, these three kinds of men ought to engage in coitus with young women because their youthful "masculinity" made their body heat more intense than the temperature of feminine women.

Some physicians suggested corporeal similarity and overlap when they asserted that women and men were physiologically alike. For example, after he defined coitus and described its benefits, Juan de Aviñón declared that men's and women's genitalia only differed qualitatively, since men's were long and round and women's were flat. Unlike the strict genital difference that marks gender definition today, Aviñón indicated that genitalia did not constitute the site of gender distinction for late medieval medical writers, and he equated the shape of the neck of the uterus ("el cuello de la madre") to the shape of the penis:

> [Y] [los genetivos] son redondos y llanos: y cada uno dellos sobre si en su bolsa del cuello de la madre que esta junta con los genetivos. Y es de figura de la verga del ome: y non ay diferencia ninguna: salvo que la del varon es luenga: y redonda: y el de la muger es llano.[64]

> [The genitals are round and flat, and each one is on top of the other in their sack at the neck of the uterus, which is adjacent to the genitals. And it has the same shape as the man's penis; there is no difference whatsoever, except that the man's is long and round, and the woman's is flat.]

Aviñón stressed the similarity rather than the division of men and women's anatomy and further supports the one-sex model of genital makeup that was prevalent throughout the Middle Ages.[65] The anatomical correspondence between women and men extended to medical beliefs about the equal functioning of the genitalia. Like many physicians of his day, Aviñón believed that female and male genitalia worked equally to move seed to the right place in the uterus.[66]

In accordance with conventional medical theory, he also attested to the dual role of female and male seed in fetal development. He seemed to refute Abenrruyz's (probably Averroes's) theory that women's seed played no part in the development of the fetus because many women conceived without reaching orgasm:

> [P]ero Abenrruyz dize que la muger non obra nada con su simiente en la criatura ca la razon dize que muchas mugeres se empreñan sin aver talante con el ome: y ambos se deleytan en su obra.[67]

> [But Abenrruyz says that the woman does not work at all with her seed on the baby, because the reason he says is that many women become pregnant without reaching orgasm with men; and both take pleasure in their work.]

Abenrruyz rejects women's seed as a force in procreation, a statement that Aviñón seems to contest with his earlier declaration about the contributions of female and male seed to fetal development. Aviñón's final statement on their shared enjoyment serves to support the direct effect of women's seed on the fetus, since he suggests that women's pleasure injects their seed with a creative force that is weaker than, yet similar, to men's. Aviñón's assertion about the role of women's seed parallels similar discussions throughout antiquity and the Middle Ages, and his conclusion about its effect on the fetus agrees with many other medical writers.[68] He also bolsters women's auspicious capacity in coition and conception, since he acknowledges their largely comparable roles with men, that is, their shared pleasure and their identical salutary need to release seed.[69]

Aviñón's ideas agree with widespread late medieval concepts of sexuality, human conception, and gender. While these relatively favorable descriptions of women and men were by no means universal in late medieval Iberian medical treatises, their predominance offered healers and patients mostly positive models of men's and women's behavior in heterosexual coition. Sixteenth-century literature altered these somewhat egalitarian norms of sex and gender because of an early modern need for sexual paradigms that increasingly established more concrete distinctions between women and men. Sixteenth-century medical treatises largely continued to reinforce many features of medieval sexual models, such as the salutary need for the expulsion of seed, but changes also started to prevail. Early modern medical writers began to inject their works with intensified moralizing about sex and the body due to the church's increasing influence and its alignment with the state during the reign of the Catholic Kings (1479–1516). The rise of the Castilian polity and the progressively intimate relations between church and government were among the late medieval, early modern events and institutional coalitions that set the stage for a revision of medical ideas on gender and sexuality in sixteenth-century medical treatises.

The emergence of syphilis in the 1490s also influenced the review of medical norms about sexual practice, since the disease was linked to sex and posed a serious health risk.[70] Its connection to prostitution, and thus to nonconjugal coition, also was contrary to early modern moral and domestic values about marriage, sex, and reproduction. Syphilis contributed to the Castilian polity's implicit demand for concepts of sexuality and gender that would supply authorities with more clearly defined corporeal models. Starting in the sixteenth century, medical treatises responded to this urgency, particularly since male physicians became part of society's professional classes, which aided in regulating the social order.[71] Their ideas about gender and sexuality assumed a stronger moral dimension than in the medieval period, and women frequently were overtly denigrated in early modern medical writings.

The Early Modern Medical Body

The rise of syphilis in the late fifteenth century was crucial to the medical revision of models of sexuality and coitus because it was immediately characterized as a sexual disease that caused severe bodily deterioration and frequent death. Syphilis constituted a grave threat to public health, since it was debilitating and difficult to cure. It was even partially responsible for the sixteenth-century shift in disease theory, from a focus on an imbalance of the humors to the belief that disease was spread by corrupt air.[72] Known most commonly in Castilian realms as *bubas* (syphilis), *mal francés* (French disease), or *morbo gallico* (Gallic disease), doctors throughout the sixteenth century speculated on its etiology and spread, which they often attributed to sexual relations with women, especially prostitutes.[73] But sex was not considered the disease's only cause, since physicians also believed that it proliferated through kissing, bad air, sleeping in bed with the afflicted, and using the same bath water as the sick.[74] Yet, Castilian treatises such as Ruy Díaz de Ysla's *Tractado llamado fructo de todos los auctos* (Treatise called the fruit of all acts), composed in Seville in 1542, and Pedro de Torres's *Libro que trata de la enfermedad de las bubas* (Book that deals with the disease of syphilis), written in Madrid in 1600, emphasized that the most common means of transmission was coitus with contagious women.[75]

In his treatise on syphilis, *Secretos de chirurgia* (Secrets of surgery), composed in Valladolid in 1567, Pedro Arias de Benavides used strong terminology to describe men's infection by "women who are unclean" ("que no esten limpias").[76] In another example, the doctor Ruy Díaz de Ysla recounted from his own experience how he treated nine or ten men from a small town who were contaminated by the same woman:

> Yo me acente en una villa pequeña y cure en ella nueve o diez hombres que todos vinieron a pelar a un tiempo y de todos me fue dicho como tal mujer les avia apegado la tal enfermedad, y la misma muger tambien me vino a las manos que la curalle.[77]

> [I settled in a small town, where I cured nine or ten men who began to lose their hair at the same time. And all of them told me how a woman had given them the disease, and the same woman approached me to cure her.]

These men all suffered from alopecia, or hair loss, which they attributed to sex with a prostitute. Díaz de Ysla talked with and treated the woman and asked her how all those men had contracted both syphilis and alopecia at the same time; she attributed the conditions to sex during her menstrual cycle. In his later treatise of 1600, Pedro de Torres repeated the same story, highlighting the sheer number of sick men while laying the blame on one diseased "public woman," or prostitute.[78]

Women in sixteenth-century medical literature on syphilis became targets of denunciation, since physicians increasingly attributed the disease to them (especially to prostitutes) and fashioned its cause as contact with women, largely in nonconjugal sexual activity.[79] Although physicians did not claim that sex was the only cause of syphilis, the relation between infection and sex took on a more resounding tone in the early modern period with the disease's spread and its difficulty of cure. Sixteenth-century Castilian literary works such as Francisco Delicado's *La Lozana andaluza* (1528), which recounted the exploits in Italy of the syphilitic prostitute Lozana, emphasized the association of syphilis, sex, and women. Even though disease and sex were always connected in the Middle Ages through leprosy, syphilis reinforced the links between illness, sex, and women in the sixteenth century. Men's well-being tacitly gained importance over women's, since early modern medical treatises on syphilis implicitly and explicitly warned male readers of women's contagious and infectious threat. Such descriptions represent a change in women's equal, and often favorable, roles in medieval models of sex.

In general, women's relatively auspicious position in coition began to disappear and was replaced by depictions that cast them not as partners in heterosexual coitus, but as objects to employ for men's benefit. The title of the physician Francisco Núñez de Coria's treatise from 1572, *Tractado del uso de las mugeres* (Treatise on the use of women) clearly bears this out, since the title emphasizes women's use rather than the general topic of coitus.[80] Juan de Aviñón used this phrase a century earlier in references to the act of "usar con muger," literally, "using with a woman," as did Alfonso Chirino in approximately the same period.[81] Chirino warned male readers about "el uso de las mugeres" during the fall, the most harmful and dangerous time of year for coitus, and during times of plague.[82] But the phrase assumed a greater and more pejorative significance in the sixteenth century when it became the title of Núñez de Coria's treatise. Around one hundred years before Núñez de Coria's *Tractado*, in fifteenth-century Catalonia, an anonymous handbook on coition directed toward male readers, the *Speculum al foderi*, stressed the benefits of coition and did not explicitly objectify women as tools to be used for men's advantage. Chapter 8, entitled "Lo vuitè capítol que parla en les maneras e les custumes de les fembres" ["Which Treats of the Manners and Customs of Women"], emphasized the importance of tapping into women's desire:

> Lo seu grau és alt e firm e amat e durable a les fembres, e con més a les males. Cor null hom no pot aconseguir la amor d'elles si no cumple lurs voluntats, si no lurs maneres, si no ab sobilea e ab manera e usant ab ells e ab grans maneres. . . . E si l'om fos lo pus noble e lo pus gallart e el pus rich e el millor en sos nodriments del món, e no sabia ço de què ha voluntat e sabor la fembra, e si no ho fa de obra, no porà aconseguir sa amor.

[In women the desire for coitus is strong, firm, and persistent—even more so for bad women. But no man can win a woman's love if he doesn't know her ways and doesn't satiate her desires with persistence and skill.... The richest, most gallant, and noblest man who owns the best the world can offer will fail to win a woman's love if he doesn't recognize that women experience sexual desire and take great pleasure in coitus.][83]

Despite the fact that the *Speculum* underlined men's salutary advantage in successfully evoking and fulfilling women's desire, it did not denigrate women's sexuality. In contrast to this passage in the *Speculum*, Núñez de Coria demonized women in the sixteenth-century *Tractado* when he likened their vaginas to fire and the mouth of hell:

[Las mujeres] naturalmente son de apetito insaciable, pues como dize Salamon en el treynta y nueue de sus prouerbios, tres cosas son que nunca se hartan, la boca del infierno, la vulua, y el fuego.[84]

[Women naturally are of an insatiable appetite, because as Solomon says in Proverb 39, three things are never satisfied, the mouth of hell, the vulva, and fire.]

Not only did Núñez de Coria degrade women's sexuality as excessive and insatiable, but he linked women to fire and hell, which indicated their worrisome proximity and connection to the devil. He reserved the salutary gains of coitus for men and connected those benefits to Catholic ideology and morality. If women were close to the devil, then their sexuality was evil. Núñez de Coria reinforced the patriarchal social order by favoring men's well-being above women's and by warning men about women's threat. Medieval medical treatises in general and specifically those on coition did not usually describe women in this disparaging way. Many sixteenth-century medical treatises attempted to influence domestic and familial conditions through a gender division that often emphasized men's sexuality and well-being, and negated or denigrated women's. Although medieval concepts of gender and sexuality were by no means absolute in their descriptions of men, women, and sex, medieval medical writers usually did not deride and disparage women in the same way as Núñez de Coria. Their relatively inclusive concepts of sex and the body generally abetted a medieval social order that was more variable than early modern Iberia's.

Women's active, independent role in coition started to disappear from general sixteenth-century medical treatises on health written in Castilian realms, such as Juan Huarte de San Juan's popular and widely translated *Examen de ingenios para las ciencias* (The Examination of Men's Wit).[85] Unlike medieval medical treatises, *Examen de ingenios* reduced women's role in coitus to its reproductive function, and it unquestionably privileged men and the male gender over women. In his final chapters on coition and reproduction, Huarte's main concern was the engendering of male subjects for the good of the republic or the state. This is evidenced by the title given to chapter 20 in the treatise of 1594, "Qué diligencias se han de hacer para que salgan varones y no hembras" (Procedures for procuring males instead of females). This chapter title shows the superior cultural value given to male over female children, a gender preference and hierarchy that Huarte reiterates when he declares that women's cold and humid complexion prohibited them from possessing a profound intellect:

> Los padres que quisiesen gozar de hijos sabios y que tengan habilidad para letras han de procurar que nazcan varones; porque las hembras, por razón de la frialdad y humidad de su sexo, no pueden alcanzar ingenio profundo.[86]

> [Parents who want to enjoy intelligent children who have a talent in letters should strive for them to be born male; because females, for reasons of the cold and humidity of their sex, cannot achieve profound wit.]

Hence, in the same way that the physician Núñez de Coria extended conventional beliefs about women's sexual pleasure to cast them pejoratively as sexually voracious and close to hell, Huarte injected traditional corporeal concepts about women's constitution as cold and wet with antifeminist meaning and value. Huarte further cited extraordinary biblical women who could ably teach and speak publicly. But the vast majority of women could not engage in men's professions, since those vocations were contrary to their intellect:

> Pero quedando la mujer en su disposición natural, todo género de letras y sabiduría es repugnante a su ingenio. Por donde la Iglesia católica con gran razón tiene prohibido que ninguna mujer pueda predicar ni confesar ni enseñar; porque su sexo no admite prudencia ni disciplina.[87]

> [But woman being in her natural state, all types of literature and wisdom are repugnant to her wit. This is where the Catholic Church with good reason

prohibits any woman from preaching, serving as confessor, or teaching because her sex does not admit prudence or discipline.]

Huarte clearly enlists the support of the church in order to reinforce his misogynist
claims about women, and he expressly attests to the intimate relation between religion and medicine in the devising of the social order. Yet his ideas on corporeal variation are not absolute, since he continues to characterize bodies according to a varying scale of heat and cold and of wet and dry, which he discusses in chapters 17 and
18 of the 1594 Castilian edition.[88] He seems to attribute great elasticity to men, some
of whom may have a bodily combination of cold and damp that makes them wise,
and who have a high voice and no bodily hair. But because their seed is watery and
weak they are incapable of reproduction.[89] Huarte insists that women can never be
too warm or they would have been born male, although a woman's failure to procre-
ate indicates that she has a warm body.[90] Despite the recognition of a varying scale of
human bodies in the *Examen de ingenios,* the majority of the work attempts to cate-
gorically divide men and women through depictions of men in professions and social roles outside the home and of women as wives and mothers.

Huarte's treatise diminishes women's portrayal with regard to their physiology,
their role in conception, and their social value. Instead of maintaining the broader
range of topics on women's well-being that often characterized late medieval medical writing, in many chapters Huarte limits the medical debate on women to their
reproductive abilities in producing males. His treatise largely avoids the more comprehensive accounts in late medieval tracts on gender, sexuality, and conception,
since it does not include chapters on genital disorders and women's illnesses, as does
Ketham's or Chirino's. Instead, Huarte infuses conventional arguments on coitus
with a more intensified preoccupation about the patriarchal social order, as evidenced by his descriptions in many chapters of the appropriate men for certain occupations in the republic, such as lawyers, doctors, and priests. Women's contribution to this revised patriarchal state becomes narrowly defined by their reproductive
function, and the emphasis on procreation greatly informs the discussion on bodily
scales in the aforementioned chapters 17 and 18.

In general, women are converted into little more than conduits for the production of males, who were destined to occupy a variety of professions that serviced the
management and regulation of the state. *Examen de ingenios* devotes chapters 8
through 17 to different kinds of men's faculties, as determined by their body type,
and to the diverse occupations that men should pursue depending on the quality of
their wit. Huarte makes explicit the relation between such professions and the well-

being of the state in his description of the qualifications that would ensure the military man's success:

> Pero es la guerra tan peligrosa y de tan alto consejo, y tan necesario al Rey saber quién ha de confiar su potencia y estado que no haremos menos servicio a la república en señalar esta diferencia de ingenio y sus señales que en las demás que hemos pintado.[91]

> [But war is so dangerous and of such high counsel, and it is so necessary that the king know to whom to entrust his power and status that we shall do no less a service to the republic in pointing out this difference in wit and its signs than in doing so for the rest (of the professions) we have described.]

Thus, Huarte links these professions to the king and the republic and shows that the correct matching of male bodies and vocations is a medical concern with important consequences for the state. In chapters 17 through 22, he further highlights the connection between professions, the monarch, the state, and medicine when he addresses human reproduction. Coitus, reproduction, and sexuality become functions of the state for the engendering of male children, who will become its regulators and rulers.

Yet, Huarte's discussion of corporeal matters in chapter 17 also admits the widespread Galenic belief in bodily mutability and the one-sex theory of genital correspondence. He concurs with Galen on the sameness of men and women's genitalia, asserting that they differ only in their interior and exterior placement:

> Y es que el hombre, aunque nos parece de la compostura que vemos, no difiere de la mujer, según dice Galeno, más que en tener los miembros genitales fuera del cuerpo. Porque si hacemos anatomía de una doncella hallaremos que tiene dentro de sí dos testículos, dos vasos seminarios, y el útero con la mesma compostura que el miembro viril sin faltarle ninguna deligneación.[92]

> [Man, although it does not seem so from the physique we see, does not differ from woman, according to what Galen says, except than in having his genitals outside his body. Because, if we explore a young woman's anatomy, we will find that she has inside two testicles, two seminal tubes, and the uterus with the same shape as the male member, without lacking any detail.]

Huarte later discusses how this sexual assignment could change in the uterus, depending upon the amount of heat that has developed in the fetus. He says that the change would be noticeable after birth, since males who were females while *in utero* would display effeminate characteristics and have a soft, sweet voice, while females who were once males would exhibit masculine qualities in their voice and manner of movement or walking. Huarte further attests to corporeal shifts when he describes men who became women, and women who became men when their genitalia fell out. For the sake of his incredulous readers, Huarte declares that he knows of one such case that occurred in Spain.[93]

Thus Huarte continues the medieval idea that body temperature constitutes the element that distinguishes the genders, which he explains following the section on people whose genitalia contracted or fell out.[94] As shown above, Huarte uses heat and cold to explain such hybrid subjects as effeminate men and masculine women, but he also adopts those qualities to show men's superiority and women's inadequacy. Women's cold complexion was a basis for misogynist interpretation because it meant they lacked physical and moral strength, as well as wit. Presumably, anomalous holy women such as Deborah and Judith were successful orators and leaders because their body temperature was warmer than ordinary women's, but they constituted exceptions to the rule about women's corporeal and vocational inferiority.[95] Huarte tries to instill in his readers a wish for unquestionably male children as the ideal reproductive end. In contrast to his derisive handling of traditional medical concepts about the body, late medieval Iberian medical treatises did not generally use the distinctive feature of body temperature to divide, deprecate, and aggrandize people.

Although Huarte does not absolutely condemn all genital and sexual variation, such as that of eunuchs, hermaphrodites, and homosexuals, the explicit religious and civic framework of the *Examen de ingenios* demonstrates the new link between ambiguous sexual and gender traits, pejorative theological and moral value, and the state. Huarte's descriptions of eunuchs, hermaphrodites, and homosexuals in chapter 20 are rational and impassive in his discussion on how to ensure the birth of male children, although he strongly advises to avoid their births through the mediations of diet and exercise.[96] Some of his discussions illustrate the new, early modern connection between genital ambiguity in hermaphrodites and theological, Counter-Reformation morality, while other proclamations show Huarte's ambivalence. It is likely that his varied ideas on sex and gender are due to similar cultural concerns as those described by Lorraine Daston and Katharine Park in their discussion about hermaphrodites in early modern French treatises. Daston and Park show that "hermaphrodites came to stand for sexual ambiguity of all kinds," particularly in seventeenth-century tracts. They also believe that the change in value of "intermediate sex" responded to social anxieties about sodomy, sexual crime, and the lack of boundaries between women and men.[97] Even though Huarte recognizes corporeal variation and mutability in the *Examen de ingenios,* his insistence on the separation of women's and men's social roles probably addresses the social tensions that Daston and Park mention. It is likely that Huarte's link between church, state, medicine, and body type sets the stage for an increased divide in early Spanish discourse and society between normative men's and women's bodies and nonnormative ones.

Social conditions such as the emergence of syphilis and the consolidation of orthodoxy during the Counter-Reformation demanded new domestic and social values. Although the early modern social order was not monolithic, Huarte's and Núñez de Coria's ideas on gender and coition addressed in different ways the need for more homogeneous social principles. For Núñez de Coria, women were sexual objects whose role in coitus was one of service to men to increase men's sexual well-being. According to Huarte, men were explicitly more important and worthy than women in intimate domestic relations, as well as in civic life. Women's physiological and biological deprecation in sixteenth-century medical treatises, such as Huarte's, Núñez de Coria's, and Díaz de Ysla's, paralleled shifts in women's depiction in other kinds of public writings.

Sixteenth-century discourses coincided and overlapped in their didactic efforts to fashion women as "ladies" of the home, and to describe them as swooning, diseased, and enclosed. For instance, conduct manuals for women (*manuales de conducta*) were controlling, discursive devices that instructed women on appropriate behaviors. These manuals went hand in hand with the newly revised medical models of women's participation in coition, because both demonstrated the consolidation of medicine, religious morality, and the state in the instruction of the citizenry.[98] One of the most popular manuals for women was Juan Luis Vives's *Formación de la mujer cristiana* (*The Instruction of the Christian Woman*), which was written in Latin in 1523 and translated into Castilian in 1528.[99] Originally composed for the queen of England, Catalina of Aragon, and her daughter, Vives extricated women from the realm of sexuality and created a female paradigm that rendered them virtually bereft of desire as Christian wives and mothers. Vives's domestic model reinforced the same characteristics and values attributed to women and described in sixteenth-century medical treatises; generally, women were weaker and less able than men, and they needed to be contained in their homes. Vives limited women's work domain to the domestic sphere, while conduct manuals for men presented them with a variety of occupational alternatives.[100]

Laurinda S. Dixon shows a similar constriction of women's agency in her study of the social implications of "wandering womb" in the miniatures of the late-thirteenth-century English medical manuscript "Ashmole 399." Although she treats an earlier time period in a different locale, Dixon illuminates the relation of medical concepts of the female body and Christian moral values, a link that did not predominate in Iberia until about the sixteenth century: "The selective reinterpretation of ancient gynecology within a Christian matrix emphasized marriage and motherhood as socially-mandated ways for women to attain and maintain their health."[101] Dixon demonstrates that medical literature relegated women in England to the home in part because of a selective focus on medical concepts that stressed their weakness and need for rest. In contrast to Dixon's conclusions about thirteenth-century England, Iberian medical treatises and other historical evidence show that the topic of women's containment did not prevail in the Middle Ages as it did in the early modern period. Unlike many early modern women, medieval Iberian women worked extensively in the public sphere and were not subjected to the same early modern domestic models and regulations of female idleness and enclosure.[102] Hence, despite the fact that the sixteenth-century conduct manuals relied on conventional, antifeminist ideas about women that certainly existed in the medieval period, the early modern cultural emphasis on marriage, chastity, and ordinary women's containment represented new areas of focus in Castilian discourse.

In the *Formación de la mujer cristiana* Vives indicated that all aspects of women's domestic and public lives had to be regulated. He started the treatise with a prologue and then divided it into three books on the Christian woman as young and single, married, and widowed. The first book included instructions on how the young, unmarried woman should dress, what books she should read, and how she should speak outside the home. The indoctrination of the married woman entailed topics such as the wife's main virtues, how she should act with her husband, and how she should behave in public. The widowed woman's education comprised discussions about her mourning and public comportment. The manual's emphasis on matrimony, chastity, and women's service to their husbands helped to circumscribe female gender and sexual roles within the institution of marriage.

Vives went to great lengths to delimit the gender and sexuality of the ideal female subject. For example, in his lengthy chapter 8 on cosmetics and dress in the first book, on single women, Vives discouraged his audience from wearing men's clothing:

> Y aun pienso que es amonestación superflua la de advertir que la mujer no se ha de vestir de hombre ni se ha de poner ropa alguna de varón, porque la conducta contraria fuera inequívoco indicio de que en pecho femenino se alberga osadía de varón e insigne y descarada desvergüenza. La diferencia del vestido conserva el pudor, padre nutricio de la pureza.[103]

[And I even think that it is an excessive admonition to advise that a woman not dress like a man, nor wear any piece of man's clothing, because this contrary behavior would be a clear indication of the fact that in a woman's bosom lies a man's boldness, as well as famous and impudent shamelessness. Difference in dress conserves modesty, the nourishing father of purity.]

These instructions against cross-dressing evidently derived from cultural anxiety about the topic and were intended to divide women from men through the wearing of appropriate apparel. Vives went on to quote the Old Testament and to stress that clothing bore the same characteristics of absolute gender distinction that nature had created.

Vives's discussion of cosmetics intersected with medieval medical treatises that contained instructions to women on the same topic.[104] Medical literature on cosmetics included directives on hair care, the whitening of teeth, depilatories, skin care, and fissures of the lips.[105] But, in consort with the humanist project to rightly instruct the Christian populace, Vives transferred cosmetics from medical literature to his conduct manual and expanded its traditional discussions by enjoining women to avoid wearing men's garments. Medieval works on cosmetics usually did not include this prescriptive mandate on clothes.

Vives's construction of the female subject further included much discussion on the maintenance of chastity. In a section on how to reject zealous suitors, he recounted the negative strategy of an ideal single woman from Barcelona who ate uncooked cabbage and carried rotten cabbage in her armpits in order to repel a young man's improper attention. When the young woman approached the eager young man as if she wanted to tell him a secret, the stench from her breath and body made him feel so nauseated that he quickly fled.[106] The woman thus made herself abject in order to preserve her bodily integrity, which suggests a continuation of the auspicious medieval value of the *via negativa,* since her conduct served moralizing, Catholic ideals about romance and sex. But the early modern social role of the *via negativa* was different from that of the medieval period, and the young woman's repelling behavior indicates three ways in which Vives contributed to and reflected its change. First, her abnegation was not considered complementary to a hypothetically positive behavior, but was meant to create an impassable affective and gendered divide between her and her male suitor. Second, her conduct shows that the *via negativa* often became embedded in a system of Catholic morality that sought to assign unequivocal negative or positive value to amorous and sexual behaviors. And, third, her strategy strengthens the early modern link between the *via negativa* and the female gender, which came to disparage and cast mundane women as other. As we saw in chapter 2, early modern ordinary women no longer corresponded to the Virgin as they did in the medieval period; instead, they resembled sinful Eve. Vives's example implicitly reinforces the early modern gap between the dignified, holy Virgin and base, ordinary women because in the same way as the woman from Barcelona the latter adopt negative strategies for their own gain.

These passages from the *Formación* demonstrate how early modern conduct manuals shifted the medieval principles of alterity and changed medieval models of sexuality and coition. Vives described women as "ladies" of the home who served their husbands according to Christian principles about chastity, sex, and sexuality. His moralizing model of the ideal Christian mother and wife coincided with the sixteenth-century medical paradigms that emphasized the link between prostitutes (and by extension perhaps sexually active women with multiple partners in general), contagion, and syphilis, and that maligned women's gender and sexuality through degrading references to their genitalia. These changes to medieval models of sex and coition reflect early modern cultural ideals that privileged men over women and rendered women subjects in need of containment and control. Christian women served their husbands while contained at home, and prostitutes increasingly were subjected to corrective measures in convents and prisons.[107]

The narrow depictions of women in early modern medical treatises and their reduced social role in conduct manuals led to women's almost complete erasure from cultural discourse in the late sixteenth and seventeenth centuries. Emilie Bergmann has shown that women increasingly disappeared as cultural protagonists after the Council of Trent (1545–1563) and the development of educational institutions in the late sixteenth century.[108] She also demonstrates how the *Formación de la mujer cristiana* contributed to their disappearance by casting the ideal woman as chaste and silent and by fashioning the consummate mother as absent.[109] Bergmann argues that later peninsular writers accentuated and continued not the grave misogyny found in the *Formación*, but Vives's "near-erasure of the positive role of women in family life."[110] As Bergmann shows, Vives blamed mothers for faulty child rearing, and he discouraged them from contact with their children. These criticisms show how Vives advocated women's individual and societal negation. Women's intimate link to silence and absence in the *Formación* further indicates how Vives changed the medieval esteem of the negative, from its frequent medieval embrace to its early modern function as a tool of denigration and erasure. Vives's stipulations on women's conduct in the domestic sphere paralleled their decreased role in many early modern medical treatises and in medical concepts of sexuality and coition. Their portrayal as a group of others to avoid and deride, as well as their association with absence and the negative, bolstered newly categorized ideals of gender and sex that lacked the fluidity of many medieval medical beliefs about the body.

The link between women and the negative, as well as the degrading of the negative itself, will become even more apparent in chapter 5 on the monstrous *medianera* Celestina. Fernando de Rojas portrays his main character as a monster in order to equate her with all that is unfavorable and despicable. Like the monsters of medieval maps and iconography, Celestina resides on the edge, where she mediates two realms of value for her clients. But her duplicity blinds many people to the danger signaled by her deformed body, and she incompetently negotiates her clients' well-being. With Celestina's portrayal, Rojas contributes to the changing value of the monstrous and deformed, from its medieval embrace to its early modern marginalization. Like the cartographic monsters of early modern maps, Celestina becomes a deformed other to be exiled and disempowered.

CHAPTER FIVE

The Monstrous Body

Fernando de Rojas's *Tragicomedia de Calisto y Melibea* (1502; *La Celestina*) features the wily, multivocational main character Celestina, a *medianera* (mediator, or intercessor), who negotiates her clients' well-being as a go-between, former prostitute, healer, and brothel owner. Celestina is hired on behalf of the noble Calisto to intervene and heal his lovesickness. But instead of relieving his illness she augments it by arranging his union with his beloved Melibea. Celestina's evil mediations eventually bring about her own death, Calisto's and Melibea's demise, and the deaths of Calisto's servants, Sempronio and Pármeno. Rojas deprecates Celestina as the implied force behind all these deaths, and he denigrates her with a series of strategies that include her link to witchcraft and prostitution, her duplicity, and her loquaciousness. Through this negative portrayal Rojas tries to dissuade readers from seeking the services of *medianeras* or other women workers in everyday society.

Rojas's attack is particularly directed toward women healers, whose legitimate medieval status increasingly eroded in the fifteenth and sixteenth centuries with the professionalization of medicine. Physicians and civil authorities sought to dignify male physicians and medical practice and thus created laws to marginalize popular healers, including women, from the licit exercise of medicine.[1] Fifteenth- and sixteenth-century writers such as Rojas who were complicit with the incipient professionalization of medicine reinforced the movement's goals through disparaging portrayals of traditional women healers. Rojas was aligned with the tacit values that propelled the elevation of medicine and demeaned Celestina in order to suggest her resemblance to women healers in his readers' society.[2] He probably knew about the changes in healing practice and the marginalization of traditional women practitioners, since as a law student at the University of Salamanca at the end of the fifteenth century he was active in a community of students and scholars who undoubtedly participated in debates on women's worth, medicine, literature, and philosophy.[3] His participation in this elite group, which included Francisco López de Villalobos, the royal physician to the Spanish king after 1509, demonstrates his close connection to the social classes that increasingly attempted to regulate Castilian society. His probably *converso* background may have caused him to detach himself from maligned groups such as women, if he wanted to prove his allegiance to the church and crown and not to early modern others. Rojas seems to achieve this distance with *La Celestina*.

One of his most disparaging techniques against the *medianera* Celestina is her portrayal as a deformed, aberrant monster. Although her monstrosity is never explicitly stated as such, her bodily deformations and her reprehensible actions signal a monstrous deviation from the conventional order. Celestina defies corporeal norms of gender and sexuality in her dreadful bodily features, including her beard, old age, and facial scar, along with her presumably single status and her intimate relations with women and Pármeno as a child. True to Isidore of Seville's explanation of the monster's etymological derivation from the Latin *monstrare* and *monitus*, Celestina's monstrous bodily signs and her disruptive actions show something beyond themselves, a second level of meaning that Rojas seeks to establish for readers as the *medianera*'s unfettered duplicity and corrupt intentions.

Celestina's monstrous qualities are signifiers to encourage readers to perceive her as disruptive and to interpret her relations with others as treacherous and dishonest. Just as Isidore claimed that monsters could be signs of disastrous future events such as someone's death, *La Celestina* warns readers that the *medianera*'s monstrous signs foretell ruinous outcomes.[4] Rojas demonstrates that readers must avoid the mistakes made by nobles who trust Celestina and overlook or misinterpret the certain danger of her monstrous signals. Celestina's grotesque characteristics mislead Calisto and others from discerning her true motives, which are to undermine the social order and take advantage of Calisto's lovesickness for her personal gain.[5] Lovesickness was a valid disease in the Middle Ages and was dealt with extensively in fourteenth- and fifteenth-century medical treatises as an affliction of the mental faculties that was produced by excessive meditation on the beloved.[6] Its cure was thought to be psychological distraction, but Celestina prescribes the opposite remedy and prolongs Calisto's illness by uniting him with Melibea. She further capitalizes on his deranged mental state by devising a plan with his servants, Sempronio and Pármeno, to benefit financially from his sickness. Instead of interpreting

Celestina's monstrousness as a warning against interacting with her, Calisto and others disregard it and are drawn to her.

At the same time that Celestina's aberrant characteristics are intended to subvert the medieval legitimacy of women healers, her abjection also relates to the changing cultural value of the monster. In the Middle Ages the monster was both favored and derided, but it became increasingly disparaged in the late medieval and early modern periods. Medieval people potentially understood monsters in a propitious way, just as Calisto and other characters favorably interpret Celestina in what Rojas suggests is an anachronistic manner. The monster's ambivalence was due to its paradoxical esteem in the mode of reasoning and deduction known as the *via negativa*, the negative route to knowledge. Its presence in medieval society extended from philosophical tracts to sacred iconography and cartography.

Early Christian writers such as Augustine greatly influenced the early medieval embrace of the monstrous and deformed and contributed to the sanctioning of the *via negativa*.[7] As I showed in chapter 1, Augustine asserted that the monstrous races such as the dog-headed cynocephali constituted legitimate parts of God's divine and worldly schemes. Augustine confirmed the simultaneous wholeness and diversity of God's creation and admonished those who did not perceive the meaning and worth of variance. He highlighted the value of the aberrant and deviant and considered them among regularly formed subjects and things. The monster's esteem faded by the late fifteenth century, but as Calisto demonstrates, some continued to mistakenly interpret the deformed in positive ways. Celestina's grotesque depiction bolsters the increasing loss of the monster's auspicious medieval worth, and it encourages the early modern predominance of its pejorative value. In contrast to the monster's simultaneously favorable and denigrated medieval value, Rojas tries through Celestina's deformity to consolidate the monster's worth in order to make it signify in an unquestionably negative way.

Traditionally scholars have focused on the monster's negative meaning and contrasted it with human beings to demonstrate human superiority.[8] Indeed, monsters have pejorative value in a variety of medieval discourses, such as chronicles and romance literature, which frequently equated degraded subjects and groups, including Muslims and Jews, with debased monsters.[9] For example, in medieval Iberia Alfonso X's *cantigas* and historical prose occasionally deprecated Muslims and Jews, who were depicted as monstrous deviations from accepted norms. *Cantiga* 4 portrays an evil Jewish man, who tosses his son into an oven, and *cantiga* 108 shows that the Virgin causes the son of a Jew to be born with his head on backward. One miniature of *cantiga* 185 portrays a Muslim accused of adultery burning in fire, with his ostensibly Christian woman lover seated beside him, untouched by the flames.[10] Images of Jews and Muslims, as well as depictions of wayward Christians, served as monstrous examples in contrast with Christian goodness. But it is misleading to argue that Jews and Muslims constituted the only denigrated others in the *cantigas*, since deviant Christians were also vilified. They all deviated from the regular order, and the exemplary *cantigas* tacitly encouraged them all to raise their status by repenting or converting to Christianity.

The enigmatic medieval monster also assumed a decorative role and sometimes was used for didactic purposes.[11] John Block Friedman affirms that it often constituted the object of moralizing, homiletic exegesis as an unsavory figure for readers and listeners to reject.[12] Friedman largely views the monster as unequivocally negative and other, a deformed figure to be marginalized and rejected by social groups seeking to dignify themselves in contrast. Other scholars also focus on the monster's derogatory value, such as Anthony Weir and James Jerman, who in their provocative study of Romanesque sexual imagery assert that the grotesque reinforced the church's moral teachings and served as negative example to keep viewers away from the corporeal and base.[13]

Jeffrey Jerome Cohen's seven theses evidence a broader understanding of the monster's medieval significance. For example, his third thesis shows that at times the monster was the representative of an ontological category crisis, since it constituted a third term that mediated and undermined binary extremes, such as the female and male genders, or the hetero- and homosexual domains of eroticism and sexuality. At the same time that the monster determined cultural norms about the body, it also presented further corporeal possibilities. In this context Cohen interprets the monster as marginalized, since in the intervening role of crisis it was not assimilated into ontological schemes, but was relegated to the limits and margins of corporeal plausibility.[14] Cohen's sixth thesis is also remarkable because it emphasizes what David Williams calls the medieval monster's most appropriate characteristic, which is paradox.[15] Cohen focuses on the psychological in his assertion that "fear of the monster is really a kind of desire," suggesting that the monster ironically attracts at the same time that it repels.[16] Cohen shows that medieval monsters were not always derided as creatures worthy of banishment, but they sometimes unconsciously drew medieval people to them, or held contrastive value. Medieval philosophy, art, and literature show that at times monsters were esteemed not for their adverse capacities, but because they were crucial to the making of meaning as part of the *via negativa*. The apophatic way was a legitimate mode of medieval understanding and deduction, and writers perceived the monstrous as paradoxically auspicious in its deformity because it provided the most effective way to reach uncontaminated knowledge or the divine.[17]

In Rojas's work, Celestina's grotesque portrayal is intended to undermine the monster's favorable medieval value and to disparage *medianeras* in everyday society. Her denigration coincides with the disappearance of the monster's positive cultural role and with the simultaneous civic and religious identification of societal others in women, Muslims, Jews, and converts, who became early modern society's new monsters. Thus *La Celestina* contributed to the shift in the monster's worth because it assigned to the freakish and malformed a contemptuous charge that was uncharacteristic of many medieval monsters. The book wielded extensive cultural influence in the sixteenth and seventeenth centuries in numerous Spanish, French, and German editions, and it served as a model for a variety of early modern books, such as Francisco Delicado's *La Lozana andaluza* (Venice, 1528) and Alonso J. de Salas Barbadillo's *La hija de Celestina* (Zaragoza, 1612). *La Celestina*'s cultural sway further suggests that it played an important role in reinforcing the erosion of the medieval tenets of alterity, since Celestina's fluid subjectivity was portrayed as dangerous and duplicitous, and her adverse features made her expendable rather than embraced.

Monstrous Mediation

Celestina resembles the deformed in her monstrous bodily characteristics, as well as her gender and sexuality, which are the very features that frequently characterized mediating medieval monsters. As scholars such as Claude Kappler, John Block Friedman, and David Williams have shown in their taxonomies, monsters exceeded the conventional limits of the human body, since they often had excessively large ears or feet, multiple arms, or misplaced body parts.[18] This is particularly evident in medieval iconography in churches and monasteries, where deformed beings often defied corporeal boundaries. Creatures such as hermaphrodites, pygmies, giants, and half-human, half-animal figures on exterior columns and capitals throughout Romanesque iconography in Spain today attest to the pivotal role of medieval Iberian monsters. With regard to sexual imagery, churches in towns such as San Pedro de Cervatos (Santander), Santillana del Mar (Santander), Mens (La Coruña), and many in Segovia depict copulating couples, male and female exhibitionists, and a wide range of images related to genitalia. Many of the figures deviate from corporeal norms, including a face on a corbel that resembles a vulva at the church in Barahona de Fresno in Segovia.[19]

Celestina is linked to such excessive, deformed creatures through her grotesque physical characteristics. For example, she calls her old age a "mesón de enfermedades" (an inn of illnesses) (4.154), a description that connects her to deteriorating disease rather than to bodily integrity and health.[20] Her negatively masculine beard further defies women's gender norms when she is described as *barbuda* (bearded) (1.103; 3.138). Her beard is a grotesque marker of the male gender, which links her to suspicious social roles. In act 1, Calisto's servant Sempronio refers to it at the same time that he emphasizes her roles as a witch and healer:

> Días ha grandes que conozco en fin desta vezindad una vieja barbuda que se dize Celestina, hechizera, astuta, sagaz en cuantas maldades hay. (1.103)

> [For a long time I have known a bearded old crone who lives in the outlying parts of our district here. Her name is Celestina. She is a witch, and she's shrewd and instructed in every evil that exists.] (1.28)

Sempronio depreciatively connects Celestina's gender aberration and old age to her evil talents in witchcraft. She also bears a facial scar left by a knife, which further reinforces her questionable gender status, since women were not commonly portrayed in altercations with knives (4.152). Celestina's scar connects her to a low social class that resolves disputes with weapons.

Celestina's dubious gender and sexuality always figure prominently in her monstrous portrayal. Her implicit and explicit relations with other women are meant to show her abjection and deviation, proving that she crosses gender and sexual boundaries. Rojas depicts Celestina as a monstrous, masculine seducer of women in an effort to equate women's mediating work with contemptible sexual and erotic practices, and to warn readers that *medianeras* threaten the integrity of the patriarchal social order. He shows that Celestina's meetings with women are duplicitous because they occur not for healing purposes, but for the *medianera*'s own enjoyment. Rojas demonstrates this in act 7 when her interventions to heal the young prostitute Areúsa of *mal de la madre* (wandering womb, suffocation of the womb) are blurred with her own erotic desire. Celestina wishes she were a man in order to seduce and take pleasure in the young woman.[21] Her monstrous gender and sexuality are further heightened by her suggested relations with Pármeno's deceased mother, Claudina, and with Elicia, a young prostitute who lives with Celestina at her house.[22] For example, Celestina exalts Claudina's "manliness" when she describes her as *varonil* (7.196), and in act 3 she fondly recalls how the two women ate together, slept together, shared each other's pleasure, and lived together like two sisters. From the beginning of act 3,

Celestina's transgressive beard and gender are plainly linked to her possible sexual infraction with Claudina, when Sempronio refers to her as "*la barbuda*" (the bearded one) (3.138). Rojas upends medieval alterity's precept of heterogeneous subjectivity, since he deprecates Celestina's fluctuating between the male and female genders, along with her intimate connections to other women, suggesting that she threatens the patriarchal social order because of her sexual and gender indeterminacy. His denigrating rendering of Celestina's multifaceted identity is a far cry from the fluid, complex subject affiliations that marked, for instance, the Andalusi *muwashshah*s and *zajal*s.

Rojas further casts Celestina as a deviant sexual monster through her suggested pedophiliac relations with Calisto's servant Pármeno, which are alluded to in act 1 when Pármeno reminisces about her care for him when he was a child. He remembers how she used to pull him into bed and hold him tight:

[Y] algunas vezes aunque era niño, me subías a la cabecera y me apretavas contigo, y porque olías a vieja, me huya de ti. (1.120)

[Sometimes (*although I was a boy*) you'd haul me up to you (*into bed*) and squeeze me tight—but I'd always get away from you because you had an old-woman smell about you.][23] (1.43; my emphasis)

Even though Pármeno does not make sex explicit in his remarks, the phrase "aunque era niño" (although I was a boy) suggests a relation beyond that of a platonic, tender one between an adult and a child. Thus Rojas links Celestina to the monster in her physical deviations and dubious activities with women and a child. Her physical monstrosities, her gender and sexual ambiguity, and her anomalous actions with others are meant to reveal the truth about *medianeras*, namely, that they are always duplicitous and diverge from the established patriarchal social order.

As we have seen, monsters in medieval society were not always deprecated in this way. Like Celestina they were mediators between people or realms of value. They were conduits between the sacred and profane, or between binary corporeal categories, such as those discussed above by Cohen. But their abject mediation was highly important in the Middle Ages, as shown by their omnipresence in medieval society. Michael Camille suggests that monsters played a legitimate and necessary role in delimiting the territory of the sacred and profane in Romanesque domains. Their presence on exterior columns and interior cloisters did not emphasize their exclusion from the sacred. Instead, the monstrous underscored the interdependence of the sacred and the profane as it circumscribed their respective terrains.[24] At the same time that monsters pointed out the boundaries of the secular and the holy, they also revealed their connection. The mediating monster showed that while the sacred and profane were different, they also were linked through their interdependent differentiation—the sacred could not exist without the contrasting profane, and vice versa. Finally, medieval monsters were conduits for meshing the two realms, since, as Camille suggests, Romanesque representation often highlighted fluidity rather than stasis. Secular and sacred terrains were not always absolutely divided in the medieval period, as Camille indicates in stressing the "flux of 'becoming' rather than 'being'" in Romanesque iconography.[25]

Visual images of medieval monsters often centered on the physical and corporeal in the same way that Rojas makes Celestina deformed through her bodily monstrosity. Romanesque monsters negotiated meaning for viewers and readers just as Celestina mediates her clients' experience and readers' understanding of the text. Monsters did not only demonstrate the limits between distinct realms of value, such as the sacred and profane, but they showed their connection, or they blurred them. It is precisely the blurred, obscure intercession that Rojas tries to warn readers about in his book, since the monstrous Celestina attracts clients, but causes their demise. Instead of maintaining a distance between the realms of health and illness, Celestina worsens Calisto's lovesickness. Rather than sustaining a distinction between nobles and workers, Celestina connects them in pernicious ways. The main characters of the working classes, Pármeno, Sempronio, and Celestina have open access to Calisto's household and witness the symptoms of his lovesickness, but they take advantage of these intimate relations to Calisto's detriment. And, rather than heal women or provide them other services, Celestina wishes to seduce them. Rojas shows readers that Celestina should be avoided because she does not produce the positive results that her clients expect. Her monstrous signs ought to be taken at face value, since only disaster lies beyond them.

Rojas's criticism of the mediating monster contrasts with the auspicious, legitimate role of the intervening deformed in the Middle Ages. This is illustrated nowhere more clearly than in the fifth-century negative theology of Pseudo-Dionysius, the Areopagite, and in the commentaries of his medieval followers.[26] From approximately the eighth through the fourteenth centuries, the deformed was crucial to epistemological and ontological examinations of substance, existence, and form.[27] The Pseudo-Dionysian model provided a most influential context for the medieval embrace of the monster because it held that one had to know the negative as well as the affirmative in order to transcend them both and reach the divine.

These concepts were related to medieval Neoplatonism and determined that contrary figures best revealed the highest form of knowledge, or the transcendent. The monster was a mitigating conduit through which human subjects could reach greater realms of understanding. The Pseudo-Dionysian theory sought to purify human thought and to overcome the Neoplatonic idea that all knowledge (according to the Neoplatonic model—forms) was anthropomorphized when human beings created or apprehended it. In order to arrive at purer forms and avoid their inevitable human corruption, the theory suggested that one lower oneself to their antithesis, that is, to the monstrous negative and abject. A subject paradoxically accumulated a plethora of "ideas" (knowledge, or forms) in the descent to the deformed (negation) and, from there, ironically denied them in the affirmative ascent to the divine. One transcended the affirmative and the negative in order to arrive at uncorrupted knowledge. Pseudo-Dionysius explained the tripartite process of descent, ascent, and transcendence in "The Mystical Theology":

> In the earlier books my argument traveled downward from the most exalted to the humblest categories, taking in on this downward path an ever-increasing number of ideas which multiplied with every stage of the descent. But my argument now rises from what is below up to the transcendent, and the more it climbs, the more language falters, and when it has passed up and beyond the ascent, it will turn silent completely, since it will finally be at one with him who is indescribable.[28]

In this passage Pseudo-Dionysius contrasts overwrought accumulation (affirmation) in the descent with the supposed nothingness (negation) of the deformed, and he opposes the shedding of forms (negation) in the ascent to the affirmative divine. This scheme was based on a tripartite structure of descent, ascent, and transcendence, in which the deformed mediated between the sacred and the profane, and the human subject and the divine. The Pseudo-Dionysian model shows that the intervening deformed was incorporated into epistemological and ontological schemes and was not always considered worthy of expulsion.

The monster constituted the most propitious vehicle for reaching the ideal because both were paradoxically opposite and analogous. The monstrous and the divine opposed one another in their evident contrast, but they paralleled each other because they were believed to exist and not exist simultaneously. The Pseudo-Dionysian negative theology held that the divine could best be known as a paradox, as something that is-not, or rather, that concurrently is and is not. The monster paralleled the divine because it also was believed to be and not to be at the same time. It paradoxically "existed" even though it defied form, and it challenged logical and linguistic relations that held being apart from its representation.[29] Like the transcendent, the monster was purely figurative and symbolic because it had no grounding referent. But at the same time it was also knowable like the divine. The deformed monster best illuminated the divine, since it could never create difference through form; it was thus seamless and limitless like the transcendent. Pseudo-Dionysius believed that the most disjointed shapes were foremost in demonstrating the divine precisely because they could not be delimited or classified:

> Then there is the scriptural device of praising the deity by presenting it in ut-
> terly dissimilar revelations. He is described as invisible, infinite, ungraspable,
> and other things which show not what he is but what in fact he is not. . . . God
> is in no way like the things that have being, and we have no knowledge at all
> of his incomprehensible and ineffable transcendence and invisibility.[30]

The most aberrant or monstrous shapes most closely paralleled the ideal because in their deformation they took no form. Hence, like the transcendent, they both *were* and *were not.*

The monster's auspicious value was not limited to philosophical and theological paradigms. Rather, in the medieval period the Pseudo-Dionysian concepts were extended to poetics and became what Williams calls a symbolic language that demonstrated the insufficiency "of human cognition in containing the limitlessness of the real."[31] In the face of the inadequacy of human cognition, medieval artists postulated that the deformed and monstrous elevated the mind to a higher understanding of the real, just as Pseudo-Dionysius believed that it raised the individual to reach the divine. In the same way that Pseudo-Dionysius regarded paradox as the fundamental element of knowledge, many medieval writers and artists ironically posited the affirmative and the negative as complementary modes of understanding.[32] They sustained the Pseudo-Dionysian principle of interrelation between the positive and the negative rather than their division. This is evidenced by a variety of allegorical representations, such as medieval riddles and stories that use dark or enigmatic language to veil another entity or level of meaning.[33] Paul Zumthor extends this principle beyond the allegorical and claims that all medieval poetic forms, however they may be defined, bear a twofold meaning:

> One might maintain, not too paradoxically, that every medieval poetic form
> (on whatever level one may define it) *tends* toward double meaning: and I don't
> mean the doubling deciphered by an allegoristic reading but, superimposing
> or complexifying its effects, a perpetual *sic et non*, yes and no, overse/reverse.
> Every meaning, in the last analysis, would present itself as enigmatic, the

enigma being resolved into simultaneous and contradictory propositions, one of which always more or less parodies the other.[34]

According to Zumthor, medieval poetry aims to capture something of the ordinary world that is otherwise obscure or difficult to perceive.[35] In order to carry this out, medieval writers and artists embraced the complex relations of enigma and paradox rather than the simple, straightforward alliances between similar qualities and things.

Pseudo-Dionysius addressed the idea of paradox in "The Mystical Theology," where he declared that negative and affirmative modes were mutually connected because they derived from the same source:

> What has actually to be said about the Cause of everything is this. Since it is the Cause of all beings, we should posit and ascribe to it all the affirmations we make in regard to beings, and, more appropriately, we should negate all these affirmations, since it surpasses all being. Now we should not conclude that the negations are simply the opposites of the affirmations, but rather that the cause of all is considerably prior to this, beyond privations, beyond every denial, beyond every association.[36]

Pseudo-Dionysian thought strove toward the return to the ideal source, which could only be achieved through contact with the complementary *via negativa* and *via affirmativa*. Arrival at this origin represented the return to perfection, before the breakup of signification and the creation of forms.

This paradoxical relation of the positive and negative is prevalent in a variety of medieval Iberian textual discourses, such as hagiography and devotional literature.[37] Devotion to a saint depended upon the holy person's integrity as manifested through her or his abjection. For example, Mary of Egypt changed into a veritable deformed monster by living forty-seven years in the desert with only three loaves of bread. After emerging from her ascetic quest, her chin was like a piece of charred wood ("cabo de tizón") and her nipples were completely dried up ("eran secas"). This grotesque description is implicitly contrasted to the sensual portrayal of her beauty close to the beginning of the hagiography. Not only did Mary's negative depiction depend upon the affirmative recounting in order to make exemplary meaning of her conversion, but her monstrous self also had favorable value.[38] Her positive beauty and her negative deformity were intrinsic to her story's objective, which was to inspire Christian devotion and conversion.

Paradox is also central to Juan Ruiz's fourteenth-century *Libro de buen amor*, where sacred contact with God and profane sexual relations represent two correlative versions of love, each mutually dependent on the other for their cultural worth. The *Lba* does not absolutely deprecate carnal love. Rather, it shows that the significance of sacred and profane love depends on particular contexts and on the reader's ethics and interpretation.[39] Ruiz's leading *medianera*, Trotaconventos, also constitutes a crucially paradoxical figure as the secular mediator contrasted to the holy Virgin. Both intervene on behalf of others; Trotaconventos's men clients seek a connection with women, and the Virgin's faithful look for divine relief. The *Lba* does not denigrate Trotaconventos, but demonstrates that her mediations are esteemed, since the Archpriest grieves her loss when she dies. The *Lba* does not separate the profane love of the *via negativa* from the sacred love of the *via affirmativa*, but shows their correspondence.

In contrast to *Lba*'s reception of the negative, *La Celestina* seeks to undermine the auspicious value of the deformed. This is demonstrated in the comparison of the works' main *medianeras*, since Celestina is depicted as more grotesque and vile than Trotaconventos.[40] With the early modern Celestina, the textual *medianera* is cast as highly distorted because monsters in general develop into creatures to deprecate and malign. Rojas subverts their medieval esteem by portraying Celestina as homologous to them, and as duplicitous. Monsters were paradoxically negative in the Middle Ages, but their complexity was embraced rather than cast as duplicitous.

The monstrous Celestina is similar to the deformed shapes that mediate the sacred and profane in Pseudo-Dionysius's negative theology, for she links two subjects, Calisto and Melibea, and two realms of value, illness and health, and suffering and joy. Just as the Pseudo-Dionysian idea of the negative and deformed allows for passage from the ordinary world to the divine, Celestina promises Calisto a similar ideal in her effort to relieve his lovesickness, unite the two young nobles, and effect their reaching a kind of godly bliss. Calisto and Melibea's relationship is based on the consummate model of courtly love, which parallels the Pseudo-Dionysian paradigm because it permits the same pattern of descent, ascent, and transcendence. Calisto symbolically lowers himself to the monstrous Celestina, who then arranges a supposedly transcendent union with the beloved Melibea.

Calisto's desire to unite with Melibea is analogous to the Pseudo-Dionysian wish to reach the divine, and both the courtly and the Pseudo-Dionysian systems seek the services of a mediating monster. Calisto deifies Melibea in act 1 when in a discussion about Calisto's desperate state of lovesickness his servant Sempronio asks him: "¿Tú no eres cristiano?" [Are you not a Christian?]. Calisto replies, "¿Yo? Melibeo só, y a Melibea adoro, y en Melibea creo, y a Melibea amo" [I? I am a Melibean. I worship Melibea, I believe in Melibea, and I devoutly love Melibea] (1.93, 1.20). Critics have long shown that Melibea's sanctification in this episode corresponds to the elevation of women in courtly love discourse.[41] But it also points to the ideal state that Calisto desires and that Celestina's mediations implicitly assure.

The tripartite relation between Calisto, Melibea, and Celestina resembles not only the Neoplatonic model of ideal union and transcendence, but also the Christian relation of the earthly and the divine.[42] In the same way that ascent to God is reached through a descent to his human son, Jesus Christ, so is courtly transcendence realized in *La Celestina* by way of the grotesque mediator Celestina. Just as Jesus paradoxically incarnates the divine in his human deformity, so does Calisto believe that Celestina embodies transcendent bliss in her heinousness. Calisto's consecration of Melibea and his employment of Celestina enact the conditions of courtly love, they correspond to the triadic Christian principle, and they closely resemble the Pseudo-Dionysian model of negative theology. In accordance with the Pseudo-Dionysian paradigm, the interceding monster Celestina arranges an alliance with Melibea that is supposed to represent an unmitigated state of purity. Yet, Celestina's negative intercessions do not paradoxically lead to divine knowledge, like the interventions of the Pseudo-Dionysian monster. Rather, they propel characters from all social classes to their own destruction. Calisto and Melibea unite intimately, but it is clear that the monstrous Celestina has schemed the meeting and that her machinations will ultimately bring about their deaths. Calisto dies falling from a ladder while leaving the garden at Melibea's house, and Melibea commits suicide, probably by throwing herself from a window. In her final words, Melibea describes to her father, Pleberio, her fall: "Pon tú en cobro este cuerpo que allá baxa" [Now gather up the shattered body of your child, who plunges down] (20.335, 20.245). Calisto and Melibea fall, not to ascend later to an ideal realm, but to descend to their destruction. Pleberio's mournful *planctus* in act 21 confirms the seeming meaninglessness of their deaths because not even a belief in God comforts him or explains his daughter's demise. Thus Celestina's failure to propel Calisto and Melibea to a transcendent state and her instigation of their deaths demonstrate that the monster is no longer favorable in its negativity.

Celestina's duplicity, her incapacity as a *medianera,* and her connection to the medieval monster are closely connected to language. Her loquaciousness is more than a misogynist strategy to discredit her; rather, it corresponds intimately to the deformed, as Pseudo-Dionysius indicates above in the quote from "The Mystical Theology." He states that the ascent to the transcendent entails the linguistic denial of all the excess forms that were assumed in the deformed. One reaches an ideal state of silence in the union with the divine, who is indescribable and outside the linguistic realm.[43] The Pseudo-Dionysian theology shows more than the mere limitation of language: it affirms the ideal that subsists beneath and beyond words.[44] In contrast to this scheme, whose final goal is the transcendent nothingness or silence beyond language, Celestina creates a linguistic cornucopia in which she seduces people through her manipulation of words. She is truly monstrous because she embodies all possible linguistic articulations like the deformed. The characters in Rojas's work do not escape her linguistic interventions by denying or shedding them as they would in the Pseudo-Dionysian ascent; rather, they are drawn into her linguistic web. Instead of rising from this deformation, many characters fall to their deaths.

The mediating Celestina resembles the deformed in the obscurity of her verbal manipulations. She says one thing but means another, and she hides her true motives behind a linguistic veil, such as in act 4, when she links Melibea and Calisto by fabricating a story about his toothache.[45] Celestina's indefinite speech is intended to show her duplicity and dissuade readers from women like her in their own society. Yet, what is cast as linguistic duplicity in *La Celestina* constituted in the Middle Ages common beliefs about language and signs. Medieval writers held that obtuse language and writing were the best ways to reach perfection, perhaps because the written word embodied paradox like the monster and the divine. Medieval people recognized that language simultaneously revealed and concealed, and they believed that the ethical reader had to uncover correctly and follow the path to transcendence.[46] Isidore of Seville wrote that letters (*litterae*) opened roads to readers:

> Se las llama *litterae* (letras), que viene a ser como *legiterae*, porque van abriendo camino al que lee (*legenti iter*), o porque se repiten a lo largo de la lectura (*in legendo iterari*).[47]

> [They are called *litterae* (letters), which comes to be like *legiterae*, because they open roads to a reader (*legenti iter*), or because they are repeated throughout the reading (*in legendo iterari*).]

Isidore showed that language presented audiences with multiple ways to read or interpret. Readers could access the ideal if they chose the right path, but language ironically obscured the transcendent in the imperfect, outer representation of the signifier or word.[48] Early modern writers generally lost confidence in this perspective on language, writing, and interpretation, although in the same way as their medieval predecessors many authors recognized language's capacity to reveal and conceal. This is exemplified by the Baroque topos of *desengaño* (disillusion), which demonstrates seventeenth-century doubt about clear interpretations of signs. Writers such as Baltasar Gracián and Pedro Calderón de la Barca often posited the world of appearances (the dream, the stage) as the real, a "condition" to which subjects had to accommodate themselves: "If we all dream reality, this means that we must adequate our mode of behavior to this condition of the real."[49] The disillusioned individual's adaptation to this world carried with it a moral imperative.

José Antonio Maravall argues that the distance between "*appearance* and *essence*" was crucial to the Baroque point of view and resulted in a moral and political emphasis on the "tactic of accommodation," that is, the need for the individual to align his or her behavior with the world of appearances.[50] In contrast, medieval listeners were to interpret exterior signs in order to conform their behavior to the inner ideal. What distinguished these early modern notions generally from medieval ones was the injection of doubt into the belief that all signifiers pointed to the same unwavering ideal. As *La Celestina* and other sixteenth-century works show, it became important for readers to be able to divide negative and affirmative signs and make categorical separations between them. While it is clear that early modern beliefs about language and interpretation were not homogeneous during the sixteenth and seventeenth centuries, Rojas's work shows how medieval confidence wavered in the reader's abilities to choose the right path to goodness and transcendence, since Calisto, Melibea, and others evidently erred in their interpretation of Celestina's linguistic interventions and her material actions. Because of the possibility of monstrous linguistic and semiotic mediation, early modern authorities and writers such as Rojas encouraged readers to sharply distinguish stable, affirmative language and signs from duplicitous, negative ones.

Thus Celestina's monstrous mediation manifests in her grotesque physical depiction, her deviant sex and gender, her duplicitous intercessions, and her twisted language. Her dismal image marks a change in the role of the medieval deformed, which is apparent in her resemblance to an abject *medianera* in Bernard of Gordon's fifteenth-century medical treatise, *Lilio de medicina*. Gordon's *medianera* contains and demonstrates the various levels of denigration that Celestina suffers in Rojas's book, but Gordon's intercessor is embraced rather than expelled. Gordon urges readers to seek the able, yet monstrous, interventions of an old, haggard woman like Celestina when all other attempts failed in remedying a man's lovesickness:

Porende busque se una vieja de muy feo acatamiento con grandes dientes y barvas y con fea y vil vestidura.[51]

[Therefore look for an old woman with a hideous countenance, big teeth, a beard, and ugly, vile clothing.]

This contemptible healer should present the afflicted man with a rag soaked in the menstrual blood of his beloved and say to him: "[M]ira que tal es tu amiga commo este paño" [Look! Your beloved is just like this cloth!].[52] As farfetched as this remedy may seem today, its inclusion in Gordon's treatise indicates that it constituted a legitimate medical intervention in the later Middle Ages. Since the cure for lovesickness was psychological distraction, Gordon believed that the physical and verbal image of the beloved as a blood-soaked cloth in the hands of the hideous woman healer would dissuade the lovesick man from his excessive cogitation on the beloved.

According to Gordon, the monstrous woman healer had a favorable, authorized role in the medical healing of lovesickness. Celestina resembles Gordon's healer in her age, beard, and use of language in seeking to heal Calisto of the same ailment. But unlike her deformed model, Celestina's interventions intensify the nobleman's thoughts instead of distracting them. Celestina takes advantage of Calisto's deranged mental state, deceptively compels him, and eventually leads him to his death. Unlike the paradoxical mediations of medieval monsters such as Gordon's *medianera*, Celestina's intercessions only produce disastrous results.

Rojas's critique of Celestina's monstrous mediation is closely connected to the late medieval and early modern decline of the *via negativa*. As demonstrated above, the monstrous and deformed had an important intermediary function in medieval society, which is apparent in Romanesque art and tripartite epistemological models, such as the Pseudo-Dionysian negative theology. Just as the role of the monster waned in the later Middle Ages, so did triadic paradigms that incorporated the deformed yield to binary schemes of speculation that abolished the mediating third term. The shift from complex, triadic models of being and thought to binary paradigms is evident in the late medieval rise of the scholastic ideas of Thomas Aquinas and his followers.[53] Whereas the Pseudo-Dionysian paradigm centered the basic nature of being in paradox, the scholastics viewed it in a logical principle. Based on the binomial concepts of Aristotle, scholasticism approached phenomena according to either their being or nonbeing, and not their capacity for both. Entities could not simultaneously exist and not exist as they did in the thought of Pseudo-Dionysius and its medieval proponents, since Scholasticism sought affirmative knowledge through analytical reasoning and logical deduction.[54] Scholasticism rejected the Neoplatonic metaphysics of the negative, which relied on the monstrous and deformed to more adequately apprehend worldly knowledge and arrive at transcendent understanding of the divine. Late medieval people began to rely on empirical, logical approaches, which asserted the affirmative intelligibility of being and knowledge.[55] Binary epistemological modes surpassed tripartite paradigms, and confidence waned in the medieval principle that the *via negativa* and the *via affirmativa* advanced "complementary understandings of the same reality."[56] Instead, they came to represent opposite, hierarchical renderings. Celestina manifests the gradual erosion of the correlation between affirmative and negative modes.

Dual models largely replaced tripartite ones, and they displaced the mediating third term, which is apparent in the late medieval loss of the deformed, which was part of the triadic Pseudo-Dionysian scheme of descent, ascent, and transcendence. Other tripartite paradigms declined from about the twelfth century on, such as Peter Abelard's *sic et non,* an early triadic example that originated in monastic exegetical tradition. This paradigm held that the meaning derived from textual interpretation was not based on a simple affirmation or negation of yes *or* no, but depended upon both yes *and* no. A simultaneous affirmation and negation of yes and no was crucial to the hermeneutic generation of truth:

> Instead of an *either/or* semiotics of difference and minimal pairs (bit/bat, *siccus/succus*) medieval exegesis runs under the aegis of *both-and,* where an image can be both dry and juicy, and equally true in both constructions.[57]

The yes and no equation mitigated and connected the affirmative and the equivocal, and it necessitated multiple, contradicting interpretations for the production of meaning and truth. Not all exegetes accepted this approach, and some were concerned about its "ethico-hermeneutic effect" on monks and laypersons. However, many early monastic writers, such as Hugh of St. Victor, believed that faith and humility would ably guide readers and listeners in their understanding of the text.[58] Like the Pseudo-Dionysian negative theology, the *sic et non* model affirmed the mutual dependence of the three terms "yes," "no," and "yes and no."

The shift to dual models of deduction and speculation shows that the negative and deformed did not disappear from early modern society. Rather, it became separate from regularity, instead of correlative. Early modern methods usually excluded the mutual dependence of unlike positive and negative elements, since the increasing reliance on empiricism and logic largely posited affirmative apprehension of the real. By the eighteenth and nineteenth centuries, with the rise of science and reason, these concepts were inculcated to such a degree that falsity became disquieting and uniformity in nature was endorsed over irregularity.[59]

Celestina's resemblance to mediating monsters is closely related to the exclusion of the obscure, intervening third term and the rise of binary models of speculation and thought. The late medieval purging of the mediating third term and the prohibitions against women healers in ordinary society arose at approximately the same time and suggest a mutual affinity between developments in cultural paradigms and circumstances in the everyday world.[60] It is possible that until the fourteenth and fifteenth centuries women's legitimate status as *medianeras* paralleled triadic frameworks, which in turn reinforced women's roles as connectors. Perhaps the mediating third term, such as the abject medieval monster and the equation "yes *and* no," supported the work of *medianeras*.

The elimination of the interceding third term suggests that mediation itself faltered and changed in worth. Relations between subjects and things came to be appreciated not when they were mediated by women, but when they were seen as direct and unmitigated. Men began to represent the purveyors of direct intervention in various parts of Europe, as they displaced *medianeras* from traditional jobs as healers and from positions in other fields.[61] The late medieval, early modern importance of the unmediated is demonstrated by the fact that civic authorities implicitly and explicitly sought to equate male physicians directly with competence in healing, thereby subverting the interventions of women healers. As male physicians replaced *medianeras* in healing practice, they became arbiters of the Iberian moral and corporeal orders.[62] Men replaced *medianeras* in different areas of civic life as the Castilian male body came to be seen as the direct, originating source of power, knowledge, and efficacy, and not as a third term whose negative interventions led to affirmative outcomes. Jean Leclercq notes that the Pseudo-Dionysian emphasis on divinely enlightened intermediaries became a later principle of civil and religious political power.[63] Late medieval and early modern male ecclesiastical authorities, municipal and royal leaders, and physicians filled the Pseudo-Dionysian mediating role not as deformed conduits, but as ideal originators of knowledge and social practice. *La Celestina* demonstrates this shift in mediation and reinforces the idea that women's interventions originate in negative duplicity, while educated men's supposedly derive from whole goodness. It underlines the late medieval, early modern separation of the positive and negative in its suggestion that they do not derive from the same source, as the early works of Augustine and Pseudo-Dionysius asserted, but from different ones.

Celestina's monstrous body was to forewarn readers about the negative source that lay behind her physical signs. It was to foretell the disastrous results of her interventions, while the pure male body instantiated rather than portended positive outcomes. The male body became directly equated with efficacy and goodness, while the female body signified duplicity and mutability. These early modern efforts to oppose men to women (which we have seen in lyric and medical discourse) coincided with the rise of binary systems, which were founded on a gap between contrasting pairs and relied on the affirmative apprehension of knowledge and being. Binary paradigms esteemed unmediated, direct connection and implicitly devalued women's traditional, mediating purpose, thereby allowing no place for their conventional roles as *medianeras.*

Monstrous Margins

The monster's early modern decline was part of the general loss of the ironically auspicious medieval value of the negative and deformed. Sixteenth- and seventeenth-century writers and artists often denigrated the deformed and relegated it to the exiled margins, a change that Valerie I. J. Flint verifies in her study of the medieval and early modern descriptions of the faraway, imagined lands of the Antipodes. She shows that Augustine's embracing of the monstrous races yielded to terror and fear in the early modern period. Although gloom and despair were also associated with medieval monsters, Flint believes that those sentiments did not "triumph" in the Middle Ages, as they did in the sixteenth century.[64] Rudolf Wittkower concurs in his remarks on humanism's reception of the monster "as a foreboding of evil," and not as acceptable according to the Augustinian tradition.[65]

The negative and deformed increasingly became disposable rather than embraced, especially from the late fourteenth century on. This change resulted in the creation of the modern other in Jews, Muslims, converts, women, and, later, indigenous peoples of the Americas, who became late medieval and early modern Iberia's newly denigrated deformed. Medieval monsters often disappeared from early modern churches, manuscripts, and maps and were incarnated in groups of people. The monster's waning in early modern society is apparent in its infrequent presence on Gothic capitals and other exterior surfaces and, as I will demonstrate in this section, on early modern maps. Writers and artists who were aligned with the ideals of the Catholic Kings sought to establish the early modern other not as a mediator of value and meaning like the medieval monster, but as opposed to the homogenizing goals of the Castilian nation-state. The demand for more rigid hierarchies of worth between subjects in the Castilian polity created a civic divide between the worthy bodies of Christian men and the unworthy bodies of monstrous others.

Even when early modern artists seemed to treat different cultures in less pejorative ways, the other was often dignified only when she or he conformed to Christian ideals. This is evident in the seeming conciliatory gesture toward the *morisco* (converted Muslim) in the anonymous sixteenth-century work *El Abencerraje,* where the Muslim Abindarráez is ennobled because he adapts to Christian values in his similarity to Rodrigo de Narváez. The men's amicable relationship illustrates the friendship that traditionally existed between Muslims and Christians in the medieval period, but Abindarráez's assimilation into a Christian realm of value elides rather than embraces cultural difference.[66] *El Abencerraje* reinforces the sixteenth-century social effort to integrate *moriscos* into Castilian society, although it supports their assimilation only if they acquiesce to Christian ideals. Sixteenth-century Iberia often assimilated ethnic and cultural difference into dominant Christian frameworks, but instead of meshing or accepting diverse cultures, those efforts subsumed Muslim and Jewish cultures to Christian modes and values. This is demonstrated by late sixteenth-century laws directed toward the dress, habits, language use, and social and religious practice of *moriscos*. When *morisco* communities failed to follow laws entreating them to speak Castilian and forego traditional, Arabic clothing, they were expelled from the peninsula for a final time in 1609.[67]

Social policy such as the purity of blood statutes (*limpieza de sangre*) contributed to the establishment of the monstrous other, since they demonstrated the esteem of an immaculate, old Christian ethnicity over new Christians, Muslims, and Jews. This ideology persisted into the nineteenth century, as evidenced by the use of the terms "old" and "new" Christian during the French invasion of 1808.[68] The early modern effort to regulate Spain and rid it of ethnic and religious non-Christian others was so extensive that outsiders in the sixteenth and seventeenth centuries ironically described the territory as implicitly Jewish. Early modern Spain's Christianizing attempts backfired at times, since foreigners and travelers tended to use the derogatory epithet *marrano*, a term associated with "pig," to generally describe Spain as Jewish. This term ironically was due to the Inquisition's pursuing of Judaizers, a practice intended to free Spain of heretics rather than to classify it pejoratively as non-Christian.[69] Thus, the institutional mechanisms erected to combat the early modern other, such as laws, medical boards, and the Inquisition demonstrate that the negative and deformed became disparaged, conquered, and combated. Difference, the monstrous, and the deformed became worthy of deprecation, marginalization, and exile.

Celestina's marginal status demonstrates the newly disposable value of the monstrous and deformed, as well as of societal others. According to Pármeno's description in act 1, she lives in a decrepit house on the outskirts of her city, in a fringe neighborhood near a river. Evidently, she has recently moved there, away from the urban center where the nobles live, since she tells Melibea's servant Lucrecia in act 4 that her move to her current neighborhood prohibited her from visiting Melibea and Melibea's mother, Alisa (4.151). In act 1, Pármeno describes the dilapidated condition of her marginal house:

Tiene esta buena dueña al cabo de la cibdad, allá cerca de las tenerías, en la cuesta del río, una casa apartada, medio cayda, poco compuesta y menos abastada. (1.110)

[This good lady now has a house that stands off by itself down there at the edge of town near those tanneries along the river bank. It is half falling down, in bad repair, and furnished even worse.] (1.34)

Celestina is geographically peripheral and lives in decaying conditions, but Pármeno relates in the same act 1 that her house has been a center of activity in prostitution, healing, and the restoration of young women's virginity. As Calisto waits to meet her in that scene, Pármeno indirectly warns him about the sordidness of her healing mediations and about her clients' mistakes in relying on her services:

Venían a ella muchos hombres y mujeres, y a unos demandava el pan do mordían, a otros, de su ropa; . . . a otros, pintava en la palma letras con açafran. . . . Pintava figuras, dezía palabras en tierra. ¿Quién te podrá dezir lo que esta vieja hazía? Y todo era burla y mentira. (1.112–13)

[Many men and women came to her. Of some she requested the bread they were actually eating, of others their clothes; . . . she painted the palms of other people's hands with saffron. . . . She painted figures and said spells. Who could ever tell you all the old creature was able to do? And it was all falsehood and trickery.] (1.36)

Pármeno's narration in the past tense calls into question Celestina's current popularity, especially since he avers that she offered clients false promises and duplicitous remedies for their ills. He also indirectly suggests that her deceptive remedies justify her peripheral location and eroding home, although Calisto insists on seeing her (1.113).

Celestina's nefarious position on the margins sharply contrasts with the auspicious value of medieval monsters on the edge. We have seen that medieval artists often placed monsters on the borders of Romanesque architecture, manuscripts, and maps, which did not signify their exile and disempowerment, but demonstrated their central medieval role as mediating connectors. They negotiated the space of the sacred and profane in Romanesque churches, and they mediated meaning in the margins of medieval manuscripts. Monsters such as serpents, monkeys, animal-human beasts, and sciapodes with large feet that became umbrellas for shade commented on the manuscript's central text in dialogue with the written word. John Dagenais has speculated on the meanings of the marginal drawings of animals in the Salamanca manuscript of the *Libro de buen amor,* proposing, for instance, that a hook-beaked bird beside verses 721–22 (folio 42v) provides a lesson on the ethics of human speech.[70] Dagenais suggests that the drawing glosses the text and illuminates its meaning.

Camille shows that the margins related to the center in another way when he explains that hybrid exotic figures on manuscripts, such as a face-footed bird with a human body, did not merely illuminate the texts they accompanied. Rather, they also subverted them: "[M]arginal images are *conscious* usurpations, perhaps even political statements about diffusing the power of the text through its unraveling."[71] Camille indicates that marginal figures commented on the central text and sometimes undermined its force. While the subverting of the text's dominance was only one of the functions of marginalia, both Camille and Dagenais emphasize that in medieval manuscript culture meaning was made through the interdependent dialogue between the text and its margins.

Monsters also were clearly visible on the margins of popular world maps, or *mappae mundi,* which included figures such as the dog-headed cynocephali, sciapodes, and bisexual hermaphrodites. World maps known as "T-O" or "T-in-O" portrayed the world as a circle, or an "O," which usually contained three major continents, divided in a "T"—Africa, Asia, and Europe—as well as important bodies of water and sometimes Jerusalem at the center. These maps often illustrated the circle's outer limits as the land inhabited by deformed monsters, suggesting that the farther one traveled from the central, known world, the more distorted the margins' inhabitants became. These monsters included the large-footed sciapod reproduced on a map by Beatus of Liébana (1086) in the Cathedral at Burgo de Osma (ill. 1), the earless, noseless, big-lipped, headless, and dog-headed men on the Psalter map, probably made in London in 1265 (ill. 2), and the grotesque figures on the edges of the map at Hereford Cathedral made in 1285.[72] Sometimes deformed figures on the edge were associated with the marginalized biblical figures Gog and Magog, who derived from Greek and Roman sources.[73] With their maps, medieval cartographers frequently sought to represent both cosmological and physical interpretations of the world, which is evidenced by the presence of rivers and continents, by Adam and Eve in Paradise, and by Jerusalem at the map's center.

Monsters were part of this physical and spiritual design, although, like the grotesque figures in Romanesque iconography, scholars tend to interpret them as banished outcasts. For example, Friedman asserts that medieval world maps often give

Illus. 1, MS p. 326.
World map by Beatus of Liébana (1086), Cathedral of Burgo de Osma, Cod.1, fols. 34v–35.
Courtesy of the Cathedral of Burgo de Osma.

"a theological turn to geography," since they show that monsters reside farthest from God, as well as from Jerusalem at the map's center.[74] He views monsters as disempowered and marginalized, far removed from the sacred center and the divine. Williams has recently demonstrated, however, that in their deformity monsters occupy the outer limits of the universe close to the divine, since God cannot be contained within the limits of the world. Monsters are not located beyond the world of order; rather, they frame it and contain and organize what lies within. Williams indicates that the edge connotes fluidity rather than stasis, and he contends that the frame of a map or manuscript folio orients "the viewer to beginning, end, and continuity." He suggests that traditional interpretations inaccurately view the monstrous races pejoratively as expulsed: "In this light the threshold position of the races suggests, perhaps, a greater importance for their locus than does the simple

Illus. 2, MS p. 326.
Psalter world map, c. 1625. British Library Add. MS 28681, fol. 9. Courtesy of the British Library.

historical explanation that it is a sign of exile."[75] Cartographic monsters were not necessarily exiled, but they mediated access to the divine in their deformity. The divine
was considered most visible in its antithesis, a contradiction that linked the ideal and
deformed on the cartographic edge. Monsters straddled the limits of the social order
in their proximity to the ideal, suggesting that ordinary subjects reached the transcendent through them. Thus monsters in the Christian map-making tradition had
affirmative value in their deformity and abjection because they showed that the divine and the monstrous were aligned in their variation. They were believed to be and
not to be, and the divine was considered most visible in its antithesis. This paradox
binds the ideal and the monstrous and, by extension, the negative and the positive.

Celestina resembles the cartographic monsters, since, like them, she is supposed
to mediate two spheres of value. She is pivotal to the well-being of her townspeople
in the same way that monsters are crucial to the mapping of medieval space. Her
clients are supposed to ameliorate their physical condition by way of the monstrous
medianera just as human subjects reach the divine paradoxically through the cartographic and Romanesque monster. Celestina is a signifier like the medieval monster,
although, instead of pointing enigmatically to a higher order, she paves the way to
disaster. In calling her interventions mendacious in act 1, Pármeno demonstrates
that Celestina's deformed exterior conforms to her twisted intentions and actions.
Celestina's deceitful healing ministrations and her outlying house constitute monstrous signs that clients do not recognize as ominous.

Rojas inverts the monster's auspicious value by indicating that Celestina's liminal interventions lead people not to a higher realm, but to misery and death. His
spatial organization equates Celestina's marginal location in her Castilian town with
the need for her elimination, since the monstrous Celestina shows that indecorous
people inhabit the late medieval, early modern margins and are worthy of expulsion. Celestina may once have been pivotal to sexual, salutary, and business transactions in her town, but her monstrousness is not shown to currently enhance or
correspond to the social order. Rather, it destroys it.

Cartographic monsters were treated in a similar way, since unlike the auspicious
mediating role that they played on the margins of medieval *mappae mundi*, European expansion and the rise of nation-states caused early modern mapmakers to
sometimes convey deprecatory information about monsters in the margins. The inhabitants on the edges of the world became at times grotesque others who resided
alarmingly close to Europe and the Americas, and not close to God, which is evidenced by a map by Muhyīddīn Pīrī Re'īs, drawn in 1513 (ill. 3). Re'īs was a sea captain
in the imperial Ottoman navy (*re'īs* means "sea captain" in Turkish), who consulted a
variety of Greek and Muslim sources, as well as Portuguese maps and one believed

Illus. 3, MS p. 329.
Fragment of the world map of Pīrī Re'īs, 1513. By permission of the Topkapi Sarayi
Müzesi Kütüphanesi, Istanbul (R. 1633 mūk).

to have been made by Christopher Columbus in constructing his world map. The
only part to survive is the fragment drawn on parchment of the Iberian Peninsula,
West Africa, the Caribbean, and America.[76] Re'īs's map is historically significant because it demonstrates the sharing of Muslim and Christian information and reveals
a familiarity with geographic places before they were thought to be known.[77]

But it also shows how the understanding of the margins changed in the early sixteenth century, since early modern cartographers sometimes disparaged them as the
geographic home of barbarous others. Re'īs demonstrates that the Iberian Peninsula
and western Africa were home to many kings and different kinds of animals, while
the Americas on the other side of the Atlantic were inhabited by ordinary animals
that stood on four legs and by anthropomorphized beasts that danced together and

sat in human positions; one scene shows a large dog dancing with what appears to be a smaller one. These humanlike animals accompanied animal-like humans, such as the headless blemmye with its face on its chest, complete with eyes, nose, and mouth, and its full head of hair on its shoulders. The blemmye sat on a mountain next to an anthropomorphized dog, which sat like a human while holding an object that resembled a drinking cup. Hence, Re'īs's rendering of the two sides of the Atlantic depicted the Americas as the land of monsters and beastly others, in contrast to the familiar land of normal animals and kings on the shores of the eastern Atlantic.

The cultural significance of Re'īs's early sixteenth-century portrayal of monsters is further illuminated when compared to a Spanish world map made by Juan de la Cosa in 1500, where the blemmye resides with other monsters in the marginal land of Gog and Magog on the upper right quadrant (ill. 4).[78] De la Cosa continues the common medieval placement of monstrous races and deformed figures in the geographic regions on the edge, while Re'īs no longer links the blemmyes and humanlike animals to the legendary marginal terrain of Gog and Magog, but to the Caribbean and the American coast. While his representation of monsters in the Americas is not overtly pejorative, their location in a known geographic space created and reinforced the association of otherness and difference with the indigenous peoples of America. It is well known that Europeans often portrayed indigenous people in derogatory ways, such as in the diaries of Christopher Columbus or in Bernal Díaz del Castillo's chronicles.[79] Pīrī Re'īs echoed these depictions by associating familiar medieval monsters with indigenous Americans. Sixteenth-century readers would have interpreted this link negatively because early modern artists and writers changed the legitimate role of medieval monsters and imbued them with a new, solely pejorative value.

Re'īs's map suggests that monsters no longer mediated the mundane and divine in the early sixteenth century, but became negative markers of ethnic and corporeal difference. It demonstrates that the medieval cosmological world view changed in the early modern period, since the monstrous blemmyes and anthropomorphized animals no longer resided close to the divine, but inhabited the American territory that became a site of conquest. The exploration and exploitation of the New World necessitated new geographic models for navigation and domination, which early modern cartographers provided. Monsters increasingly disappeared from early modern maps because they became verifiable in the women, Muslims, Jews, and converts who populated Iberian domains. Their cartographic function thus came to an end.

Monsters such as the blemmyes were associated with indigenous Americans, as well as with *medianeras* such as Celestina, who were transformed into early modern Iberia's monstrous others. Sixteenth-century world maps demonstrate a change in value of the late medieval, early modern Iberian margins, which increasingly

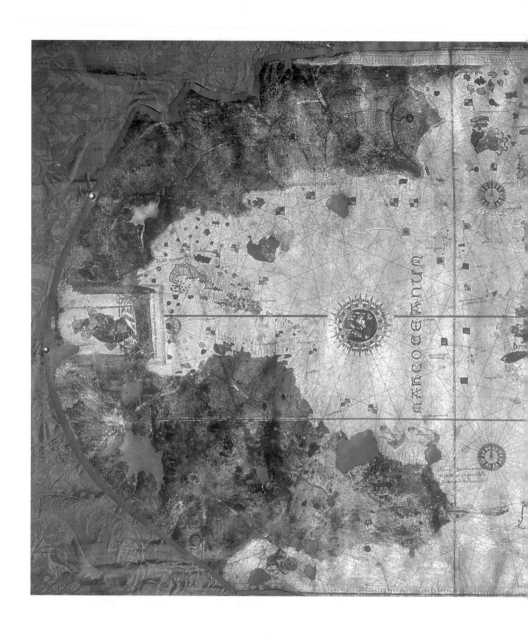

Illus. 4, MS p. 331.
World map of Juan de la Cosa, 1500. Courtesy of the Naval Museum, Madrid.
Detail: The marginal land of Gog and Magog in the upper right quadrant.

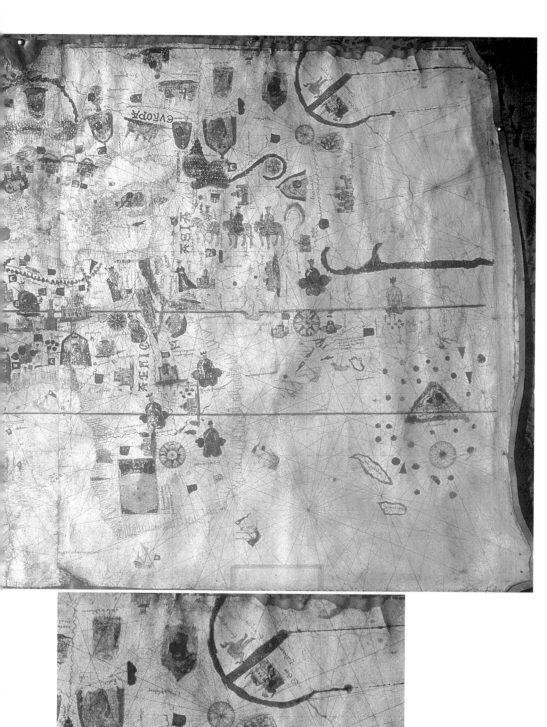

constituted a pejorative terrain divided from the center, and not interdependent with it. They also show the change in value of the monstrous and deformed, from its paradoxically auspicious medieval worth to its conversion into an early modern threat. Artists, writers, and civic authorities began to identify everyday people as monstrous and deformed, and they advocated their exile to society's margins. The creation of monstrous others in late medieval and early modern literature and everyday society marks a change in medieval alterity. Instead of integrating contrariety, opposites, and variance into epistemological and social models, early modern authorities used them as means to disparage and degrade others who threatened consistent social integrity. Hence, changes in the role of the negative and the relation of contrasts and opposites in philosophical and theological paradigms contributed to alterations in the making of individual and social meaning. The disparagement of the *via negativa* paralleled ontological changes in the value of ordinary subjects, so that monstrous others became expendable rather than culturally enmeshed. *La Celestina* augmented the early modern creation of women as monstrous others, since readers would have made parallel connections between Celestina and the women she resembled in Castilian society.

Conclusion

Medieval Iberia was characterized by a complex mixture of conflict, discord, cultural agreement, and political negotiation. Its pliable social organization, which allowed for ways of incorporating diversity, eroded from approximately the fifteenth century on, as evidenced by changes in the sociopolitical order and by the shifts in Iberian lyric, medical concepts of the body, and discourse on the monster. But no historical age is a monolith. Although the social order shifted with the establishment of the Castilian nation-state, this effort alone did not create an instantly consistent and homogeneous society. As I demonstrated in chapter 1, many historical events show the tenuousness of social and political integrity in the early modern period. Despite the early modern attempt to establish political hierarchies and social divisions, the Castilian nation-state contained diverse communities and a variety of ways to make difference.

Furthermore, as I have indicated, the differences between the medieval and early modern periods were not always absolute. It may even be argued that certain medieval Iberian kingdoms were "nations," according to Benedict Anderson's definition of the nation as "an imagined political community—and imagined as both inherently limited and sovereign."[1] This is apparent in Alfonso X's (1252–1284) historical works, the *Estoria de Espanna* and the *General Estoria,* and in his legal writings in the *Siete Partidas.*[2] Alfonso evidently saw himself as the ruler of reconquered territory and of peoples who constituted a *regno,* or "nation,"[3] but he also was highly concerned

about placing himself and his kingdom within a providential and divine order: "[H]is-
toria did not seek to describe events as they were, but to transform them into texts
paralleling those of Scripture and theology in order to complete the dialectic of Revelation."[4] Since medieval historiography usually did not consist of a positivist retelling
of past events, but of ordering those events to show how they elucidated both divine
organization and present affairs, Alfonso aimed to incorporate his "nation" into the
broader scheme. The Estoria de Espanna showed that his Castilian kingdom repeated
and imitated the great dominions of Hercules and Julius Cesar, while their resemblance justified and made inevitable the transfer of Hercules's and Cesar's kingdoms
to Alfonso in the process of translatio imperii.[5]

But Alfonso's concept of the nation differed from the early modern Castilian polity,
mainly in the early modern effort to regulate and constitute society according to
previously unforeseen religious, ethnic, and linguistic divisions.[6] Furthermore, early
modern institutions such as the church, universities, and the crown made unprecedented alliances to inculcate a selective, categorical social order in everyday society.
As we have seen in chapter 1, despite the fact that early modern political and social
consolidation was not complete, extraordinary links were forged between Castilian
monarchs and writers and artists, who became purveyors of the ideals of the early
modern polity. This is evident in the changes to the discourses analyzed in the previous chapters.

Alfonso's idea of the nation also differed from the early modern nation-state in
its relation to past events. While Alfonso viewed his kingdom and himself as fitting
into a historical pattern of divine repetition, early modern writers sometimes injected historical change with the idea of "progress." Early modern people did not see
themselves as illuminating and imitating past events; rather, they often viewed their
distance from them. José Antonio Maravall believes that the early modern emulation of classical and ancient culture was not meant to demonstrate the rebirth of the
ancients, but of the moderns themselves. In contrast to the medieval interlocking of
present and past in a providential order, early modern people often dissociated themselves from the past and placed themselves in an ascendant, superior present.[7] The
modern idea that historical progress dignifies the present and removes it from an inferior past is an early modern invention that reinforces the ruptures and gaps that
characterized Iberian ideology and alterity from about the fifteenth century on.

Yet, it is evident that the early modern relation to the past was multifaceted and
that the idea of "progress" was not common to all perspectives on historical change.
At the same time, however, early modern writers and artists often emphasized categorical division more than many of their medieval counterparts. The variety that exists in any historical period suggests that all epochs may be examined not through the

linear, chronological master narrative of traditional historical and literary studies, but according to the idea of the meshwork, that is, the mutable historical processes of amalgamation and merger similar to a text or a woven garment.[8] The vast heterogeneity and vacillating social conditions of medieval Iberia match the meshwork's supple, interwoven quality, while the permeable meshwork further complements the pliant tenets of medieval Iberian alterity.

And just as the Middle Ages are more consistent with a web than with an unyielding structure, so can modern periods be described in nonlinear, fluid ways. Manuel De Landa believes that the early modern establishment of the individual nation was crucial for Europe's control of much of the world by 1500, since it was precisely the lack of European centralization that allowed for European domination of many regions. De Landa believes that Europe's failure to form a "homogeneous empire" made dominance possible over the more prepared empires of Islam and China, whose centralized forces better controlled the "turbulent" dynamic processes that "raged unobstructed in the West." De Landa points to an excessive dependence in Eastern empires on "skills of their elites," which led at times to bungled management by incompetent leaders. In contrast to this centralized, empirical model, De Landa calls European nations to the present day "meshworks of hierarchies."[9] His description suggests that the early modern changes toward categories and hierarchies are not completely inconsistent with the idea of society as an interlocking meshwork.

The persistent diversity of early modern Iberia is evident, for example, in the continued presence of the negative. The negative did not disappear from early modern society; rather, it continued to exist in complex ways, such as in mystical discourse. Sixteenth-century mystical writers such as Teresa de Jesús and Juan de la Cruz demonstrate the vestiges of the negative's auspicious medieval triadic role. This link to the mediating function of the negative is illustrated by the fact that both early modern mysticism and the negative theology of Pseudo-Dionysius were associated with anagoge, or an uplifting. Anagogical thought is believed to be mystical or mysterious because it relies on paradox to surpass the material and arrive at the ideal.[10] This trust in paradox may explain why the poetic subject of Juan de la Cruz's "Noche oscura" leaves her house enigmatically disguised (*disfrazada*), assuming a multiplicity of possible identities and meanings through the wearing of outer layers. Often presumed to be the soul, this mysterious, unidentified subject overloads herself with clothes and signification, that is, with as much of the mundane as she can "wear," and then renounces all worldly things to finally reach a union with the transcendent.

In "Noche oscura," the journey toward the ideal takes place through a series of negations and obscurities, a realm of value that was intimately associated in the medieval period with the transcendent and divine: "[S]alí sin ser notada" [I left without being noticed]; "en secreto que nadie me veía" [in secret so that no one saw me]; "en parte donde nadie parecía" [in a place where nobody was].[11] The marginalized early modern mystical discourse incorporates the negative into its scheme of arriving at a perfect relation with the divine, and it enacts an uplifting that carries the subject beyond multiplicity to union with a consummate origin. Like medieval negative theology, mystical discourse achieves through the negative the complete reunion of the symbolic and the real, of the signifier and the sign, and of form and content. It continues to demonstrate the problem that Pseudo-Dionysian theology articulated in the medieval period, that human cognition is flawed and that transcendent knowledge may best be attained in paradox.

But the decline of the negative resulted in mysticism's status as "a separate, inferior category" of theology in the early modern period.[12] While the negative was marginalized in mystical discourse and clearly did not disappear from early modern society, it was increasingly seen as opposing the affirmative rather than complementing it. The division between the negative and affirmative contributed to the efforts to homogenize society through ethnic, religious, gender, and linguistic separation, which changed prevailing medieval concepts of alterity. The idea that medieval alterity was constituted differently than early modern otherness moves beyond the anachronistic modern construct of the other that is often attached to the Middle Ages.

The questioning of modern assumptions about medieval alterity and the characterization of all historical periods as complex, diverse meshworks contribute to the current critical dialogue on modern perceptions of the past. They also offer a view of history that contradicts the narrow vision of many political and religious leaders today. As María Rosa Menocal's recent work suggests, the religious, political, and ethnic tensions that plague the Middle East and Mediterranean regions nowadays were not always so violent and extreme.[13] These conflicts do not originate necessarily in rigidly divided medieval groups, but are largely the product of an aggressive modern present. Powerful fundamentalist religious and political leaders around the world today see the past through a mythic lens, which they use to induce whole groups of people to return to a supposedly more pristine era when religious doctrine determined the civic order and delimited people's social roles. Medieval Iberia demonstrates the erroneousness of such a perspective on the past, since its frequent lack of religious identification flies in the face of the ostensibly strict medieval religiosity of Muslims, Christians, and Jews.[14]

Literature, scientific discourse, and art played important roles in the creation and reinforcement of medieval and early modern cultural values. Medieval artists and writers often demonstrated the flexible principles of medieval alterity, while artists and writers who bolstered the goals of the Castilian polity evidenced their shift. Art and textual production readily became tools of the early modern nation-state because of institutional consolidation between the church, professional groups, municipalities, and the crown, as well as technological advances such as the printing press. The direct political link between art and the state was forged during the rule of the Catholic Kings in the late fifteenth and early sixteenth centuries. While this relation was never absolute, it contrasts with the arrangement between art and institutions in the medieval period. Although medieval cultural production was used at times as an ideological tool and often was connected to the church or to the courts of monarchs and nobles, the discourses I have analyzed demonstrate more malleable ways of making difference than their early modern counterparts. Because the medieval Iberian political order and its institutions were even more in flux than those of the early modern period, writing and art did not necessarily bolster institutions as they often did in the late fifteenth and sixteenth centuries. Lyric, medical literature, and discourse on the monster show that texts and art began to affirm new cultural values more widely during the fifteenth century, when they strengthened the hierarchical principles of the Catholic Kings and the Castilian polity. Early modern works such as Fernando de Rojas's *La Celestina* or Juan Huarte de San Juan's *Examen de ingenios para las ciencias* became highly popular in their time, and many of their depictions of the body and their frequently categorical approach to difference contributed to the forging of newly predominant precepts of early modern alterity.

APPENDIX

Poems and Translations

These translations are offered to facilitate access to poems that may not be available otherwise to non-Spanish, Arabic, and Hebrew readers. They are not meant to be an artful contribution to literary studies in translation and thus have been rendered literally. I extend my deepest gratitude to my friend Lisa Dillman, without whose professional expertise my translation efforts would have suffered greatly. I have arranged the poems according to their order in the book and occasionally have reproduced footnotes from the Spanish when I thought them useful to readers.

I. *Muwashshah* originally in Hebrew, with a *jarcha* in Romance (except for the word *habīb* [amigo; friend]), by Yosef el-Katib, "the scribe." Solá-Solé explains that it is a panegyric dedicated to Abu Ibrahim Šemuel, who is probably Samuel Ibn Nagrila, vizier to the kings of Granada, Habus (1025–1038) and Badis (1038–1077), and also to his brother Ishaq. The *muwashshah* was probably composed before 1042, the year that Ishaq died, making the Romance *jarcha* the oldest one known.[1]

1. Alegra tu voz, hija de las olas,[2] / y multiplica las alabanzas; / alaba y tañe bien, / con cantores y danzarines, / a Dios que tan prodigiosamente ha hecho por ti, / multiplicando las recompensas. / Te ha engrandecido por medio de tu salvador, / el

príncipe, el *rab* de muchas acciones buenas, / el *rab* Šĕmuel, adalid de la asamblea. / Su rango es elevado, / y, en cuanto a la transgresión, a causa de su favor, / la cubrirá el amor.

2. El señor afable reúne / la gloria con el esplendor. / El corazón de todos los reyes está conquistando, / por lo que mi brecha ha reparado.[3] / Es un príncipe en cuya mano ha florecido la parra, / de donde salió la uva. / Con las bondades hacia el pobre se inclina / para pagar lo que prometió. / Regala su mano derecha la ofrenda / a mil y a diez mil. / Incluso, en cuanto a mí, mi esperanza, que de él viene, / no me ha sido denegada.

3. Son amables y buenos los hermanos / cuando están juntos. / Los príncipes y el pueblo / ciertamente no pueden ocultar / la redención del pueblo de Dios que ha sido ungido, quitando todo temor. / El que fue atado[4] y el hombre de Ramá[5] / son amigos del Dios único. / Las dos manos del primero son el fruto / y la corona de la asamblea; / el otro, para luchar sale y entra, / apaciguando la querella.

4. Es fuerte en mi interior el amor hacia él: / en mi corazón hay una llama. / Para el deseo de toda su congregación, / que sobre él se asienta . . . no hay en todo el universo semejante a él / en esplendor y en carruaje, / . . . por su mano / cesó la opresión. / Mi amigo es puro y rosado, / prominente entre diez mil.

5. Se levantaría su pináculo de Israel / muy alto y alto; / ya que a través de su aviso la paz es otorgada / para enderezar la senda. / Hará desaparecer al que divide la casa de Dios, / uniendo a la congregación. / Es hombre de temor de dios, cuya mano levanta a Dios / para construir un templo de plegaria. / Por su mano derecha heredaré bondad, / mientras esté sobre el arca sinagogal. / El fortificará con su fuerza mi sendero, / mediante una carta escrita.

6. Príncipe, mi señor, hijo de la majestad, / escucha, pues, mi canto, / y apiádate y cura mi herida: / galardona el regalo de mi tributo. / Por mi parte, yo imploraré por ti a mi Dios, / que es mi salvación y mi luz, / y clamaré mi amor / con la mejor de mis palabras. . . .

Amended version
tnt 'm'ry tnt 'm'ry   hbyb tnt 'm'ry
'nfrmyrwn wlywš (n)ydš   ydwln tn m'ly

Modern Spanish version
"¡Tanto amar, tanto amar, / amigo, tanto amar! / ¡Enfermaron unos ojos brillantes / y duelen tan mal!"

Translation

1. Gladden your voice, daughter of the waves, / and multiply the praises; / praise and play well, / with singers and dancers, / to God who so prodigiously has acted on your behalf, / multiplying the rewards. / He has extolled you through your savior, / the prince, the *rab* of many good actions, / the *rab* Samuel, chief of the assembly.[6] / His rank is elevated, / and, with respect to transgression, on account of his favor, love will cover it up.

2. The affable lord joins / glory with splendor. / All the kings' hearts he is conquering, / which has repaired my breach. / He is a prince in whose hand the grapevine has flourished, / from where grew the grape. / With kindness toward the poor he is impelled, / in order to pay what he promised. / With his right hand he gives offering to a thousand and to ten thousand. / Even, with regard to me, my hope, which comes from him, / has not been denied me.

3. All people are kind and good / when they are together. / The princes and the people / certainly cannot hide / the redemption of God's people, who have been anointed, removing all fear. / He who was bound and the man from Ramah / are friends of the one and only God. / The first man's two hands are the fruit / and the crown of the assembly; / the other goes off to fight and returns, / pacifying the complaint.

4. My love for him is strong inside me: / in my heart there is a flame. / For the desire of his whole congregation, which is seated above him . . . / in the entire universe there is none equal to him / in splendor and in personal carriage, / . . . by his hand / oppression was ended. / My friend is pure and rosy, / prominent among ten thousand.

5. His pinnacle of Israel would be raised / very, very high; / since through his counsel peace is granted / to straighten the path. / He shall make disappear whoever divides God's house, / uniting the congregation. / He is a man fearful of God, whose hand lifts God / to construct a temple of prayer. / By his right hand I will inherit goodness, / while he is over the arc of the synagogue. / With his strength he will fortify my path, / through a written letter.

6. Prince, my lord, son of majesty, / listen, then, to my song, / and take pity and cure my wound: / reward the gift of my tribute. / For my part, on your behalf I will implore God, / who is my salvation and light, / and I will cry out my love / with the best of my words. . . .

"So much loving, so much loving, / friend, so much loving! / Some bright eyes became ill / and they hurt so badly!"

II. *Muwashshah* in Arabic by Yahyà al-Ğazzar, which consists of a prelude and five strophes, and a final *jarcha*. Al-Ğazzar wrote until the end of the eleventh century. Solá-Solé calls the poem amorous and believes that the poet recites the final *jarcha* to a friend who calls on him.[7]

¡Oh mis ojos! / ¿Acaso los asuntos / el fuego del corazón / inflaman, / o bien el ardor de mi sed / empuja el correr / de mis lágrimas?

1. ¡Oh mi censor! / ¿Cómo a aquél censuras / que presenta la extenuación manifiesta? / A mi asesino / yo le adoro, / incluso si yo / no tengo / de lo que deseo / sino la pena. / ¿Qué cosa / podría ser como yo? / Hasta que mi enfermedad / desaparezca, / no tendré otra insignia / que mi palidez.

2. Hay en mí una pequeña gacela / —¡oh sus dos trenzas / que yo cogí!— / y mis entrañas / escondieron mi amor por ella, / pero luego lo revelaron. / Si lo revelan, / ¡cuánto las entrañas lo han escondido / para que no sea divulgado! / ¡Y qué manera de esconder! / No hay nadie que pueda ayudarme / salvo el abundante correr de lágrimas, / presente en mí. / No hay victoria posible, / salvo mis sollozos.

3. Y la realización de mi deseo / puede ser el medicamento del que es experimentado, / si jamás se consigue . . . / ¿Qué debo hacer? / He aquí que mis penas / —¡oh mi ser venerado ante quien yo me arrepiento!— / operan / el efecto de agudos sables / sobre el herido maltratado.

4. El deseado / por mis ojos, pasa ahora / por el odio violento / ¡Puede ser que / un día se ponga contento / o, quizás, se aleje! / ¡Ofrécele a mi ojo / un momento en que esté satisfecho / de él, o, en todo caso, sombrío como la noche! / ¡Oh pequeña gacela! / Aquellos párpados / para los corazones / operan / el efecto de agudos sables / en tiempo de guerras.

5. ¡Qué malo es lo que / el censor ha dejado / y lo que ha querido hacer! / Cada vez que / aparece el bien amado / se presenta también él. / ¡Cuántas veces / canto yo para responder / a quien llama . . . !

Transcription

kd'my	flmwly 'lbyn	'đl mb
kđl	myt t'ry	sr'lrqyb

Modern Spanish version

"Amé / a un hijito ajeno, / y él a mí; / lo quiere / captar (apartar) de mí / su espía (guardador)."

Translation

Oh my eyes! / Perhaps events / inflame / the fire of my heart, / or maybe the ardor of my thirst / impels the flow / of my tears?

1. Oh my censor! / How do you censure him / who presents manifest exhaustion? / I adore / my assassin, / even if I / do not have / that which I desire / but only grief. / What thing / could be like me? / Until my illness / disappears, / I will have no other insignia / than my paleness.

2. There is in me a little gazelle / —oh, her two braids / that I pulled!— / and my entrails / hid my love for her, / but then revealed it. / If they reveal it, / how much the entrails have hidden it / so that it would not be divulged! / And what a way of hiding! / There is no one who can help me, / except the abundant flowing of tears / present in me. / There is no possible victory, / except my sobs.

3. And the fulfillment of my desire / can be the medicine of that which is experienced, / if ever it is attained . . . / What must I do? / Here are my sorrows / —oh my venerated one before whom I repent!— / that have / the effect of sharp sabers / on the ill-treated wound.

4. The desired one / passes now, before my eyes, / to violent hate. / It could be that / one day he becomes contented / or, maybe, he will go away! / Let my eye behold / one moment in which I am satisfied / with him, or, at the least, gloomy like the night! / Oh, little gazelle! / Those eyelids / for hearts / have / the effect of sharp sabers / in time of war.

5. How terrible is that which / the censor has left behind, / and what he wanted to do! / Every time / the beloved appears, / the censor presents himself as well. / How many times / do I sing to respond / to him who calls . . . !

"I loved another's little boy, and he loved me. His guardian wants to separate him from me."

III. *Zajal* that Ibn Quzmān (d. 1160) fashioned as a love poem in which he asks his patron, Abu al-Hasan 'Ali al-Baiyani, to provide things for his house, since the holidays are approaching. Solá-Solé says that the *jarcha* is sung by a young woman (*doncella*) who is equally in love with Ali.[8]

1. Me trata con orgullo, me tiraniza, me esclaviza / conforme quiere. El mismo ve con sus propios ojos que mi corazón derrite, / y aumenta el tormento. / Si me matara, y en torno a eso anda, / mataría a un esclavo. / Mas imposible es que mi amado se vea / cogido por mi venganza.

2. Le pregunté en mi amor hacia él por el motivo de su huida: / "¿por qué te alejas?" / Me dijo: "enamorado, tonto e insistente, / mueres por mi causa. / Por Dios que te inquietas, te pones miserable y agitado / hasta verme. / Y, a causa de tu amor por nuevas de mí, / te vuelves amoroso de mi vecino."[9]

3. ¿Cómo va a esperar uno la unión o la constancia (en el amor) / o la vida que yo deseo, / de quien tiene en la cintura un cuchillo / (que es) como un rayo que brilla? / Al decir: "¿quién (está) por este mezquino / (a quien) tú matas? ¡Oye!" / de un golpe prodigó mi mosto / (que era) mi vecino.

4. Error grave sería matar a mi Quzmán, / pues su vida es muy preciosa; / y ello, sobre todo, al tiempo que la fiesta viene; / pues, ¿cómo voy a celebrarla? / El elogio de Abu-l-Hassan al-Baiyani / es para mí el más firme. / Así pues, en dirigirme a él a través de mis poemas / veo mi inclinación.

5. La fiesta está cerca y basta lo que ves / de la proximidad de esta fiesta. / Y los desvanes en toda fiesta, ciertamente se rinden / al arreglo y a la renovación. / Y no es cuestión de una pequeña cosa en la compra, / pues ello no sería bueno. / Así pues, ¡compra para mí según me aprecias / cosas para mi casa!

6. ¡Oh quién, cuando no tengo un chavo / le pido un chavo, / y cuando le cojo por la vía del provecho, / consigo el provecho! / Dame a aquél cuyo poder es aceptado / y reúneme con él: / rubio, hermoso, por él pasan mis cuidados, / (y que tiene) el color de mis patillas.[10]

7. Movióme a que hiciera versos / en este ritmo, / una muchacha bonita, dulce, que cantaba / un canto bello; / y no había agravio para él que nombró / con pelos y señales. . . .

Vocalized, reconstructed version
'ašiq(a), *ay mamma, yo de ešte* al-ǧārī
'Alī al-ḥumārī

Modern Spanish version
"Locamente enamorada estoy, ay madre, yo de este vecino mío / Alí, el morenazo."

Translation

1. He treats me with arrogance, he tyrannizes me, he enslaves me / at will. He himself sees with his own eyes that my heart melts, / and my torment grows. / If he were to kill me, and that is what he is doing, / he would kill a slave. / But it is impossible that my beloved see himself / caught by my revenge.

2. In my love for him, I asked him the reason for his flight: / "Why do you leave?" / He told me, "Lover, silly and insistent, / you die for me. / By God, you get upset, you become miserable and agitated / until you see me. / And because of your love of news about me, / you fall in love with my neighbor."

3. How is one going to expect union or consistency (in love), / or the life that I desire, / from him who has a knife at his waist, / (which is) like a ray that shines? / Upon saying, "Who (is) in favor of this wretch / (whom) you kill? Listen!" / with one stroke my frenzy proved / that he was my neighbor.

4. A grave error it would be to kill my Quzmán, / since his life is very valuable; / to do so, especially, as the holiday approaches; / anyhow, how am I going to celebrate it? / The praise of Abu-l-Hassan al-Baiyani / is for me the most unswerving. / So then, addressing him through my poems / I see my calling.

5. The holiday is close and what you see abounds / in the proximity of this holiday. / And attics in all holidays certainly lend themselves / to repair and renovation. / And it is not a question of a small thing to shop for, / because that would not be good. / So then, buy for me according to how you esteem me, / things for my house!

6. Oh, he whom, when I do not have a *chavo* [*ochavo,* an old copper coin, valued at two maravedis] / I ask for a *chavo,* / and when I catch him on the way of gain, / I obtain profit and gain! / Give me over to him whose power is accepted, / and unite me with him: / fair, handsome, because of him I am so tormented, / (and who has) the color of my sideburns.

7. A young girl, pretty and sweet, who was singing / a lovely song, / moved me to write verses / in this rhythm; / and there was no offense toward him whom she named / chapter and verse. . . .

"Crazy in love, o Mother, am I with my neighbor, / Ali, the big brown man."

IV. Twelfth-century Hebrew *muwashshah* by Abraham Ibn Ezra (c. 1089–1167), with a Romance *jarcha*. Sáenz-Badillos and Targarona Borrás say that it includes the "conventional topics" of the beauty of the beloved and the grief produced by his absence.[11]

¿Cómo se apaciguarán / en mi corazón mis entrañas, /
      que gimen como el mar?

Amigos míos, por favor cogedme de la mano,
que quema como el fuego de mis vísceras
por la ausencia del corzo gracioso, mi amigo.

Con amargura lloran / mis ojos, destilan rocío, /
      y no se acallan.

Huerto de amor, y ciervo
en el que se juntan gracia y belleza.
¡Sea mi alma su liberación y rescate!

Por ello se multiplican / todas mis bendiciones en su honor, /
      y no se acaban.

Pomo de mirra y escogido ciervo,
su aroma es como el nardo y las alheñas.
Los que le conocen de todas partes

a él acuden, / para encontrar el bálsamo de los dolores /
      cuando enferman.

¡Qué admirable es su amor,
para mí, cuando contemplo su figura!
Su esplandor es como el del sol cuando sale;

si vieran / quienes bajan al *šĕ'ol* su imagen /
      y su belleza, revivirían.

Lloro en mi alma por una doncella
que gime con voz amarga como cierva

por su amado que marchó al destierro:
"bajaré con pena al mundo de los muertos,

Dime ¿qué he de hacer? ¿(cómo viviré)? A este amigo espero,
    por él moriré."

Translation

How will they calm down / my heart's entrails, / which howl
    like the sea?

My friends, please take me by the hand,
which burns like the fire of my entrails
at the absence of the graceful brown deer, my friend.

With bitterness they cry, / my eyes exude dew, /
    and they are not stilled.

Orchard of love, and deer
where grace and beauty meet.
Let my soul be his liberation and rescue!

Thus are multiplied / all my blessings in his honor, /
    and they do not end.

Bouquet of myrrh and chosen deer,
his fragrance is like the tuberose and henna.
Those who know him from all over

approach him / to find the balm for their pains /
    when they are sick.

How admirable is his love,
for me, when I contemplate his figure!
His splendor is like the sun's when it rises;

if they saw / those who lower to the *šĕ'ol*[12] his image /
    and his beauty, they would be revived.

I cry in my soul for a maiden
who moans with a bitter voice like a doe
for her [male] lover who left for exile:
"I will descend with sorrow to the world of the dead,

Tell me, what am I to do? (How shall I live?) I await this
    friend; for him I will die."

V. Two non-*muwashshah* and *zajal* love poems by Yishaq Ibn Jalfun, an eleventh-century writer from Cordova.[13]

1.

Con falaz cortesía, boca halagadora y hablar tierno
       engañarme quieres y aplacarme;
mi corazón robar pretendes con lisonjas,
       te finges hermoso y no lo eres.
Te acercas sonriente, con corazón perverso,
       cual plata a la arcilla recubriendo.
Parece que hay remedios en tu boca,
       mas herida de víbora no cura con conjuros.

Translation

With fallacious courtesy, a flattering mouth, and tender words
       you want to deceive and placate me;
my heart with flattery you attempt to rob,
       you [male beloved] pretend to be handsome and you are not.
You approach smiling, with a perverse heart,
       like silver coating clay.
It seems that there are remedies in your mouth,
       but the viper's wound does not cure with spells.

2.

Me despierta el amor y brinco,
       cual ciervo, para mirar los ojos de mi amada.
Me acerco, y junto a ella está su madre,
       su padre, su hermano y su tío.
La miro y vuelvo la espalda,
       como si no fuera su amigo ni amante.
Me asustan, aunque mi corazón sienta por ella
       lo que la mujer al morir su único hijo.

Translation

Love wakes me and I leap
      like a deer to look at my [woman] lover's eyes.
I approach, and next to her is her mother,
      her father, her brother, and her uncle.
I look at her and I turn my back,
      as if I were neither her friend nor her lover.
They scare me, although my heart feels for her
      what the woman feels who loses her only child.

VI. This poem by the eleventh- or twelfth-century Andalusi woman poet Hamda Banāt Ziyād de Guadix is identified as "Poema, que compuso Hamda cuando fue al río con una joven. Y cuando ésta se desnudó completamente dijo . . ." [A poem that Hamda composed when she went to the river with a young woman. And when that woman was completely naked, Hamda said:]

> Las lágrimas revelan mis secretos en un río
> donde hay tantas señales de belleza:
> es un río que rodea jardines,
> y jardines que bordean al río;
> entre las gacelas hay una humana
> que posee mi alma y tiene mi corazón;
> cuando entorna los ojos por alguna razón,
> esa razón me impide a mí dormir;
> cuando suelta sus bucles sobre el rostro,
> parece la luna en las tinieblas de la noche;
> es como si a la aurora se le hubiese muerto un hermano
> y de tristeza se hubiese vestido de luto.

Translation

> Tears reveal my secrets in a river
> where there are so many signs of beauty:
> it is a river that surrounds gardens,
> and there are gardens that border the river;
> among the gazelles there is a woman
> who possesses my soul and holds my heart;
> when she half closes her eyes for some reason,
> that reason impedes my sleep;
> when she loosens her curls over her face,
> she looks like the moon in the night's darkness;
> it is as if the aurora's brother had died,
> and, from sadness, she had dressed in mourning.[14]

VII. *Muwashshah* by Ibn ʿUbada al-Qazzaz, "the poet from Málaga," with a prelude and five strophes. Solá-Solé describes it as a panegyric dedicated to a king who goes unnamed, but who is probably Muʿtasim of Almería (1051–1091). He further declares that the *jarcha* is narrated by war, but that it is based on a young, desperate girl's song. In a footnote that I have not reproduced (note 28), Solá-Solé suggests two interpretations for the relation between the *muwashshah* and *jarcha*: first, it transmits the poet's fear and sadness in the face of the king's absence; and, second, the *jarcha* ironically mocks the poet, who will lose the king's patronage when the latter leaves for war. He bases his second interpretation on the *jarcha*'s constructed (*artificioso*) character, which derived, perhaps, from another poem. Solá-Solé's second asseveration is in my view difficult to sustain.[15]

Codicia el vaso de vino tinto / y escucha las cuerdas musicales. / No te preocupes de las penas: / ¡sea lo que ha determinado el Creador!
1. Rechaza a los locos / que se nos han opuesto en cuanto a la religión (del amor), / y canta para nosotros, / ya que la realización de mis afanes / está en que logre mis necesidades / de vino cálido / y el clamor de cuerdas musicales.
2. Favoreció una lluvia pródiga / a una mansión junto al río, / y no cesará por ello mi gratitud. / He aquí que yo arrastro la cola de mis vestidos / por tal morada, entre lunas, / y ella ha honrado mi indulgencia / y ha menospreciado mis dineros.
3. He aquí que la luz se derrama / por el favorecido de Dios, el victorioso; / y su elogio es perfumado / en mis mañanas y en mis tardes, / cantándole en mis poemas, / sobre el árbol de mi conocimiento / y sobre la rama de mi recuerdo.
4. Rey es que siempre ha resuelto / todos los eventos por completo; / que ha extendido la justicia a todas las criaturas. / Si se generalizan las noches / —que son oscuras para los ojos—, / entonces él será una luna perfecta, / por la que se guiaría el viajero nocturno.
5. Cuántas veces le cantó la guerra, / cuya victoria es penosa, / el canto de quien está afligido.

Amended version
'ls'm m(w) h'l   (brq)y h'ly qd b'r
k fry ymm   f'nq bd lb'r

Modern Spanish version
"La muerte es mi estado, / porque mi estado (es) desesperado. / ¿Qué haré, oh madre mía? / El que me mima va a marcharse."

Translation

Covet the glass of red wine / and listen to the musical chords. / Do not worry about sorrows: / let it be as the Creator has determined!

1. Reject the crazy ones / who have opposed us as to the religion (of love), / and sing for us, / since fulfilling my duties / lies in my fulfilling my need / for warm wine / and the plaint of musical chords.

2. A prodigal rain favored / an abode next to the river, / and my gratitude for that will not end. / Look! See how I drag the train of my robes / by the house, from one moon to the next, / and the rain has honored my indulgence / and has scorned my money.

3. Here is the light that spreads / around God's favored one, the victorious; / and his praise is perfumed / in my mornings and in my afternoons, / singing to him in my poems, / the tree of my knowledge / and the branch of my memory.

4. He is a king who always has resolved / all possible events completely; / who has extended justice to all creatures. / If nights were forever / —which are dark to the eyes—, / then he would be a perfect moon, / by which the nocturnal traveler would be guided.

5. How many times did War, / whose victory is arduous, / sing him the song about the one who is afflicted.

"Death is my station / because my station is desperate. / What will I do, / o Mother? / He who pampers me is headed off to war."

VIII. Poem from the *Cancionero de Stúñiga* by the noble Lope de Stúñiga (c. 1414–1480), who spent the last few years of his life in Toledo.[16]

Señora, grand sinrazón
me fezistes, en buena fe,
condenarme sin porqué.

Todo hombre se enamora
a fin de ser amado,
e por ser yo enamorado
vos amé a vos, señora,
e segund paresce agora,
aunque yo vos dé mi fe,
condenáisme sin porqué.

Ruego a los amadores
que aman sin ser amados,
que sientan los mis cuidados
e plangan los mis dolores,
pues saben que son amores
que siempre mudan la fe,
e condenan sin porqué.

Fin
Vuestra muy linda figura
yo siempre desearé,
pues de vos me cativé.

Translation

My lady, a grave injustice
you committed, in good faith,
by condemning me without reason.

All men fall in love
in order to be loved,
and because I am in love,

I loved you, my lady,
and as it seems now,
even though I give you my faith,
you condemn me without reason.

I beg lovers
who love without being loved
to feel my suffering
and bewail my pain,
because they know that love affairs
always change faith
and condemn without reason.

End
Your very beautiful figure
I will always desire,
because I was captivated by you.

IX. Anonymous poem from the *Cancionero general* (1511). According to the descriptive title in the edition, the poem describes a woman who left her house and walked down a street, where many officials were watching her.[17]

Tan gentil os vieron ir,
que depués, en el tornar,
unos hezistes morir,
y a otros maravillar.
Todos estavan atentos,
todos d'una voluntad,
maravillados, contentos,
heridos de pensamientos
de vuestra mucha beldad.

Las damas hezistes mustias
y a los hombres sin denuedos,
los amantes con angustias,
los oficios estar quedos.
Y todos los que labravan
de su arte y jumetría,
con sus ojos os miravan
y de las lenguas loavan
la vuestra gran loçanía.

Fin
Y tras vos, yo, sospirando,
iva cual nunca os halléis,
aquella tierra adorando
do poníades los pies.
Iva con mucha tristura,
puestos mis ojos en vos,
quexando por mi ventura
del valer y hermosura
que vos quiso poner Dios.

Translation

So genteel they saw you go
that later, upon returning,
you made some die,
and others marvel.
All were attentive,
all were of one will,
amazed, happy,
wounded by thoughts
of your great beauty.

You made the ladies gloomy
and the men without bravery,
the lovers with anguish,
the professions still.
And all who were working
on their trade and burdensome task
with their eyes looked at you
and with their tongues praised
your great beauty.

End
And behind you went I, sighing,
though you will never know,
adoring that ground
where you put your feet.
I went with great sadness,
my eyes fixed on you,
lamenting my fate
of the worthiness and beauty
that God granted you.

X. From the *Cancionero de Stúñiga,* a poem by Carvajal or Carvajales, who probably spent time at the court of Alfonso V in Naples. Carvajal was alive at the time of the king's death in 1460.[18]

Passando por la Toscana,
entre Sena y Florencia,
vi dama gentil, galana,
digna de gran reverencia.

Cara tenía de romana,
tocadura portuguesa,
el aire de castellana,
vestida como senesa
discretamente, no vana;
yo le fize reverencia
y ella, con mucha prudencia,
bien mostró ser cortesana.

Así entramos por Sena
fablando de compañía,
con plazer haviendo pena
del pesar que me plazía.
Si se dilatara el día
o la noche nos tomara,
tan grand fuego se encendía
que toda la tierra quemara.

Vestía de blanco domasquino,
camurra al tovillo cortada
encima de un vellud fino
un luto la falda rastrada,
pomposa e agraciada
una invención traía
por letras que no entendía
de perlas la manga bordada.

Item más traía un joyel,
de ricas piedras pesantes:

un balax y, en torno d'él,
çafís, rubís e diamantes,
firmado sobre la fruente
con muy grande resplandor;
pero dávale el favor
su gesto lindo, plaziente.

Fin
En su fabla, vestir e ser
non mostrava ser de mandra;
queriendo su nombre saber,
respondióme que Casandra;
yo, con tal nombre oír,
muy alegre desperté
e tan solo me fallé,
que, por Dios, pensé morir.

Translation

Passing through Tuscany,
between Siena and Florence,
I saw a genteel lady, fine-looking,
worthy of great reverence.

She had the face of a Roman,
her headdress, Portuguese,
the air of a Castilian,
(she was) dressed as a Sienese
discretely, not frivolous;
I paid her reverence
and she, with great prudence,
proved herself to be a lady of the court.

Thus we entered Siena,
talking together,
with pleasure having grief
from the sorrow that pleased me.

If the day were prolonged
or the night seized us,
so great a fire would start
that the whole world would burn (down).

She was dressed in white damask,
in sable cut to the ankle
over a fine velvet,
a crepe the dragging skirt,
splendid and graceful,
she wore a design
with letters I did not understand,
the sleeve embroidered with pearls.

She also wore a small jewel
of rich, heavy stones:
a balas (a kind of ruby) and, around it,
sapphires, rubies, and diamonds,
affixed to her forehead,
shining so brightly;
but she gave it her touch
with her lovely, pleasing expression.

End
In her speech, dress, and appearance
she showed she was not from the hills;
when I wanted to know her name,
she responded to me, Cassandra;
I, upon hearing that name,
very happily awoke
and found myself so alone
that, by God, I wanted to die.

XI. "Cutting poem" from Hernando de Castillo's *Cancionero general* of 1511 about a cloth shearer, called a *tondidor*. Grey says that the poem is placed in the section called "Obras menudas," or "Worthless Works." The first and last stanzas are uncut, while the rest of the poem can be read in uncut and cut versions. Grey notes the clever insertion of "marcado de niño" in the opening stanza, which refers to circumcision, and believes that it demonstrates the poet's ill favor toward the *tondidor*: "One wonders if the poet wished to point out that the *converso* was 'marked' whether or not he sincerely accepted his new faith."[19] The poem is published without a division, but Grey includes it for ease of reading. Translation note: Parenthetical additions within the translation refer to changes that readers must make in order to understand the second, cut version of the poem. There are occasional irregularities in the move from the uncut to the cut version.[20]

> Tondidor maestro de buenos maestros
> marcado de niño por mucha excelencia
> para que diga los hechos tan vuestros
> enestos renglones presentes no diestros
> demando perdon y tomo licencia

> Vos soys muy sabido   de cosas divinas
> de males del mundo   soys apartado
> vos soys guarnescido   de buenas doctrinas
> del rayo profundo   soys bien desuiado
> Vos soys sabidor   delo ques verdad
> delos torpes males   no soys vos amigo
> vos soys obrador   de toda bondad
> de pecados mortales   mortal enemigo

> De vanas nouelas   soys trassechador
> dezis toda via   delo ques verdad
> de falsas cautelas   no soys sabidor
> vsays compañía   de honestidad
> Soys muy amador   de cosas gentiles
> delas viles cosas   soys muy apartado
> teneys desamor   a gentes ciuiles
> a gentes graciosas   soys muy allegado

Soys muy furioso
ala humildad
soys muy desdeñoso
dela caridad
Alos honrrados
teneys por rehenes
delos malhechores
dezis muchos bienes

Ala gente loca
honrrays de bondad
jamas vuestra boca
no dize verdad
Soys de quistiones
muy gran causador
de santos sermones
soys blasfemador

Soys de agarenos [Muhammad]
pariente y amigo
de ayunos muy buenos
soys gran enemigo
De forma de juda [Judas]
servis de verdad
enla trenidad
poneys mucha dubda

Siempre hezistes
burlas de pobres
de alma creystes
los dioses de cobre
De nuestra senora
soys perseguidor
dela vieja tora
soys gran seruidor

Tenes por bendita
la eretica secta

contra los furiosos
soys muy allegado
alos mentirosos
soys aficionado
honrrays por ygual
alos maliciosos
dezis mucho mal
delos virtuosos

tractays con gran yra
aquien vos bien dize
no dize mentira
quien malde vos dize
muy apartado
de cosas perfectas
soys muy arreado
de falsos profetas

gran perseguidor
delos defensores
soys gran causador
de blasfemadores
cerrays vuestra puerta
a Dios y alos reyes
teneys fe muy perfecta
enlas falsas leyes

limosna a cristianos
jamas las hezistes
los papas romanos
jamas los creystes
soys aficionado
de toda eregia
renegays de buen grado
de santa maria

la inquisicion
por descomulgada

teneys por maldita   la mala opinion
nuestra fe perfecta   por bien aprouada
Teneys desamor   alos lisongeros
con nuestros perlados   teneys aficion
tractays con rigor   alos hechizeros
los templos sagrados   con gran devocion

Fin
No es la muestra verdadera
que al pie de la letra glosada
bien consiento
mas dalde dela tisera
quenel medio esta la celada
delo cierto

Translation

Cloth shearer, master of good masters,
marked as a child for great excellence,
in order to tell of the facts about you
in these unskilled, present verses
I request pardon and I take license.

You are very knowledgeable   of (from) divine things
from (of) the evils of the world   you are separated
you are full   of (from) good doctrines
from (of) deep unseen misfortune   you are well deviated
You are very knowledgeable   of the truth
of lewd evil   you are not a friend
you are a laborer   of all goodness
of mortal sins   mortal enemy

From (of) vain novellas   you are diverged
you still speak   of (from) what is true
of false cunning   you are not knowledgeable
you employ companions   of honesty
You are a great lover   of (from) genteel things

from (of) base things
you have an indifference
to gracious people

You are very furious
to (about) humility
you are very disdainful
of charity
Honored people
you hold as prisoners
about malefactors
you say many good things

Crazy people
you honor with goodness
your mouth never
does not tell the truth
You are from (of) fights
(the) very great cause
by (of) sacred sermons
you are a blasphemer

Of Muhammad you are
relative and friend
of very good fasts
you are a great enemy
On the way of Judas
you serve in truth
in the trinity
you put much doubt

You always gave (made)
scoffing (fun of) the poor
you believed with your heart
the copper gods
Of the Virgin
you are a persecutor

you are quite separated
to mean people
you are very close

against furious people
you are very close
of liars
you are fond
you honor equally
malicious people
you say many bad things
about virtuous people

you treat with anger
whomever you well say
(does not) tell(s) a lie
he who speaks badly of you
very separated
of (from) perfect things
you are very driven
of (by) false prophets

a great persecutor
of the defenders
you are a great cause
of blasphemers
you shut your door
(to) God and the kings
you have most perfect faith
in false laws

alms to Christians
you never did (gave)
the Roman popes
you never believed
you are fond
of all heresy

(of) the old Torah
you are a great servant

You hold as blessed
the heretical sect
you hold as evil
our perfect faith
You have indifference
for our prelates
you treat with rigor
the sacred temples

you deny with vigor
of Saint Mary

the Inquisition
as wicked
bad opinion
as excellent
for flatterers
you have fondness
(for) sorcerers
with great devotion

End
It is not the true indication
That, literally glossed,
indeed do I permit;
rather, give it a cut with scissors,
as the trap is in the middle
of the truth

XII. Five "cutting poems" from the fourteenth century by Ibn Játima de Almería (Abū Ya'far Ahmad ibn Jātima).[21]

1. Ahí te va esta página llena de las quejas de un enamorado
   triste, que ha caído en el infierno del amor:
   No las ha escrito con aire en vano,
   sino para decirte la inmensidad de su cariño.

2. Pasea tus ojos por mi trazado, y verás
   una escritura donde la tinta es aire.
   El que me escribió se parece a mí en dos cosas:
   en que tenemos cuerpo, pero perdimos el corazón.

3. Cuando mi deseo me llenó de tristeza, escribí
   el secreto de mi amor bordándolo con la tijera,
   pues, si hubiera querido escribirlo de otro modo,
   el cálamo habría ardido entre mis manos.

4. ¡Oh aquél por cuyo amor estoy celoso
   de él, de mí y de todo el mundo
   hasta el punto de que, si quiero escribir un secreto,
   he de hacerlo en la página del aire!

5. Escucha, amado de mi corazón, la voz de un enamorado,
   a quien la pasión extenuó, o, más aún, derritió.
   Quiso declararte sus sentimientos,
   y, al hacerlo, ardieron las letras del escrito.

Translation

1. Here, for you, a page full of a sad lover's complaints
   who has fallen into love's inferno:
   He has not written them in air in vain,
   but rather to tell you the immensity of his affection.

2. Cast your eyes on my design, and you will see
   a composition where ink is air.

He who wrote to me resembles me in two things:
in that we have a body, but we lost our heart.

3. When my desire filled me with sadness, I wrote
the secret of my love, embroidering it with scissors,
because if I had wanted to write it in another way,
the pen would have burned in my hands.

4. Oh, he for whose love I am envious
his, mine, and everyone's,
to the point that if I want to write a secret,
I have to do it on the page of air!

5. Listen, [male] lover of my heart, to the voice of a [male] lover,
whom passion wore out, or, what is more, melted.
He tried to declare his feelings to you,
and, upon doing so, the letters of the text burned.

XIII. From the first half of the thirteenth century, a "cutting poem" by the 'Abd Allāh al Ansārī al-Qurtubī, a resident of Málaga, who emigrated to the east and died in Cairo in 1254.[22]

Es un calígrafo que adorna a maravilla el papel,
pues no lo hace con tinta ni con pluma,
sino con una tijera, que lo deja tan bello
como el jardín regado por generosa lluvia.
Recortándolas, da existencia a letras inexistentes:
maravíllate de una cosa cuyo ser es el no ser.

Translation

He is a calligrapher who marvelously adorns paper
because he does it with neither ink nor pen,
but with scissors, which makes it as lovely
as a garden watered by generous rain.
Cutting them out gives existence to nonexistent letters:
marvel at a thing whose existence does not exist.

XIV. A final "cutting poem" by the Valencian poet al-Rusāfī (Abū ʿAbd Allāh Muhammad b. Gālib al-Rusāfī), who died in Málaga in 1177.[23]

> ¡Por tu vida! ¿viste antes unas letras
> escritas con el agua de la belleza en los bordes de la flor?
> Es un trozo de papel, al que dobló, como ves,
> el juego de la tijera, línea tras línea.
> ¿No es asombroso que su autor haya cambiado
> el papel con su alcanfor, por el amizcle de la tinta?

Translation

> On your life! Have you ever before seen letters
> written with the water of beauty on the edges of the flower?
> It is a piece of paper, folded, as you see,
> by the scissors game, line after line.
> Is it not astonishing that its author has exchanged
> the paper with its camphor, for the musk of the ink?

Notes

Translations are mine, except where noted otherwise.

•

Introduction

1. Castro, *España en su historia*. Castro analyzes the *Lba* in chap. 9, 355–446.
2. Sánchez Albornoz, *España*. Many scholars have studied the debate and its link to reconquest ideology, such as Dodds, *Architecture*, 2–3; Menocal, *Shards of Love*, 41–42, 211–12, 242–43; and, most recently, Hutcheson, "Sodomitic Moor," 99–122.
3. González Jiménez, "Frontier and Settlement," 49–52.
4. Nirenberg, *Communities of Violence*.
5. Tolan, *Saracens*.
6. Said, *Orientalism*; and Bhabha, *Location of Culture*.
7. Meyerson, Introduction, xii–xiii.
8. Ibid., xiii.
9. Ibid., xiii–xiv.
10. Young Gregg, *Devils, Women, and Jews*. Ora Limor also questions Young Gregg's assumptions in her review of the book in *The Medieval Review*. Available at http://www.hti.umich.edu/t/tmr, TMR ID: 99.01.04.
11. Goodich, *Other Middle Ages*, 7, 17.
12. Brown, *Contrary Things*; and Burke, *Desire against the Law*.
13. Foucault, *Order of Things*, 47.

14. Ibid., 50.

15. José Antonio Maravall concurs in *Antiguos y modernos*, 285, where he claims that continuity and simultaneity characterized the medieval period, while ruptures and fractures define modern society.

Chapter One.   Identity and the Limits of Iberian Alterity

1. For biographical information on Samuel Ibn Nagrila, see *Poetas hebreos de al-Andalus*, 71–72; and Scheindlin, *Wine, Women, and Death*, 11.

2. Manuela Marín discusses the variable character of Iberian society in *Al-Ándalus*, especially 9–26.

3. Menocal, *Ornament*, 86–87.

4. Brann, "Arabized Jews," 442. Raymond P. Scheindlin further demonstrates the Andalusi cultural meshwork in *Gazelle*, 3–12.

5. Phillips, *Enrique IV*, 86–88. Enrique's establishment of the Inquisition in Castile might seem to refute his court's impartiality. Yet Phillips believes that through its founding Enrique sought to invalidate the societal criticism about Christian converts (*conversos*), 86–87.

6. Menocal, *Ornament*, 49, 244–45.

7. Nirenberg, "Religion and Sexual Boundaries," 144.

8. Edward W. Said demonstrates the effects of colonization on the creation of the modern other in *Orientalism*. N. Katherine Hayles argues that it is unlikely that local identities and divisions will disappear today amidst destabilizing, globalizing processes, in "Complexities," 119.

9. Glick, *Islamic and Christian Spain*, 46–47, 49.

10. Larsson, *Ibn García's shu'ūbiyya Letter*, 133.

11. Glick, *Islamic and Christian Spain*, 209.

12. Ibid., 47, 210.

13. For an account of Muslim-Christian relations into the ninth century, see Baxter Wolf's "Christian Views," 85–108. Baxter Wolf shows that the mid-ninth-century case of the Cordovan martyrs' movement attests to the anxiety of some Christians about Christian attachments to Islam, 95–102.

He further shows that Iberians in the eighth century probably did not view the North Africans as "Muslim" or "Islamic," suggesting that religion did not play an initial role in North African domination. Baxter Wolf, "Muhammad as Antichrist," 4.

14. Lindberg, *Beginnings of Western Science*, especially 203–6; and Siraisi, *Medieval and Early Renaissance Medicine*, 14–15.

15. Gil, *Escuela de traductores*. No physical "school" is known to have existed, and translators probably worked in the king's *scriptorium*. Illuminations from King Alfonso X's *Cantigas de Santa María*, nos. 1, 2, 56, 138, and 156, demonstrate writing and reading practices at

his royal court and in monasteries. See the facsimile edition of the T. I.1 codex from the library at El Escorial, *Cantigas de Santa María* (Madrid: Edilán, 1979).

16. Gil, *Escuela de traductores,* 57–83. Gil argues against Claudio Sánchez Albornoz's claim that the contributions of Ibero-Jewish translators were insignificant and their ranks small in number, 57 n. 3.

17. Roth, "Jewish Collaborators," 59–71.

18. Epalza, "Mozarabs," 184.

19. Adang, *Islam frente a Judaísmo,* 15–16.

20. Marín, *Al-Ándalus,* 28, 30, 32.

21. Nederman, *Worlds of Difference,* 36–37.

22. Menocal, *Arabic Role,* 34–35.

23. Arié, *Reino nasrí de Granada,* 146.

24. Constable, *Medieval Iberia,* 91.

25. Tolan, introduction to *Diálogo,* xii.

26. Menocal, *Ornament,* 88.

27. Docker, *1492,* 12–13; and Abu-Lughod, *Before European Hegemony,* 11–12, 15–16.

28. Constable, *Trade and Traders,* 2.

29. Ibid., 62.

30. Castro, *España en su historia,* 355–446.

31. Menocal, *Arabic Role,* 30, 65.

32. López-Morillas, "Language," 34.

33. Ibid., 47.

34. Ibid., 51.

35. Carpenter, *Alfonso X,* 104–5.

36. Mackay, "Religion, Culture, and Ideology," 217.

37. Ibid., 219–20.

38. Moran Cruz, "Popular Attitudes," 61–62.

39. Menocal, *Ornament,* 45.

40. Hutcheson, "Sodomitic Moor," 104.

41. Menocal, *Ornament,* 40.

42. Burke, *Desire,* 18–19, 57.

43. Birge Vitz, *Medieval Narrative,* 64.

44. Dagenais, *Ethics of Reading*; Camille, *Image on the Edge*; and Burke, *Desire,* 54–78.

45. Birge Vitz, *Medieval Narrative,* 16.

46. Burke, *Desire,* 15.

47. Ibid., 16.

48. Dagenais, *Ethics of Reading,* 59–60. Dagenais stresses *assimilatio* as becoming when he states the impossibility of union between text, world, and reader.

49. Burke, *Desire,* 15.

50. Ibid., 54.

51. Ibid., 19.

52. Dagenais, *Ethics of Reading*, 59–61, 86–91.

53. Marín, *Al-Ándalus*, 29.

54. Ibid., 29–30.

55. Ibid., 30. For more information on the Arab onomastic system, see Marín, *Individuo y sociedad*, 177–81.

56. Marín, *Al-Ándalus*, 28, 32; and Menocal, *Ornament*, 67.

57. Marín, *Al-Ándalus*, 45–46.

58. Ibid., 46; Marín, *Individuo y sociedad*, 41–46; and al-Abbīdī, *Eslavos en España*. Al-Abbīdī emphasizes the influence of eleventh-century Andalusi kingdoms ruled by "slaves" of Slavic origin, 24–26.

59. For a recent discussion of the role of Slavs and Berbers in the transition from the caliphate to the *taifas*, see Larsson, *Ibn García's shu'ūbiyya Letter*, 114–22.

60. Shlomo Goitein discusses the documents of the Cairo *Genizah* in Mediterranean Society. Docker, *1492*, 1–19, especially 10–12.

61. Marín, *Al-Ándalus*, 45. Eduardo Manzano Moreno questions the term "slave" to describe individuals who were recruited in foreign states to serve in the Muslim armies and rose to military and administrative positions, *Historia*, 192–93.

62. Williams, *Deformed Discourse*, 4, 6, 16.

63. Kurrik, *Literature and Negation*, 4–5.

64. Vance, *From Topic to Tale*, 42.

65. Covarrubias Horozco, *Tesoro*, 770.

66. Sells, *Desert Tracings*, 3.

67. Translated by Monroe, *Hispano-Arabic Poetry*, 160.

68. Williams, *Deformed Discourse*, 6–7, 24, 39.

69. Minnis and Scott, *Medieval Literary Theory*, 165–66.

70. Williams, *Deformed Discourse*, 17.

71. Camille, *Image on the Edge*, 10.

72. Heath, *Allegory and Philosophy*; Whitman, *Allegory*; and Tiffany, "Lyric Substance," 72–98.

73. Reynolds, *Interpreting the Self*, 91.

74. For discussions of Augustine's accounting for diversity, see Flint, "Monsters," 65–80; and Wittkower, "Marvels of the East," 45–74.

75. Augustine, *City of God*, 16.8.661–62.

76. Ibid., 16.8.662.

77. Eco, *Art and Beauty*; and Behrens-Abouseif, *Beauty*.

78. Brown, *Contrary Things*, 28–35; and Menocal, *Ornament*, 11.

79. Nederman, *Worlds of Difference*, 34.

80. Williams, *Deformed Discourse*, 57.

81. Menocal, *Ornament*, 45.

82. Translated by Menocal, *Shards of Love*, 79.

83. Ibid., 73. Sells, *Mystical Languages*, 63, concurs with Menocal about the blending and obscuring in Ibn ʿArabī's poetry.

84. Menocal, *Shards of Love*, 62.

85. Sells, *Mystical Languages*, 64.

86. Menocal, *Shards of Love*, 57–90.

87. Ibid., 63.

88. Burke, *Desire*, 5.

89. Menocal, *Shards of Love*, 87.

90. Ibid., 66, where Menocal connects the confounding of human and divine love in the works of Llull, Ibn ʿArabī, and Ruiz. Castro analyzes the parallels between the *Lba* and Andalusi-Arabic literatures in "El *Libro de buen amor* del Arcipreste de Hita," in *España en su historia*, and deals with double meaning in the *Lba*, 398–401.

91. Williams, *Deformed Discourse*, 58–59.

92. Morrison, "Interpreting the Fragment," 34.

93. Williams, *Deformed Discourse*, 52.

94. Poovey, *History of the Modern Fact*, introduction and chap. 1.

95. Nirenberg, "Enmity and Assimilation," 137–55. For professionalizing efforts in medicine, see "Tribunal," 17–259.

96. Nirenberg, *Communities of Violence*, 223–30.

97. Ibid., 231–49.

98. Ibid., 228–29, 245–49.

99. Rubert de Ventos, *Nacionalismos*, 155–64; and Castells, *Power of Identity*, 31–32.

100. Rubert de Ventos, *Nacionalismos*, 219.

101. Ibid., 219–20.

102. An article of June 22, 2005 in *El País* on-line claims that birth rates in Spain reached their highest average since 1993 because of childbirths by foreign citizens. "El número medio de hijos por mujer en 2004 fue de 1,32, la cifra más alta desde 1993," available at http://www.elpais.es/articulo.html?xref=20050622elpepusoc_2&type=Tes&anchor=elpporsoc.

103. Hillgarth, *Mirror of Spain*, 160, 204–11.

104. Anderson stresses the imagined limits and sovereignty of nation-states, in *Imagined Communities*, 6–7. Glick demonstrates the distinction between the early modern polity and Andalusi political organization in chap. 6 of *Islamic and Christian Spain*, especially 194–97.

105. Hillgarth, *Mirror of Spain*, 216. Anderson suggests that the establishment of a centralized body of power is the most important element in nation building, *Imagined Communities*, 55.

106. Hillgarth, *Mirror of Spain*, 216–17.

107. Foucault, *Discipline and Punish*, specifically 231–308.

108. Anderson, *Imagined Communities*, 114.

109. Maravall, *Antiguos y modernos*, 239–77.

110. Ibid., 283.

111. Ibid., 326, 329; and Menocal, *Shards of Love*, 3–54. Juan Carlos Rodríguez describes the use of classical materials similarly to Maravall and Menocal, in *Theory and History*, 114–15.

112. Boase, *Troubadour Revival*. See documents on the establishment of the poetry contests on pp. 123–38.

113. For further information on the professionalization of medicine, see García-Ballester, McVaugh, and Rubio-Vela, *Medical Licensing*; and Lanning, *Royal Protomedicato*. For more on Spain's early modern medical board see the valuable monograph "Tribunal," 17–259. See "Mujeres y salud," 17–400, for research on the social control of women practitioners.

Chapter Two.　The Lyric Body

1. Behrens-Abouseif, *Beauty*, 182.
2. Ibid., 84.
3. Pérès, *Esplendor de al-Andalus*, 63–91.
4. Monroe, *Hispano-Arabic Poetry*, 3–71. See pp. 24–26 for information about al-Mu'tamid of Seville and his court.
5. Ibid., 9–10.
6. *Poetas hebreos*, 15–16.
7. Brann, "Arabized Jews," 440.
8. Behrens-Abouseif, *Beauty*, 84. Pérès, *Esplendor de al-Andalus*, 93–253.
María Jesús Rubiera Mata points out that Andalusi-Arabic women's poems are less numerous than men's because women did not have access to the public forums where it was presented or performed. See *Poesía femenina hispanoárabe*, 11.
9. The two most comprehensive collections of poetry by Andalusi-Arabic women are Rubiera Mata's *Poesía femenina hispanoárabe*, and Teresa Garulo's *Dīwān*. Little poetry by Andalusi-Jewish women seems to exist, although Rubiera Mata includes two poems by the twelfth-century poet Qasmūna, the daughter of Ismael, a Jewish poet, 149–51. Brann says that Qasmūna wrote at least some of her compositions in Arabic. See "Arabized Jews," 436.
10. Sells, "Love," 126.
11. The early-twentieth-century Egyptian composer Sayyid Darwīsh (d. 1923) and the renowned Lebanese singer Fayrūz perform the Andalusi style. See Reynolds, "Music," 62.
12. See Tova Rosen's overview of the *muwashshah* in "Muwashshah," 165–89.
13. Corriente, *Poesía dialectal*, 23–24; and Monroe, "Zajal and *Muwashshaha*," 404–5.
14. Corriente, *Poesía dialectal*, 25. In a related opinion about the relation of the *muwashshah* and *zajal*, Monroe believes that the *zajal* is probably older than the *muwashshah*. See "Zajal and *Muwashshaha*," especially 405–13. Reynolds concurs with Monroe in "Music," 75.
15. See Rosen, "Muwashshah," for a discussion of formal variation in the *muwashshah*.
16. Kelley, "Virgins," 21 n. 14; and Rosen, "Muwashshah," 168–69.
17. Ibid., 168.
18. Espósito, "Monkey in the *Jarcha*," 463–77.
19. This is the standard explanation for the speaker of the *jarcha*. For instance, see Emilio García Gómez's rendering throughout *Jarchas romances*; and Frenk Alatorre, *Lírica española*,

12–13. Otto Zwartjes indicates that the *jarcha* usually derives from traditional, stock imagery, suggesting a long-recognized connection between women's voices and laments about love, in *Love Songs*, 250–51.

20. *Jarchas romances*, 59.

21. Ibid., 57.

22. Espósito, "Dismemberment," 9–13.

23. *Jarchas romances*, 87–88.

24. Rosen, "Muwashshah," 175.

25. Monroe, "*Zajal* and *Muwashshaha*," 406.

26. Rosen, "Muwashshah," 166. María Rosa Menocal concurs with Rosen about the parallel between the hybridity of the *muwashshah* and Andalusi society in *Ornament*, 126–27.

27. Menocal notes the simultaneous contradiction and congruity of the *muwashshah* and *jarcha* in *Arabic Role*, 100. They are divergent but congruent as part of a unified poem.

28. The works of Andalusi-Arabic men poets can be found in a variety of collections, including Federico Corriente's *Ibn Quzmán*, Teresa Garulo's *Ar-Rusāfī de Valencia*, and *Jarchas romances*.

29. *Jarchas romances*, 191.

30. Ibid., 191–92.

31. Ibid., 192.

32. The figure of the gazelle or, in this case, the deer, is a common trope in Arabic poetry. For instance, it is found throughout the classic ode, or *qasīda*. See Sells, *Desert Tracings*, 4–6, as well as an example of the gazelle on pp. 32–44.

33. *Poetas hebreos*, 213.

34. Ibid.

35. Ibid., 214.

36. Ibid.

37. Sells, *Stations of Desire*, 20–26.

38. Ibid., "Preface," xii. Sells argues that poetry and mysticism influenced one another throughout the history of Arabic verse: "From the earliest mystical writings in Islam, poetic and mystical expressions have interacted intensely, influencing and transforming one another. In many literary texts the two expressions are so completely intertwined that it is impossible to discover where one begins and the other leaves off."

39. *Jarchas romances*, 112–19.

40. Kelley, "Virgins," 11. Rubiera Mata concurs; see *Poesía femenina hispanoárabe*, 23.

41. Haidu, "Text and History," 1–62; Burns, "Man behind the Lady," 254–70; Wack, *Lovesickness*, 164–66; and Bruckner, "Fictions," 130–31.

42. Oberhelman, "Hierarchies," especially his conclusion on pp. 70–71; Rowson, "Two Homoerotic Narratives," 158–91; and Monroe, "Striptease," especially 118–20.

43. Oberhelman, "Hierarchies," 70.

44. Kelley, "Virgins," 19.

45. Foucault, *Discipline*, 3–31, 195–228.

46. Ibid., 26–27, 201–3, and Butler, *Psychic Life*, 14–15.

47. The ever changing poetic space also characterizes Ibn ʿArabī's writings: "As in a continually turning kaleidoscope, the configuration changes before we can adequately take it in" (Sells, *Mystical Sayings*, 64). As I suggested in note 38, the similarity between the lyric space of the *muwashshah* and mystical writing probably results from the general influences and commonalities between them in the medieval period.

48. Rosen, "Muwashshah," 167.

49. Trans. Heller-Roazen, "Speaking in Tongues," 108.

50. Ibid., 107. Heller-Roazen calls the *jarcha* a dislocation in his discussion of the formal repercussions of the *jarcha*'s status as beginning and end.

51. Menocal, *Ornament*, 127. For further analysis of rhyming patterns in the *muwashshah*, see Heller-Roazen, "Speaking in Tongues," 105.

52. Kelley's and Heller-Roazen's readings of Ibn Sanāʾ's treatise inspired this connection between the formal meanings and relations of the *muwashshah* and *jarcha*, and their extension to gender, sexuality, and subjectivity. See Kelley, "Virgins," 21 n. 14; and Heller-Roazen, "Speaking in Tongues," 104–8.

53. *Poetas hebreos*, 59. For biographical information on Ibn Jalfun, see pp. 55–56.

54. Ibid., 59. The editors introduce the poem in this way: "Con expresiones convencionales del género, el poeta se queja del amado que no corresponde realmente a su afecto" [With conventional expressions of the genre, the poet complains about the male lover who does not share his affection].

55. *Poesía femenina hispanoárabe*, 137.

56. Ibid., 135.

57. Pagis, *Hebrew Poetry*, 66.

58. Ibid., 68.

59. Ibid.

60. Scheindlin, *Wine, Women, and Death*, 86–89.

61. Stone, *Death of the Troubadour*, 9, 201 n. 14.

62. "War" is a feminine noun in Arabic and Spanish.

63. *Jarchas romances*, 86.

64. Ibid.

65. Ibid., 85.

66. Behrens-Abouseif, *Beauty*, 37–43.

67. Ibid., 41.

68. Al-Jāhiz, *Singing-Girls*, sec. 35, p. 25.

69. Stetkevych, "Intoxication," 213.

70. Ibid.

71. Scheindlin, *Wine, Women, and Death*, 9.

72. Ibid., 74. Scheindlin gives both the original Hebrew and the English translation. Samuel Ibn Nagrila is called Samuel the Nagid in the English translation.

73. Ibid., 75.

74. Ibid., 26.

75. Ibn 'Ezra, *Kitāb*, 167.
76. Scheindlin, *Wine, Women, and Death*, 9.
77. Ibn 'Ezra, *Kitāb*, 272–75, 282–86.
78. Bürgel, "Ambiguity," 19–20.
79. Schimmel, *My Soul*, 23.
80. Ibid., 102–3.
81. Ibid., 25.
82. Pérès, *Esplendour de al-Andalus*, 375; and Murray, "Woman-Woman Love," 99.
83. *Poesía femenina hispanoárabe*, 105.
84. AbuKhalil, "Note," 33.
85. Walther, *Women in Islam*, 118.
86. Mark D. Johnston considers them to be one and the same, in "Cultural Studies," 235.
87. For more information on the Gay Science, see Boase, *Troubadour Revival*, 2, 123–38, passim. Many of the documents on pp. 119–50 deal with its establishment.
88. Dangler, *Mediating Fictions*, 51–58.
89. Ibid., 32–33, 185 n. 66.
90. *Trobes en lahors de la Verge Maria*. No page or folio numbers are given in the facsimile edition.
91. Dangler, *Mediating Fictions*, 54–55.
92. For more on misogyny and the *Spill*, see Solomon, *Literature of Misogyny*.
93. *Trobes en lahors de la Verge Maria*.
94. Juan Huarte de San Juan dignified men and their occupations in the sixteenth-century work *Examen*.
95. Menocal, *Arabic Role*, 103.
96. Menéndez Pidal, *Poesía árabe*, 12–78; Menocal, *Arabic Role*; and Menocal, *Shards of Love*.
97. Boase, *Origin and Meaning*, 129–30; and Boase, "Arab Influences," 459.
98. Menocal, *Shards of Love*, 154–83.
99. Boynton, "Women's Performance," 51–52.
100. Burns, *Courtly Love Undressed*, 16.
101. *Poesía de cancionero*, 187.
102. Burns, *Courtly Love Undressed*, 8–9.
103. *Poesía de cancionero*, 383.
104. For bibliography, see note 41.
105. *Poesía de cancionero*, 207.
106. Boase, "Arab Influences," 471. Boase also recognizes the complexity of the poetry of this period. Although it was less sensual, its language tended toward double-entendres.
107. Whinnom, *Poesía amatoria*, 74, 111 n. 143; and Whetnall, "Songs and *Canciones*," 197–207.
108. Goody, *Logic of Writing*.
109. Duby, *France*, 180.

Chapter Three. The Divided Body

1. Castillo, *Cancionero general*, in *Cancionero*, vol. 5, fols. 164v–165r. Reproduced in Grey, "Ingenious Portrayal," 335.

2. It is possible that the *cartas de tijera* were purely metaphorical, since at least one poet, the fourteenth-century writer Ibn Játima de Almería (Abū Ya'far Ahmad ibn Jātima), wrote his in a conventional manner. His five *cartas de tijera* are conserved in the Arabic collection at the Biblioteca de El Escorial, catalogued by Derenbourg as number 381, fol. 42a. Letters are not cut away on the paper, as one might expect, but are clearly written in ink.

3. For a description of this medieval genre, see Gibert Fenech, "Manera de escribir," 211; and Mehrez, "Cartas de tijera," 221. Gibert Fenech further alludes to the decorative quality of this form of writing in the introduction to Ibn Játima's fourteenth-century anthology, or *dīwān*, *Dīwān*, 41–42, where she mentions the fourteenth-century, fifty-nine verse *qasīda* (ode) composed with scissors by the Eastern calligrapher Yawād b. Sulaymān b. Gālib al-Lajmī.

4. For a current bibliography on this medieval tradition, see Zemke, *Critical Approaches*, 124–25 n. 179.

5. The articles by Gibert Fenech, "Manera de escribir," and Mehrez, "Cartas de tijera," are examples from this era. In 1968, Gibert Fenech also published an article on the cutting poems of the Valencian poet al-Rusāfī, "Escritura de tijera," 471–73.

6. See Julio Rodríguez Puértolas's recent essay about the antisemitic events from the mid–fourteenth century on that led up to the Jewish expulsion and the conquest of Granada in 1492, "Jews and *Conversos*," 187–97.

7. Mehrez, "Cartas de tijera," 222.

8. Gibert Fenech, "Manera de escribir," 212–13, and Ibn Játima, *Dīwān*, 136–37.

9. Behrens-Abouseif, *Beauty*, 17.

10. Ibid., 7–8. Despite the fact that Arabic constructions of beauty in realms such as secular poetry were often unrelated to religious beliefs, the religious importance of beauty in devout Muslim society likely influenced popular ideas about the significance of beauty.

11. Ibid., 19–20.

12. Ibid., 95–96.

13. Al-Jāhiz, *Singing-Girls*, sec. 34–35, pp. 25–26.

14. Behrens-Abouseif, *Beauty*, 23.

15. Ibid., 38.

16. Ibid., 41. There is no doubt that this discursive format of contrasts precedes al-Jāhiz, as shown by Galen's approach in his medical treatise "On the Secrets of Women," in which he provides pharmacological advice on a range of dualities related to women's sexuality. For instance, one rubric discusses "[d]rugs which cause women to detest sexual intercourse in a way that they ignore it and forget about it," while the next rubric considers medications with the opposite effect, "[d]rugs which excite the desire of women so that they go wandering around, leaving their homes, looking for sexual satisfaction, throwing themselves before men and searching for a good time" (Levey and Souryal, "Galen's 'On the Secrets of Women,'" 211–12).

17. Colahan and Rodríguez, "Semitic Forms," 35–42. See the English translation of al-Jāhiz's debates in Al-Jāhiz, *Nine Essays*.

18. Castillo, *Cancionero general*, fol. 226r.

19. For a related discussion of this poem, see Yovel's "Converso Dualities," 2.

20. Behrens-Abouseif, *Beauty*, 64.

21. Gibert Fenech, "Manera de escribir," 213; Ibn Játima, *Dīwān*, 136–37. It bears repeating that Ibn Játima's allusions to writing with scissors may have been purely metaphorical, since he wrote this poem in a conventional manner according to its preservation at the Biblioteca de El Escorial (see note 2).

22. Van Gelder, *God's Banquet*, 12. Van Gelder also believes that *qasīda* (the classical ode) is related to *qasada*, "to split in two," given the fact that a metrical line is often separated into two hemistichs, or halves.

23. See the editors' comments about the meaning of *astroso* in Díaz-Mas and Mota's edition of Sem Tob, *Proverbios morales*, 130 n. 40a.

24. See Díaz-Mas and Mota's recent edition for quotes from Sem Tob, *Proverbios morales*, pp. 130–31, vv. 40–44.

25. Colahan, "Santob's Debate," p. 307, vv. 886–87.

Jewish writers such as Sem Tob imitated the Arab *maqāmā*, a satiric narrative in rhymed prose. The Jewish writer al-Harizi wrote a similar pen and sword debate, "La espada y la pluma," in *Asambleas*. The origins of the pen and sword debate are Arabic, as evidenced by Ibn Burd's "Epístola de la espada y el cálamo" in Granja's *Maqâmas*, 32–44. For more information on the genre, see Amparo Alba's "Debate," 7–13. Díaz Esteban and Colahan and Rodríguez concur that Sem Tob likely adapted his pen and scissors debate from these Arabic and Hebrew sources. See Díaz Esteban, "Debate," 85–89; and Colahan and Rodríguez, "Traditional Semitic Forms," 45 n. 47.

26. Ibn 'Ezra, *Kitāb*, 2:199.

27. T. A. Perry, *Moral Proverbs*, 106–9.

28. Ibid., 151.

29. See Colahan and Rodríguez for a further discussion of this topic and for examples of the reversing of value in the *Proverbios morales*, in "Semitic Forms," 46–47.

30. Al-Harizi, "La carta de doble lectura," in *Asambleas*, 100.

31. Ibid. Sanford Shepard discusses this passage and the *cancionero* cutting poem in *Shem Tov*, 110–11 n. 10, where he transcribes the original Hebrew.

32. Joset, "Opposition," 188.

33. Sem Tob, *Proverbios morales*, 517a–517b.

34. Colahan, "Santob's Debate," p. 294, vv. 598–603. Fernando Díaz Esteban does not include this selection in his Spanish translation of Sem Tob's *maqāmā*; hence its citation in English, and not in the Spanish translation. Díaz Esteban apparently was unaware of this and other sections of the work. See Colahan's comments in "Santob's Debate," 90–91, for more on this editorial problem.

35. Ibid., p. 307, v. 893.

36. See note 21.

37. Zemke, *Critical Approaches,* 25. Perhaps the early modern *cancionero* poet derives his contradictory and entertaining cutting poem about the cloth shearer from al-Harizi's lines, which may be read in reverse, and from Sem Tob's satirical tradition.

38. Colahan, "Santob's Debate," 97. Colahan's comments on pp. 92–93 and 97 on serious and parodic debates are useful.

39. Ibid., p. 272, vv. 140–41.

40. Ibid., p. 272, v. 149. For the quote about the dual nature of the scissors, see p. 307, vv. 886–87.

41. Sanford Shepard, ed., in Sem Tob, *Proverbios morales,* 90 n. 40d.

42. In Beutler, "Enigmas," 272. For biographical information on Pérez de Herrera, see 267 n. 52.

43. Ibid., 272–73.

44. *Adivinancero culto español,* 2:50, no. 46.

45. Olson, *Literature as Recreation,* 96–100.

46. Ibid., 231.

47. Ibid., 231–32.

48. Tiffany, "Lyric Substance," 79.

49. The bibliography on these changes is extensive. For social shifts and their connection to literature, see, for instance, Nerlich, *Ideology of Adventure;* and Cruz, *Discourses of Poverty.*

50. A *protomédico* served on a board of directors to oversee the licensing and examination of physicians and the general operation of the medical profession. Like many *protomédicos,* Pérez de Herrera was also a physician, albeit not for a municipality but in a military capacity. For information on the Royal Protomedicato and the professionalization of medicine in the Spanish empire, see Lanning, *Royal Protomedicato.*

51. See Teresa Garulo's comments in *Ar-Rusāfī,* 24–25. Ar-Rusāfī's cutting poem is found in an anthology of illustrious Malagans, entitled *Al-Takmīl wāl-Itmān li kitābay al-ta'rif wāl-I'lam* and compiled by Ibn al-'Askar (d. 1226). For information on this anthology, see Vallvé Bermejo, "Fuente importante," 237–65.

52. The three final poems of section 3 of Ibn Játima's *Dīwān,* 139–40, are enigmatic. Gibert Fenech comments on the enigmas in Ibn Játima, *Dīwān,* 42.

Chapter Four. **The Medical Body**

1. Siraisi, *Medieval and Early Renaissance Medicine,* 11–13.

2. Ibid., 31–32. Luis García-Ballester analyzes the impact of Arabic treatises on Christian, Muslim, and Jewish communities in Christian Iberia from the eleventh through the sixteenth centuries in "Medical World," 353–94.

3. Siraisi, *Medieval and Early Renaissance Medicine,* 100–106; and Cadden, *Sex Difference,* 170–77, 184–85.

4. *Trotula,* 19–22; and Cadden, *Sex Difference,* 173–76.

5. Siraisi, *Medieval and Early Renaissance Medicine,* 101.

6. Cadden, *Sex Difference,* 184.

7. Siraisi, *Medieval and Early Renaissance Medicine,* 103.

8. *Liber minor de coitu,* pt. 1, chap. 1, p. 56; and *Trotula,* par. 142, 121–22. Green further comments on phlegmatic women and men on pp. 38–39.

9. Siraisi, *Medieval and Early Renaissance Medicine,* 102–4; and Cadden, *Sex Difference,* 170–77, 183–88.

10. Cadden, *Sex Difference,* 177. Thomas Laqueur elaborates on the one-sex theory in *Making Sex.*

11. Cadden, *Sex Difference,* 183.

12. Ibid., 186–88.

13. Siraisi, *Medieval and Early Renaissance Medicine,* 102, 104.

14. Cadden, *Sex Difference,* 201–2.

15. Cadden, "Western Medicine," 63.

16. Ibid., 54–55.

17. Ibid., 57–58. See Galen, *On the Affected Parts.*

18. Jacquart and Thomasset, *Sexuality and Medicine,* 64–70, 79–97, passim.

19. Cadden, "Western Medicine," 55–56.

20. See note 8.

21. Cadden, *Sex Difference,* 130, 203, 209.

22. Ibid., 279–81.

23. Ibid., 209, 214.

24. Ibid., 205.

25. Ibid., 119–30.

26. Ibid., 218. Also see pp. 218–27; and Jacquart and Thomasset, *Sexuality and Medicine,* 139–67.

27. Cadden, *Sex Difference,* 219.

28. Cadden, "Western Medicine," 51; and Jacquart and Thomasset, *Sexuality and Medicine,* 122–29.

29. Solomon, "Towards a Definition," 184.

Vilanova was born in Aragon in 1240 and died in Genoa in 1311. He studied and taught at the medical faculty in Montpellier, where he was a pivotal figure in the integration of Greek philosophy and Arabic medicine in the medical curriculum. Vilanova was known as a highly successful doctor at court who served as physician to Peter III of Aragon, to Peter's son and heir Alfonso III, and to Alfonso's successor and brother Jaume II. He translated works from Arabic into Latin by Ibn Sīnā, Galen, and Ibn Zuhr, and his own *Regiment de sanitat* was quickly translated into Catalan from Latin in the fourteenth century. *Dictionary of Scientific Biography,* 1:289–91.

Jacme d'Agramont received the highest academic degree of master in both medicine and the arts. He served the new medical faculty at the University of Lleida as full professor, starting at the latest in the academic year 1343–44, until 1348, when he died of the Black Death.

García Ballester and Arrizabalaga, *"Regiment."* Biblioteca Virtual Joan Lluís Vives, available at: http://www.lluisvives.com/FichaObra.html?portal=1&Ref=1995.

30. Dutton and Sánchez, "Introduction to Gordon, *Lilio de medicina*, 1:7–34.

Gordon was a celebrated professor in the faculty of medicine at Montpellier, where he completed the Latin *Lilium medicinae* in 1305. The treatise was translated into Castilian and published in Seville for the first time in 1495, again in Toledo in 1513, and finally in Madrid in 1697. Hernández Morejón and Sancho de San Román, *Historia bibliográfica*, 1:307–8.

31. Solomon, "Towards a Definition," 184.

32. *Mirror of Coitus.*

33. Constantinus Africanus, *De coitu*; and Montero Cartelle's edition of the *Liber minor de coitu.* For a discussion of these works as sources for the *Speculum*, see Solomon's introduction to the *Speculum*, xvi–xviii; and for information on their general influence, see Cadden's discussions in *Sex Difference*, 66–70.

34. Al-Jatīb, *Libro del cuidado*, 151–52; Gordon, *Lilio de medicina*, fols. 60v, 166v; and Aviñón, *Sevillana medicina*, fol. 109r. The anonymous author of the *Tratado de patología general* embedded salutary information on coitus in chapters on genital illnesses, such as chapter 20, "Las dolençias de las vergas" (Disorders of the penis), fols. 94v–99r.

35. Al-Jatīb, *Libro del cuidado*, 151–52.

Al-Jatīb was born to a renowned family in Granada, where he practiced medicine, wrote poetry, and composed treatises on rhetoric, history, politics, and the military. He also practiced medicine in Loja, Cordova, and Toledo. He died in 1398 while imprisoned on charges of treason. Hernández Morejón, *Historia bibliográfica*, 1:186.

36. Zuhr, *Kitāb al-Muyarrabāt.* The passages on aphrodisiacs are in sections 231 and 303, and section 264 mentions postcoital shaking.

The patronymic Ibn Zuhr belonged to a prominent family of scholars and physicians from the Arabian tribe of Iyād. Abū l-Alāʿ Zuhr served as physician to the Murābit dynasty (Almoravids, 1090–1147) in both Seville and Morrocco and was the father of the more influential Abū Marwān Ibn Zuhr (Avenzoar), whose nine medical works on a variety of topics contributed to shaping both Western and Arabic medicine. *Dictionary of Scientific Biography*, 14:637–39.

37. In contrast to this widespread command in general treatises, Solomon notes that the specialized manual on sexual well-being, the *Speculum al foderi*, offers no theory of conception and instead focuses on the salutary effects of moderate coitus, in *Speculum*, xii–xv.

38. *Speculum al foderi*, chap. 4, par. 1, p. 57; Al-Jatīb, *Libro del cuidado*, 152.

39. Ketham, *Compendio*, fol. 18v; pp. 119–20. Since Herrera's edition simultaneously gives the medieval text and the modernized version, I cite the folio and page numbers of the two accounts.

Johannes of Ketham lived and worked in Vienna in the fifteenth century. His treatise was first published in Latin in Venice in 1491, and again in that same city in 1495. The first Castilian translation was published in 1494 in Zaragoza, and the second in 1495 in Burgos. Ketham, *Compendio*, 7–9.

40. Aviñón, *Sevillana medicina*, fol. 109r.

41. Many writers cited the ill effects of immoderate coitus, such as Aviñón, *Sevillana medicina*, fols. 109r–109v; and Gordon, *Lilio de medicina*, fols. 60v, 166v–167r.

42. Aviñón, *Sevillana medicina*, fol. 110r; and *Speculum*, chap. 3.

43. Gordon, *Lilio de medicina*, fol. 167v.

44. Ibid., fol. 60v.

45. Aviñón, *Sevillana medicina*, fol. 111r.

Although originally from France, Juan de Aviñón spent so many years in Seville that historians generally include him in discussions of Iberian medicine. He arrived in Seville in 1391 and concluded his treatise in 1419, although it was not published until 1545 in Seville. Hernández Morejón, *Historia bibliográfica*, 1:286–88.

46. Gordon, *Lilio de medicina*, fol. 60v.

47. Ibid., fols. 60v, 167r. Juan de Aviñón concurs in *Sevillana medicina*, fol. 108v.

48. Ketham, *Compendio*, fol. 23r.

49. Zuhr, *Kitāb:* amenorrhea (238), excessive menstruation (244), menstrual problems after abortion (299), and sterility (249).

50. The treatise on women's illnesses in Ketham's *Compendio* begins on fol. 15r; p. 97. The chapter on their ailments in Chirino's *Menor daño de la medicina* begins on fol. 184r. See Chirino, *Menor daño de la medicina*.

It is unclear whether Chirino was born in Guadalajara or Cuenca, although it is certain that he served King Juan II of Castile as physician and medical examiner of physicians and surgeons. He wrote two treatises in the fifteenth century, *Espejo de medicina* and *Menor daño de la medicina*, which was published a century later, in 1513, in Toledo, and in Seville in 1547. Chirino was most concerned with advising readers to avoid unlearned doctors and surgeons and to rely instead on educated, licensed practitioners like him. Hernández Morejón, *Historia bibliográfica*, 1:288–93.

51. *Tratado de patología*, fols. 99v–112v.

52. Gordon, *Lilio de medicina*, fols. 165r–182r. Gordon indicates an even broader interest in women's well-being, since he assigns the final chapter of book 7 not to a genital ailment, but to the common medieval topic of women's cosmetics, entitled "De los afeytes de las mugeres" (On women's cosmetics), beginning on fol. 185v.

53. Ibid., fol. 167r.

54. Burke, "*Mal de la Madre,*" 111–12.

55. Ibid.

56. Aviñón, *Sevillana medicina*, fol. 109r.

57. Cadden discusses the lack of clarity about women's fluids in *Sex Difference*, 79. On pp. 247–48 she further cites the medical writer John of Gaddesden, who called women's sperm "a certain watery, whitened menstruum." For another facet of the discussion on women's fluids, see Jacquart and Thomasset, *Sexuality and Medicine*, 76–77, where they demonstrate that Thomas Aquinas distinguished between purified blood, which affected the embryo, and residual menstrual blood, which had to be expelled.

58. Ketham, *Compendio*, fol. 20r; p. 131.

59. Juan de Aviñón, *Sevillana medicina*, fol. 108v.

60. Ibid., fols. 111v–112r.
61. Cadden, *Sex Difference*, 201–9.
62. Al-Jatīb, *Libro del cuidado*, 203.
63. Ibid., 215, 229.
64. Aviñón, *Sevillana medicina*, fol. 108v.
65. See note 10 for the citations from Cadden and Laqueur.
66. Aviñón, *Sevillana medicina*, fols. 108r–108v.
67. Ibid., fol. 108v.
68. For a discussion of the role of women's seed in conception, see Cadden, *Sex Difference*, 93–97.
69. Aviñón, *Sevillana medicina*, fols. 108r–108v.
70. Quétel, *History of Syphilis*; and Arrizabalaga, Henderson, and French, *Great Pox*.
71. Gracia Guillén, "Judaism," 375–400.
72. Siraisi, *Medieval and Early Renaissance Medicine*, 128–130.
73. Quétel, *History of Syphilis*, 66–67.
74. Ibid., 55; and Arrizabalaga, Henderson, and French, *Great Pox*, 35–36. Arrizabalaga et al. stress the variety of theories of transmission and indicate that in the early period until about 1500 sex was not thought to be the dominant means for the spread of the disease.
75. Díaz de Ysla, *Tractado*, fol. 10r; and Torres, *Enfermedad de las bubas*, fol. 24v.
Díaz de Ysla was born in Baeza (Jaén) and also lived in Seville in the sixteenth century. He practiced medicine in Lisbon and dedicated his treatise to the king of Portugal, Juan III. The *Tractado* was published in two editions in Seville in 1539 and 1542. The *Historia bibliográfica* calls the work *Tratado llamado de todos los santos*, in reference to the hospital Todos los Santos in Lisbon, where Díaz de Ysla treated patients afflicted with syphilis. See Hernández Morejón, *Historia bibliográfica*, 2:286–90.
Pedro de Torres was born in Daroca, Aragon, and was physician to the empress María de Austria. His treatise was well known in its time, and physicians used its many cures to treat syphilis. Hernández Morejón, *Historia bibliográfica*, 3:423.
76. Arias de Benavides, *Secretos de chirurgia*, fol. 71v. *Lamparones*, or scrofula, a form of tuberculosis characterized by swelling and degeneration of the lymphatic glands, was known as "king's evil" because it was believed cured by the royal touch. The *Diccionario español* defines *miraquia*, or *mirachia*, as an abdominal disease that produces severe, intermittent pain. See Herrera, *Diccionario español*, 2:1052.
Arias de Benavides was born and lived in Toro before studying medicine at the University of Salamanca. He practiced medicine in Guatemala and at Mexico City's general hospital. Along with a discussion of syphilis and its cures, his treatise conveys information on many American plants, roots, fruits, and resins that were used as medical remedies. Hernández Morejón, *Historia bibliográfica*, 3:126.
77. Díaz de Ysla, *Tractado*, fol. 10r.
78. Torres, *Enfermedad de las bubas*, fol. 28v.

79. Arrizabalaga, Henderson, and French, *Great Pox,* argue that traditional medical historians seek to show that prostitutes were the main transmitters of the disease prior to 1530. Arrizabalaga et al. suggest, however, that historians do not acknowledge the humanitarian efforts of hospitals and convents in "the moral rehabilitation of prostitutes and later on for preventing young unprotected girls from falling into a life of sin" (168). Yet, the corrective, paternalistic posture toward prostitution evinces a moral tone that lacks respect for one of the few occupations that women could sometimes practice independently in the early modern period. Moreover, medical writers such as Díaz de Ysla and Arias de Benavides denounce prostitutes and do not express goodwill toward them or concern for their "rehabilitation."

80. Núñez de Coria, *Tractado,* fol. 290v.

Núñez de Coria was born in Casarrubios del Monte (Toledo) and practiced several vocations as physician, writer, and poet. He studied medicine at the University of Alcalá. The *Tractado* was published for the first time in 1569 along with a larger work, *Tratado de medicina,* whose bibliographic information is difficult to locate. The *Tractado* was published again in 1572 in Madrid, and a third time in 1586, where it accompanies a larger treatise by the same author, the *Regimiento y aviso de sanidad de todos los géneros de alimentos y del regimiento de ello* (Directions and health information on all kinds of food) (Medina del Campo: Francisco del Canto, 1586). Hernández Morejón, *Historia bibliográfica,* 3:148–49.

81. This phrase appears periodically in Juan de Aviñón, *Sevillana medicina,* such as "o por mucho vsar con muger mas delo que deue" [or because of having a lot of sex with women, more than one ought], fol. 107v; "vsar mucho con la muger," fols. 109r, 109v, and 110r, where it is used three times.

82. Chirino, *Menor daño de la medicina,* fols. 21r–21v and 23r–23v, respectively. For other references in Chirino, see fols. 9v, 106v–107r, 112v, and 134r. On fol. 138r Chirino declares that men are sometimes very thin because of excessive coitus with women.

83. *Speculum al foderi,* chap. 8, pars. 1–2, p. 73 (Catalan), and chap. 8, pars. 1–2, p. 29 (English translation).

84. Núñez de Coria, *Tractado,* fol. 290v.

85. Huarte de San Juan, *Examen de ingenios.* Serés's edition is based on the Castilian treatise of 1594, which was composed of twenty-two chapters and three final digressions on fire, salt, and the forbidden tree of paradise.

Huarte was born around 1529 in San Juan del Pie del Puerto (Navarra) and died in 1588. Apparently he resided much of his life in Baeza (Jaén), where he was hired on a two-year contract as a physician in 1571, but he also lived in Linares (Jaén). He probably studied medicine at the University of Alcalá from 1553 to 1559. *Examen de ingenios* was published in Castilian for the first time in 1575 and was translated numerous times in the sixteenth and seventeenth centuries into French, Italian, English, Latin, Dutch, and at least three times into German in the eighteenth century. See the introduction to Serés's edition, 13–19, 108–22.

86. Ibid., 627.

87. Ibid., 615.

88. Ibid., 607–22.

89. Ibid., 622.

90. Ibid., 611–12, 614.

91. Ibid., 526.

92. Ibid., 608.

93. Ibid., 609. See the editor's comments on this topic in *Examen de ingenios*, 609 n. 31.

94. Ibid., 610.

95. Ibid., 615.

96. Ibid., 634–35.

97. Daston and Park, "Hermaphrodite," 124, 129.

98. For more on the links between conduct, the family, and the state, see Casey, *Early Modern Spain*, chap. 9.

99. Vives, *Formación*, 2:985–1175.

100. Navarro, "Manual Control," especially 17–22. Casey concurs in *Early Modern Spain*, 192.

101. Dixon, "Curse of Chastity," 72.

102. Muñoz Fernández and Segura Graíño, *Trabajo de las mujeres*; and *Women and Work*.

103. Vives, *Formación*, 1025.

104. Green, "Possibilities," chap. 7, 35.

105. See the Latin text and translation of the twelfth-century work *De ornatu mulierum* (On women's cosmetics), in *Trotula*, 166–91. Green also deals with cosmetics in "Possibilities," 33–37, where she discusses the Catalan treatise *Libre*. Along with the *Libre*, Cabré i Pairet's dissertation includes an edition of the Latin *De ornatu*, attributed to Arnau de Vilanova, and of another Catalan work on cosmetics.

106. Vives, *Formación*, 1056.

107. Mary Elizabeth Perry, "Magdalens and Jezebels," 131.

108. Bergmann, "Exclusion of the Feminine," 127.

109. Ibid., 128–133. See Vives's arguments on motherhood in *Formación*, bk. 2, chap. 11, pp. 1136–49.

110. Bergmann, "Exclusion of the Feminine," 136.

Chapter Five. **The Monstrous Body**

1. García-Ballester, McVaugh, and Rubio-Vela, *Medical Licensing*, 60–61; Lanning, *Royal Protomedicato*; "Tribunal," 17–259; "Mujeres y salud," 17–400.

2. Dangler, *Mediating Fictions*, 84–127.

3. Illades Aguiar, *La Celestina*, 11–35.

4. Isidore of Seville, *Etimologías*, bk. 11, v. 3, 2:47.

5. Although grotesque, monstrous, and deformed can have different meanings, I use them synonymously as that which deviates from the regular order.

6. Wack, *Lovesickness*; and Solomon, "Calisto's Ailment," 41–64.

7. Flint, "Monsters," 72–76; and Williams, *Deformed Discourse*, 7–12, 323.

8. Cohen, *Of Giants*, xiv.

9. Lorraine Daston and Katharine Park describe the different kinds of literatures that portray what they call wonders and marvels, that is, things that always inhabit the margins, in *Wonders*, 24. They define wonders and marvels on pp. 13, 14, and 16–17.

10. See reproductions of these miniatures in Keller and Grant Cash, *Daily Life*, cantiga 4, pl. 13; cantiga 108, pl. 19; cantiga 185, pl. 65.

11. Williams, *Deformed Discourse*, 3.

12. Friedman, *Monstrous Races*, 123–25.

13. Weir and Jerman, *Images of Lust*, 10.

14. Cohen, *Monster Theory*, 6–7.

15. Ibid., 16–20; and Williams, *Deformed Discourse*, 6, passim.

16. In *Of Giants*, xiii, Cohen further suggests the importance of paradox in the forging of the monster when he argues that the giant exists both inside and outside human identity, thus comprising two paradoxical features.

17. Williams, *Deformed Discourse*, 4–6.

18. Kappler, *Monstres*; Friedman, *Monstrous Races*, 5–25; and Williams, *Deformed Discourse*, 105–227.

19. Ruiz Montejo, "Temática obscena," 140. Further examples of deviant gender and sexuality are found in Weir and Jerman, *Images of Lust*, such as a photograph of a female exhibitionist on a church in Mens, La Coruña, pl. 68, 121.

20. References to Rojas, *La Celestina*, and to the English version, Rojas, *Celestina: A Play*, are cited by act and page numbers.

21. Dangler, *Mediating Fictions*, 122–25; and Dangler, "Transgendered Sex," 70–72.

22. Dangler, "Transgendered Sex," 72–78.

23. Hendricks Singleton omits the crucial translation of *cabecera*, which refers to a headboard or perhaps means "bedside," and of *aunque era niño*, "although I was a boy." Their absence obscures the allusion to pedophilia.

24. Camille, *Image on the Edge*, especially chap. 2 on the monastery, 56–75; and Camille, "Mouths and Meaning," 43–57.

25. Camille, *Image on the Edge*, 9.

26. Williams, *Deformed Discourse*, 3–60.

27. Ibid., 3–4. As I explained in chapter 1, I use the term "negative" broadly as contrary to that which is deemed positive, and in its philosophical and logical meanings as a descent, denial, or absence. Hence, the negative refers to a variety of phenomena, such as the corporeal, the profane, the base, and the absent.

28. Pseudo-Dionysius, "Mystical Theology," 139.

29. Williams, *Deformed Discourse*, 59. Williams elaborates on this idea in a variety of contexts, but particularly in the study of the language of the monstrous, which John Scotus Eriugena articulated in his natural philosophy, 61–103.

30. Pseudo-Dionysius, "Celestial Hierarchy," 149–50.

31. Williams, *Deformed Discourse,* 4, 6. Jean Leclercq demonstrates the influence of Pseudo-Dionysian thought on medieval writers in "Influence," 25–32.

32. Williams, *Deformed Discourse,* 23–48.

33. Tiffany, "Lyric Substance," 72–98.

34. Zumthor, *Middle Ages,* 63.

35. Ibid., 62.

36. Pseudo-Dionysius, "Mystical Theology," 136.

37. Williams highlights the role of the deformed in saints' lives in *Deformed Discourse,* 285–322.

38. *Vida de María Egipciaca.* See Mary's positive description on pp. 55–57, vv. 205–60, and her deformed description on p. 77, vv. 720–59. Verse 735 describes her chin as a "cabo de tizón," and verse 739 calls her nipples "secas."

39. Dagenais, *Ethics of Reading.*

40. Dangler, *Mediating Fictions,* 58, 60.

41. Lida de Malkiel, "Hipérbole sagrada," 121–30; and Lida de Malkiel, "Obra maestra," 267–324. Reprinted in Lida de Malkiel, *La literatura española,* 291–309 and 179–290, respectively.

42. Guillermo Serés analyzes the similarities and differences between Platonic thought and Christian beliefs of ascent and descent in *Transformación,* chap. 1. He stresses that Christ's mediation and incarnation as human and *verbum* differentiate the Platonic and Christian traditions, 37.

43. Pseudo-Dionysius, "Mystical Theology," 139. For more on language and the monster, see Williams, *Deformed Discourse,* chap. 2.

44. Walsh, *Dark Matter,* 9–10.

45. Gaylord, "Fair of the World," 11–12.

46. Colish, *Mirror of Language,* 3. Colish contends that medieval Christian writers believed that words were signs in the knowledge of God. The study of the link between language and reality in the trivium was the most correct mode of Christian understanding and revelation and was to be applied later in teaching.

47. Isidore of Seville, *Etimologías,* bk. 3, v. 3, 1:279.

48. Robert S. Sturges attests to the dual medieval belief in language as a reliable signifier of truth and as leading to indeterminacy in *Medieval Interpretation.*

49. Maravall, *Culture of the Baroque,* 202.

50. Ibid., 194.

51. Gordon, *Lilio de medicina,* fol. 58r.

52. Ibid.

53. Williams, *Deformed Discourse,* 48–60.

54. Ibid., 49–50.

55. Ibid., 52.

56. Ibid., 57.

57. Brown, *Contrary Things,* 31.

58. Ibid., 33.

59. Daston and Park, *Wonders*, 60, 252–53.

60. For the progressive restrictions on women healers and other women workers, see Dangler, *Mediating Fictions*, 34–35, 43–49, 111–27.

61. Greilsammer, "Midwife," 287; and Dangler, *Mediating Fictions*, 111–13.

62. Dangler, *Mediating Fictions*, 177–78.

63. Leclercq, "Influence," 31.

64. Flint, "Monsters," 65–80.

65. Wittkower, "Marvels of the East," 64.

66. I am grateful to Luis Avilés for pointing out the conventionality of amicable relations between Muslims and Christians in *El Abencerraje*.

67. Hillgarth, *Mirror of Spain*, 204–11.

68. Ibid., 231. Hillgarth also cites verses by Byron from 1818, which describe Don Juan's father and attest to the lasting significance of an "untainted" genealogy.

69. Ibid., 240: "The longer the persecution of secret Jews continued, the more certain non-Spaniards became that *all* Spaniards were Marranos."

70. Dagenais, *Ethics of Reading*, 162–64.

71. Camille, *Image on the Edge*, 42.

72. Edson, *Mapping Time and Space*, 4–5, 152, and plates 2, 4, 6–10.

73. Ibid., 17.

74. Friedman, *Monstrous Races*, 37.

75. Williams, *Deformed Discourse*, 17.

76. Harley and Woodward, *History of Cartography*, bk. 1, *Cartography in the Traditional Islamic and South Asian Societies* 2:265–72.

77. Turner, *Medieval Islam*, 128.

78. Martín Merás, *Cartografía*, 78–80.

79. Colón, *Textos*; and Díaz del Castillo, *Historia verdadera*.

Conclusion

1. Anderson, *Imagined Communities*, 6. See Lesley Johnson's discussion of this point in "Imagining Communities," 6.

2. Roberto J. González Casanovas calls for a broader study of Alfonso's concept of Hispania, which would include not only the historical vernaculars of the *Estoria de Espanna* and the *General Estoria*, but also his legal writings, in "Alfonso X's Concept of Hispania," 163.

3. Ibid., 158–60.

4. Nichols, *Romanesque Signs*, 9.

5. Alfonso X, *Prosa histórica*, 45–66.

6. John Docker illuminates this change throughout his book, at the same time that he posits 1492 as "a pivotal moment of world history," in *1492*, vii.

7. Maravall, *Antiguos y modernos*, 285, 326, 329.

8. De Landa, *One Thousand Years*, especially 11–22.
9. Ibid., 50–52.
10. Williams, *Deformed Discourse*, 38, 53.
11. Cruz, *Poesía*, 261–62.
12. Williams, *Deformed Discourse*, 53.
13. Menocal, *Ornament*.
14. Ibid., 86–87.

Appendix.   Poems and Translations

1. *Jarchas romances*, 57–59.
2. Reference to Israel.
3. Isaiah 58:12.
4. Allusion to the sacrifice of Isaac, who was tied up by Abraham in order to be sacrificed (see Genesis 2:29).
5. Samuel, the biblical prophet, was from Ramah (see 1 Samuel 1:1). Here the allusion is to Samuel ibn Nagrella.
6. I have retained Solá-Solé's use of the Hebrew *rab* (*rav?*), which likely signifies "rabbi."
7. *Jarchas romances*, 87–88, 91.
8. *Jarchas romances*, 190–92.
9. Is this an allusion to the topic of the lover who seeks compensation from the neighbor (García Gómez) or a veiled reference to wine, which later appears again?
10. Reference to gold, which is golden, or blond, like the poet.
11. *Poetas hebreos*, 213–14.
12. I have opted for maintaining the Hebrew, as do Sáenz-Badillos and Targarona Borrás in *Poetas hebreos*. *Šĕ'ol* probably means "grave" here, but could also signify "underworld" or "abyss."
13. *Poetas hebreos*, 59.
14. *Poesía femenina hispanoárabe*, 137.
15. *Jarchas romances*, 85–86.
16. *Poesía de cancionero*, 187–88.
17. Ibid., 383.
18. Ibid., 206–7.
19. Grey, "Ingenious Portrayal," 337 n. 3.
20. Castillo, *Cancionero general*, vol. 5, fols. 164v–165r. Reproduced in Grey, "Ingenious Portrayal," 334–36.
21. Gibert Fenech, "Manera de escribir," 212–13, and Ibn Játima, *Dīwān*, 136–37.
22. Mehrez, "Cartas de tijera," 222.
23. Gibert Fenech, "Escritura de tijera," 473.

Works Cited

Primary Sources

Adivinancero culto español. Edited by José Luis Gárfer and Concha Fernández. 2 vols. Madrid: Taurus, 1990.

Alfonso X. *Cantigas de Santa María.* 2 vols. Madrid: Edilán, 1979.

———. *Prosa histórica.* Edited by Benito Brancaforte. Madrid: Cátedra, 1990.

Arias de Benavides, Pedro. *Secretos de chirurgia, especial de las enfermedades de Morbo Galico y lamparones y mirrarchia.* Edited by Andrea L. Arismendi. In *Textos y concordancias electrónicos del corpus médico español,* edited by María Teresa Herrera and María Estela González de Fauve. Madison: Hispanic Seminary of Medieval Studies, 1997. CD-Rom.

Augustine. *City of God.* Translated by Henry Bettenson. 1972. Reprint, with an introduction by John O'Meara, New York: Penguin, 1984.

Aviñón, Juan de. *Sevillana medicina.* Edited by Brian Taylor. In *Textos y concordancias electrónicos del corpus médico español,* edited by María Teresa Herrera and María Estela González de Fauve. Madison: Hispanic Seminary of Medieval Studies, 1997. CD-Rom.

Castillo, Hernando del. *Cancionero general 1511.* In *El cancionero del siglo XV: c. 1360–1520,* edited by Brian Dutton, 117–538. 7 vols. Salamanca: Biblioteca española del siglo XV, Universidad de Salamanca, 1991.

Chirino, Alfonso. *Menor daño de la medicina.* Edited by Enrica J. Ardemagni, Ruth M. Richards, and Michael R. Solomon. In *Textos y concordancias electrónicos del corpus médico español,* edited by María Teresa Herrera and María Estela González de Fauve. Madison: Hispanic Seminary of Medieval Studies, 1997. CD-Rom.

Colón, Cristóbal. *Textos y documentos completos.* Edited by Consuelo Varela. Madrid: Alianza, 1989.

Constantinus Africanus. *De coitu (Constantini liber de coitu).* Edited by Enrique Montero Cartelle. Santiago de Compostela: Universidad de Santiago de Compostela, 1983.

Covarrubias Horozco, Sebastián de. *Tesoro de la lengua castellana o española (1611).* Edited by Martín de Riquer. Barcelona: Horta, 1943.

Cruz, Juan de la. *Poesía.* Edited by Domingo Ynduráin. Madrid: Cátedra, 1984.

Díaz de Ysla, Ruy. *Tractado llamado fruto de todos los auctos: Contra el mal serpentino.* Edited by Patricia Gubitosi. In *Textos y concordancias electrónicos del corpus médico español,* edited by María Teresa Herrera and María Estela González de Fauve. Madison: Hispanic Seminary of Medieval Studies, 1997. CD-Rom.

Díaz del Castillo, Bernal. *Historia verdadera de la conquista de la Nueva España.* Madrid: Austral, 1989.

Dictionary of Scientific Biography. Edited by Charles Coulston Gillispie. 16 vols. New York: Scribner's, 1970–81.

Dīwān de las poetisas de al-Andalus. Edited by Teresa Garulo. Madrid: Hiperión, 1998.

Galen. *On the Affected Parts.* Edited and translated by Rudolph E. Siegel. New York: S. Karger, 1976.

Gordon, Bernard of. *Lilio de medicina.* Edited by John Cull and Cynthia Wasick. In *Textos y concordancias electrónicos del corpus médico español,* edited by María Teresa Herrera and María Estela González de Fauve. Madison: Hispanic Seminary of Medieval Studies, 1997. CD-Rom.

Al-Harizi, Judá ben Shĕlomo. *Las asambleas de los sabios (Tahkĕmoní).* Edited and translated by Carlos del Valle Rodríguez. Murcia: Universidad de Murcia, 1988.

Hernández Morejón, Antonio, and Rafael Sancho de San Román. *Historia bibliográfica de la medicina española: Obra póstuma.* 7 vols. New York: Johnson Reprint, 1967.

Herrera, María Teresa, ed. *Diccionario español de textos médicos antiguos.* 2 vols. Madrid: Arco/Libros, 1996.

Huarte de San Juan, Juan. *Examen de ingenios para las ciencias.* Edited by Guillermo Serés. Madrid: Cátedra, 1989.

Ibn'Ezra, Moše. *Kitāb al-Muhādara wal-Mudākara.* Edited and translated by Montserrat Abumalham Mas. 2 vols. Madrid: CSIC, Instituto de Filología, 1986.

Ibn Hazm de Córdoba. *El collar de la paloma (Tauq al-hamāma).* Edited by Emilio García Gómez. Madrid: Alianza, 1989.

Ibn Játima de Almería. *El Dīwān de Ibn Játima de Almería (Poesía arabigoandaluza del siglo XIV).* Edited by Soledad Gibert Fenech. Barcelona: Universidad de Barcelona, 1975.

Ibn Quzmān. *Ibn Quzmán: Cancionero andalusí.* Edited by Federico Corriente. Madrid: Hiperión, 1989.

Isidore of Seville. *Etimologías.* 2 vols. Madrid: Biblioteca de autores cristianos, 1993.

Al-Jāhiz, 'Amr Ibn-Bahr. *The Epistle on Singing-Girls of Jāhiz (Risālat al-qiyān).* Edited and translated by A. F. L. Beeston. Warminster, England: Aris & Phillips, 1980.

————. *Nine Essays of al-Jāhiz.* Translated by William M. Hutchins. New York: Peter Lang, 1989.

Las jarchas romances y sus moaxajas. Edited by Josep M. Solá-Solé. Madrid: Taurus, 1990.

Al-Jaṭīb, Muhammad B. ʿAbdallāh B. *Libro del cuidado de la salud durante las estaciones del año, o "Libro de higiene."* Edited by María de la Concepción Vazquéz de Benito. Salamanca: Universidad de Salamanca, 1984.

Ketham, Johannes de. *Compendio de la humana salud.* Edited by María Teresa Herrera. Madrid: Arco/Libros, 1990.

Liber minor de coitu: Tratado menor de andrología anónimo salernitano. Edited by Enrique Montero Cartelle. Lingüística y filología, no. 2. Valladolid: Universidad de Valladolid, 1987.

Lo Libre . . . al qual à mès nom Tròtula (The Book . . . Which Is Called "Trotula"). Edited by Montserrat Cabré i Pairet. In *La cura del cos femeni i la medicina medieval de tradicio llatina,* by Montserrat Cabré i Pairet. Ph.D. dissertation. Universidad de Barcelona, 1994.

Mirror of Coitus. A Translation and Edition of the Fifteenth-Century Speculum al foderi. Edited and translated by Michael Solomon. Madison: Hispanic Seminary for Medieval Studies, 1990.

Núñez de Coria, Francisco. *Tractado del uso de las mugeres.* Edited by Jean Dangler. Available on-line at http://parnaseo.uv.es/Lemir/Textos/Trat_mugeres/mugeres2.html.

De ornatu mulierum (On Women's Cosmetics). Edited by Monica H. Green. In *The* Trotula*: A Medieval Compendium of Women's Medicine,* edited and translated by Monica H. Green, 166–91. Philadelphia: University of Pennsylvania Press, 2001.

Poesía de cancionero. Edited by Álvaro Alonso. Madrid: Cátedra, 1986.

Poesía femenina hispanoárabe. Edited by María Jesús Rubiera Mata. Madrid: Castalia, 1989.

Poetas hebreos de al-Andalus (siglos X–XII): Antología. Edited by Ángel Sáenz-Badillos and Judit Targarona Borrás. Córdoba: El Almendro, 1990.

Pseudo-Dionysius. "The Celestial Hierarchy." In *The Complete Works,* translated by Colm Luibheid and Paul Rorem, 143–91. New York: Paulist Press, 1987.

————. "The Mystical Theology." In *The Complete Works,* translated by Colm Luibheid and Paul Rorem, 133–41. New York: Paulist Press, 1987.

Rojas, Fernando de. *Celestina: A Play in Twenty-One Acts Attributed to Fernando de Rojas.* Translated by Mack Hendricks Singleton. Madison: University of Wisconsin Press, 1968.

————. *La Celestina.* Translated by Dorothy S. Severin. Madrid: Cátedra, 1987.

Ar-Rusāfā de Valencia: Poemas. Edited and translated by Teresa Garulo. Madrid: Hiperión, 1986.

Sem Tob de Carrión. *Proverbios morales.* Edited by Sanford Shepard. Madrid: Castalia, 1985.

————. *Proverbios morales.* Edited by Paloma Díaz-Mas and Carlos Mota. Madrid: Cátedra, 1998.

Speculum al foderi. Edited and translated by Michael Solomon. Madison: Hispanic Seminary for Medieval Studies, 1990.

Torres, Pedro de. *Libro que trata de la enfermedad de las bubas.* Edited by Andrea María Bau. In *Textos y concordancias electrónicos del corpus médico español,* edited by María Teresa Herrera and María Estela González de Fauve. Madison: Hispanic Seminary of Medieval Studies, 1997. CD-Rom.

Tratado de patología general (Tratado médico). Edited by María Teresa Herrera. In *Textos y concordancias electrónicos del corpus médico español,* edited by María Teresa Herrera and María Estela González de Fauve. Madison: Hispanic Seminary of Medieval Studies, 1997. CD-Rom.

Les trobes en lahors de la Verge Maria. Valencia, 1474. Reprint, Valencia: Librerías "París-Valencia," 1979.

The Trotula: *A Medieval Compendium of Women's Medicine.* Edited and translated by Monica H. Green. Philadelphia: University of Pennsylvania Press, 2001.

Vida de María Egipciaca. Edited by Manuel Alvar. 2 vols. Madrid: CSIC, 1972.

Vives, Juan Luis. *Formación de la mujer cristiana.* In *Obras completas,* edited by Lorenzo Riber, 985–1175. 2 vols. Madrid: Aguilar, 1947.

Zuhr, Abū l-Alā'. *Kitāb al-Muyarrabāt (Libro de las experiencias médicas).* Edited by Cristina Álvarez Millán. Madrid: CSIC, 1994.

Secondary Sources

al-Abbādī, Ahmad Mukhtār 'Abd al-Fattāh. *Los eslavos en España: Ojeada sobre su origen, desarrollo y relación con el movimiento de la Su'ūbiyya.* Madrid: Ministerio de Educación de Egipto, Instituto Egipcio de Estudios Islámicos, 1953.

AbuKhalil, Asad. "A Note on the Study of Homosexuality in the Arab/Islamic Civilization." *Arab Studies Journal* 1, no. 2 (1993): 32–34, 48.

Abu-Lughod, Janet L. *Before European Hegemony: The World System A.D. 1250–1350.* New York: Oxford University Press, 1989.

Adang, Camila. *Islam frente a Judaísmo: La polémica de Ibn Hazm de Córdoba.* Madrid: Aben Ezra, 1994.

Amparo Alba, Cecilia. "El debate de la espada y el cálamo." In *Proyección histórica de España en sus tres culturas: Castilla y León, América y el mediterráneo,* edited by Eufemio Lorenzo Sanz, 7–13. 3 vols. Valladolid: Junta de Castilla y León, 1993.

Anderson, Benedict. *Imagined Communities: Reflections on the Origin and Spread of Nationalism.* 2d ed. New York: Verso, 1991.

Arié, Rachel. *El reino nasrí de Granada (1232–1492).* Madrid: Mapfre, 1992.

Arrizabalaga, Jon, John Henderson, and Roger French. *The Great Pox: The French Disease in Renaissance Europe.* New Haven: Yale University Press, 1997.

Baxter Wolf, Kenneth. "Christian Views of Islam in Early Medieval Spain." In *Medieval Christian Perceptions of Islam: A Book of Essays,* edited by John Victor Tolan, 85–108. New York: Garland, 1996.

———. "Muhammad as Antichrist in Ninth-Century Córdoba." In *Christians, Muslims, and Jews in Medieval and Early Modern Spain: Interaction and Cultural Change,* edited by Mark D. Meyerson and Edward D. English, 3–19. Notre Dame: University of Notre Dame Press, 2000.

Behrens-Abouseif, Doris. *Beauty in Arabic Culture.* Princeton: Marcus Wiener, 1999.

Bergmann, Emilie. "The Exclusion of the Feminine in the Cultural Discourse of the Golden Age: Juan Luis Vives and Fray Luis de León." In *Religion, Body and Gender in Early Modern Spain*, edited by Alain Saint-Saëns, 124–36. San Francisco: Mellen Research University Press, 1991.

Beutler, Gisela. "Enigmas y adivinanzas sobre el libro, la pluma y otros utensilios para escribir: Estudio sobre su origen, sus metáforas, su estructura." In *Homenaje a Fernando Antonio Martínez*, 244–82. Bogotá: Instituto Caro y Cuervo, 1979.

Bhabha, Homi K. *The Location of Culture*. New York: Routledge, 1994.

Birge Vitz, Evelyn. *Medieval Narrative and Modern Narratology*. New York: New York University Press, 1989.

Boase, Roger. "Arab Influences on European Love-Poetry." In *The Legacy of Muslim Spain*, edited by Salma Khadra Jayyusi, 457–82. Leiden: Brill, 1992.

———. *The Origin and Meaning of Courtly Love: A Critical Study of European Scholarship*. Manchester: Manchester University Press, 1977.

———. *The Troubadour Revival: A Study of Social Change and Traditionalism in Late Medieval Spain*. London: Routledge and Kegan Paul, 1978.

Boynton, Susan. "Women's Performance of the Lyric before 1500." In *Medieval Woman's Song: Cross-Cultural Approaches*, edited by Anne L. Klinck and Ann Marie Rasmussen, 47–65. Philadelphia: University of Pennsylvania Press, 2002.

Brann, Ross. "The Arabized Jews." In *The Literature of Al-Andalus*, edited by María Rosa Menocal, Raymond P. Scheindlin, and Michael Sells, 435–54. Cambridge: Cambridge University Press, 2000.

Brown, Catherine. *Contrary Things: Exegesis, Dialectic, and the Poetics of Didacticism*. Stanford: Stanford University Press, 1998.

Bruckner, Matilda Tomaryn. "Fictions of the Female Voice: The Women Troubadours." In *Medieval Woman's Song: Cross-Cultural Approaches*, edited by Anne L. Klinck and Ann Marie Rasmussen, 127–51. Philadelphia: University of Pennsylvania Press, 2002.

Bürgel, J. Christoph. "Ambiguity: A Study in the Use of Religious Terminology in the Poetry of Hafiz." In *Intoxication Earthly and Heavenly. Seven Studies on the Poet Hafiz of Shiraz*, edited by Michael Glünz and J. Christoph Bürgel, 7–39. Berlin: Peter Lang, 1991.

Burke, James F. *Desire against the Law: The Juxtaposition of Contraries in Early Medieval Spanish Literature*. Stanford: Stanford University Press, 1998.

———. "The *Mal de la Madre* and the Failure of Maternal Influence in *Celestina*." *Celestinesca* 17, no. 2 (1993): 111–28.

Burns, E. Jane. *Courtly Love Undressed: Reading through Clothes in Medieval French Culture*. Philadelphia: University of Pennsylvania Press, 2002.

———. "The Man behind the Lady in Troubadour Lyric." *Romance Notes* 25, no. 3 (1985): 254–70.

Butler, Judith. *The Psychic Life of Power: Theories in Subjection*. Stanford: Stanford University Press, 1997.

Cadden, Joan. *Meanings of Sex Difference in the Middle Ages: Medicine, Science, and Culture*. Cambridge: Cambridge University Press, 1993.

———. "Western Medicine and Natural Philosophy." In *Handbook of Medieval Sexuality,* edited by Vern L. Bullough and James A. Brundage, 51–80. New York: Garland, 1996.

Camille, Michael. *Image on the Edge: The Margins of Medieval Art.* Cambridge: Harvard University Press, 1992.

———. "Mouths and Meaning: Towards an Anti-Iconography of Medieval Art." In *Iconography at the Crossroads,* edited by Brendan Cassidy, 43–57. Papers from the colloquium sponsored by the Index of Christian Art, Princeton University, 23–24 March 1990. Princeton: Index of Christian Art, Department of Art and Archaeology, Princeton University, 1993.

Carpenter, Dwayne E. *Alfonso X and the Jews: An Edition of and Commentary on* Siete Partidas 7.24 *"De los judíos."* University of California Publications in Modern Philology, vol. 115. Berkeley: University of California Press, 1986.

Casey, James. *Early Modern Spain: A Social History.* New York: Routledge, 1999.

Castells, Manuel. *The Power of Identity.* Oxford: Blackwell, 1997.

Castro, Américo. *España en su historia: Cristianos, moros y judíos.* Barcelona: Crítica, 1983.

Cohen, Jeffrey Jerome, ed. *Monster Theory: Reading Culture.* Minneapolis: University of Minnesota Press, 1996.

———. *Of Giants: Sex, Monsters, and the Middle Ages.* Minneapolis: University of Minnesota Press, 1999.

Colahan, Clark. "Santob's Debate: Parody and Political Allegory." *Sefarad* 34 (1979): 87–107, 265–308.

Colahan, Clark, and Alfred Rodríguez. "Traditional Semitic Forms of Reversibility in Sem Tob's *Proverbios morales." Journal of Medieval and Renaissance Studies* 13 (1983): 33–50.

Colish, Marcia L. *The Mirror of Language: A Study in the Medieval Theory of Knowledge.* Lincoln: University of Nebraska Press, 1968.

Constable, Olivia Remie. *Medieval Iberia: Readings from Christian, Muslim, and Jewish Sources.* Philadelphia: University of Pennsylvania Press, 1997.

———. *Trade and Traders in Muslim Spain: The Commercial Realignment of the Iberian Peninsula, 900–1500.* Cambridge: Cambridge University Press, 1994.

Corriente, Federico. *Poesía dialectal árabe y romance en Alandalús.* Madrid: Gredos, 1998.

Cruz, Anne J. *Discourses of Poverty: Social Reform and the Picaresque Novel in Early Modern Spain.* Toronto: University of Toronto Press, 1999.

Dagenais, John. *The Ethics of Reading in Manuscript Culture: Glossing the* Libro de buen amor. Princeton: Princeton University Press, 1994.

Dangler, Jean. *Mediating Fictions: Literature, Women, and the Go-Between in Medieval and Early Modern Iberia.* Lewisburg: Bucknell University Press, 2001.

———. "Transgendered Sex and Healing in *Celestina." Celestinesca* 25, nos. 1–2 (2001): 69–81.

Daston, Lorraine, and Katharine Park. "The Hermaphrodite and the Order of Nature: Sexual Ambiguity in Early Modern France." In *Premodern Sexualities,* edited by Louise Fradenburg and Carla Freccero, 117–36. New York: Routledge, 1996.

———. *Wonders and the Order of Nature, 1150–1750.* New York: Zone, 1998.

De Landa, Manuel. *One Thousand Years of Nonlinear History.* New York: Swerve, 1997.

Díaz Esteban, Fernando. "El debate del cálamo y las tijeras de Sem Tob Ardutiel." Homenaje a Ramón Menéndez Pidal. *Revista de la Universidad de Madrid* 18, no. 1 (1969): 61–102.

Dixon, Laurinda S. "The Curse of Chastity: The Marginalization of Women in Medieval Art and Medicine." In *Matrons and Marginal Women in Medieval Society,* edited by Robert R. Edwards and Vickie Ziegler, 49–74. Woodbridge, England: Boydell, 1995.

Docker, John. *1492: The Poetics of Diaspora.* London: Continuum, 2001.

Dodd, Jerilynn. *Architecture and Ideology in Early Medieval Spain.* University Park: Pennsylvania State University Press, 1990.

Duby, Georges. *France in the Middle Ages, 987–1460: From Hugh Capet to Joan of Arc.* Translated by Juliet Vale. Oxford: Blackwell, 1993.

Dutton, Brian, and María Nieves Sánchez. Introduction to *Lilio de medicina,* by Bernard of Gordon, 7–34. 2 vols. Madrid: Arco/Libros, 1993.

Eco, Umberto. *Art and Beauty in the Middle Ages.* New Haven: Yale University Press, 1986.

Edson, Evelyn. *Mapping Time and Space: How Medieval Mapmakers Viewed Their World.* London: British Library, 1997.

Epalza, Mikel de. "Mozarabs: An Emblematic Christian Minority in Islamic al-Andalus." In *History and Society,* pt. 1 of *The Formation of al-Andalus,* edited by Manuela Marín, 183–204. Vol. 46, *The Formation of the Classical Islamic World.* Brookfield, Vt.: Ashgate, 1998.

Espósito, Anthony P. "Dismemberment of Things Past: Fixing the *Jarchas.*" *La corónica* 24, no. 1 (1995): 4–14.

———. "The Monkey in the *Jarcha:* Tradition and Canonicity in the Early Iberian Lyric." *Journal of Medieval and Early Modern Studies* 30, no. 3 (2000): 463–77.

Flint, Valerie I. J. "Monsters and the Antipodes in the Early Middle Ages and Enlightenment." *Viator* 15 (1984): 65–80.

Foucault, Michel. *Discipline and Punish: The Birth of the Prison.* New York: Vintage, 1977.

———. *The Order of Things: An Archaeology of the Human Sciences.* New York: Vintage, 1970.

Frenk Alatorre, Margit. *Lírica española de tipo popular.* Madrid: Cátedra, 1989.

Friedman, John Block. *The Monstrous Races in Medieval Art and Thought.* Cambridge: Harvard University Press, 1981.

García-Ballester, Luis. "A Marginal Learned Medical World: Jewish, Muslim and Christian Medical Practitioners, and the Use of Arabic Medical Sources in Late Medieval Spain." In *Practical Medicine from Salerno to the Black Death,* edited by Luis García-Ballester, Roger French, Jon Arrizabalaga, and Andrew Cunningham, 353–94. Cambridge: Cambridge University Press, 1994.

García Ballester, Luis, and Jon Arrizabalaga. "El *regiment* de Jacme d'Agramont y el *Estudi* de medicina de Lleida." In *Regiment de preservació de pestilència: (Lleida, 1348).* Biblioteca Virtual Joan Lluís Vives. Available on-line at: http://www.lluisvives.com/FichaObra.html?portal=1&Ref=1995.

García-Ballester, Luis, Michael R. McVaugh, and Agustín Rubio-Vela. *Medical Licensing and Learning in Fourteenth-Century Valencia: Transactions of the American Philosophical Society.* Philadelphia: American Philosophical Society, 1989.

García Gómez, Emilio, ed. *Las jarchas romances de la serie árabe en su marco*. Madrid: Sociedad de Estudios y Publicaciones, 1965.

Gaylord, Mary M. "Fair of the World, Fair of the Word: The Commerce of Language in *La Celestina.*" *Revista de estudios hispánicos* 25, no. 1 (1991): 1–28.

Gibert Fenech, Soledad. "La 'escritura de tijera' en unos versos de al-Rusāfī. " *Al-Andalus* 33 (1968): 471–73.

———. "Sobre una extraña manera de escribir." *Al-Andalus* 14 (1949): 211–13.

Gil, José S. *La escuela de traductores de Toledo y sus colaboradores judíos*. Toledo: Instituto Provincial de Investigaciones y Estudios Toledanos, Diputación Provincial, 1985.

Glick, Thomas F. *Islamic and Christian Spain in the Early Middle Ages*. Princeton: Princeton University Press, 1979.

Goitein, Shlomo. *A Mediterranean Society: The Jewish Communities of the Arab World as Portrayed in the Documents of the Cairo* Genizah. 6 vols. Berkeley: University of California Press, 1967–93.

González Casanovas, Roberto J. "Alfonso X's Concept of Hispania: Cultural Politics in the Histories." In *Concepts of National Identity in the Middle Ages,* edited by Simon Forde, Lesley Johnson, and Alan V. Murray, 155–70. Leeds Texts and Monographs 14. Leeds, England: University of Leeds, 1995.

González Jiménez, Manuel. "Frontier and Settlement in the Kingdom of Castile (1085–1350)." In *Medieval Frontier Societies,* edited by Robert Bartlett and Angus MacKay, 49–52. Oxford: Clarendon, 1989.

Goodich, Michael, ed. *Other Middle Ages: Witnesses at the Margins of Medieval Society*. Philadelphia: University of Pennsylvania Press, 1998.

Goody, Jack. *The Logic of Writing and the Organization of Society*. New York: Cambridge University Press, 1986.

Gracia Guillén, Diego. "Judaism, Medicine, and the Inquisitorial Mind in Sixteenth-Century Spain." In *The Spanish Inquisition and the Inquisitorial Mind,* edited by Ángel Alcalá, 375–400. Boulder, Colo.: Social Science Monographs, 1987.

Granja, Fernando de la. *Maqāmas y risālas andaluzas*. Madrid: Hiperión, 1997.

Green, Monica H. "The Possibilities of Literacy and the Limits of Reading: Women and the Gendering of Medical Literacy." In *Women's Healthcare in the Medieval West: Texts and Contexts,* chap. 7. Burlington, Vt.: Ashgate, 2000.

Greilsammer, Myriam. "The Midwife, the Priest, and the Physician: The Subjugation of Midwives in the Low Countries at the End of the Middle Ages." *Journal of Medieval and Renaissance Studies* 21, no. 2 (fall 1991): 285–329.

Grey, Ernest. "An Ingenious Portrayal of a Split Personality." *Romance Notes* 9 (1968): 334–37.

Haidu, Peter. "Text and History: The Semiosis of Twelfth-Century Lyric as Sociohistorical Phenomenon (Chrétien de Troyes: 'D'Amor qui m'a tolu')." *Semiotica* 33, nos. 1–2 (1981): 1–62.

Harley, J. B., and David Woodward, eds. *The History of Cartography*. 2 vols. Chicago: University of Chicago Press, 1992.

Hayles, N. Katherine. "The Complexities of Seriation." *PMLA* 117, no. 1 (2002): 117–21.

Heath, Peter. *Allegory and Philosophy in Avicenna (Ibn Sina)*. Philadelphia: University of Pennsylvania Press, 1992.

Heller-Roazen, Daniel. "Speaking in Tongues." *Paragraph* 25, no. 2 (2002): 92–115.

Hillgarth, J. N. *The Mirror of Spain, 1500–1700. The Formation of a Myth*. Ann Arbor: University of Michigan Press, 2000.

Hutcheson, Gregory S. "The Sodomitic Moor: Queerness in the Narrative of *Reconquista*." In *Queering the Middle Ages*, edited by Glenn Burger and Steven F. Kruger, 99–122. Minneapolis: University of Minnesota Press, 2001.

Illades Aguiar, Gustavo. *La Celestina en el taller salmantino*. México, D. F.: Universidad Nacional Autónoma de México, 1999.

Jacquart, Danielle, and Claude Thomasset. *Sexuality and Medicine in the Middle Ages*. Translated by Matthew Adamson. Princeton: Princeton University Press, 1988.

Johnson, Lesley. "Imagining Communities: Medieval and Modern." In *Concepts of National Identity in the Middle Ages*, edited by Simon Forde, Lesley Johnson, and Alan V. Murray, 1–19. Leeds Texts and Monographs 14. Leeds, England: University of Leeds, 1995.

Johnston, Mark D. "Cultural Studies on the *Gaya Ciencia*." In *Poetry at Court in Trastamaran Spain: From the* Cancionero de Baena *to the* Cancionero General, edited by E. Michael Gerli and Julian Weiss, 235–53. Tempe: Medieval and Renaissance Texts and Studies, 1998.

Joset, Jacques. "Opposition et réversabilité des valeurs dans les *Proverbios morales:* Approche du systéme de pensée de Santob de Carrión." Hommage au Prof. Maurice Delbouille. *Marche Romane* (1973): 171–89.

Kappler, Claude. *Monstres, démons et merveilles à la fin du moyen âge*. Paris: Payot, 1980.

Keller, John Esten, and Annette Grant Cash. *Daily Life Depicted in the* Cantigas de Santa María. Lexington: University of Kentucky Press, 1998.

Kelley, Mary Jane. "Virgins Misconceived: Poetic Voice in the Mozarabic *Kharjas*." *La corónica* 19, no. 2 (1990–91): 1–23.

Kurrik, Maire Jaanus. *Literature and Negation*. New York: Columbia University Press, 1979.

Lanning, John Tate. *The Royal Protomedicato: The Regulation of the Medical Professions in the Spanish Empire*. Durham: Duke University Press, 1985.

Laqueur, Thomas. *Making Sex: Body and Gender from the Greeks to Freud*. Cambridge: Harvard University Press, 1990.

Larsson, Göran. *Ibn García's shu'ūbiyya Letter: Ethnic and Theological Tensions in Medieval al-Andalus*. Leiden: Brill, 2003.

Leclercq, Jean. "Influence and Noninfluence of Dionysius in the Western Middle Ages." In Pseudo-Dionysius, *The Complete Works*, translated by Colm Luibheid and Paul Rorem, 25–32. New York: Paulist Press, 1987.

Levey, Martin, and Safwat S. Souryal. "Galen's 'On the Secrets of Women' and 'On the Secrets of Men.'" *Janus* 55 (1968): 208–19.

Lida de Malkiel, María Rosa. "La dama como obra maestra de Dios." *Romance Philology* 28 (1974–75): 267–324.

———. *Estudios sobre la literatura española del siglo XV*. Madrid: Porrúa Turanzas, 1977.

———. "La hipérbole sagrada en la poesía castellana del siglo XV." *Revista de Filologá Hispánica* 8 (1949): 121–30.

Limor, Ora. *The Medieval Review.* Available on-line at http://www.hti.umich.edu/t/tmr, TMR ID: 99.01.04.

Lindberg, David C. *The Beginnings of Western Science: The European Scientific Tradition in Philosophical, Religious, and Institutional Context, 600 B.C. to A.D. 1450.* Chicago: University of Chicago Press, 1992.

López-Morillas, Consuelo. "Language." In *The Literature of Al-Andalus,* edited by María Rosa Menocal, Raymond P. Scheindlin, and Michael Sells, 33–59. Cambridge: Cambridge University Press, 2000.

Mackay, Angus. "Religion, Culture, and Ideology on the Late Medieval Castilian-Granadan Frontier." In *Medieval Frontier Societies,* edited by Robert Bartlett and Angus Mackay, 217–43. Oxford: Clarendon Press, 1989.

Manzano Moreno, Eduardo. *Historia de las sociedades musulmanas en la Edad Media.* Madrid: Síntesis, 1992.

Maravall, José Antonio. *Antiguos y modernos: Visión de la historia e idea de progreso hasta el Renacimiento.* 2d ed. Madrid: Alianza, 1986.

———. *Culture of the Baroque: Analysis of a Historical Structure,* translated by Terry Cochran. Minneapolis: University of Minnesota Press, 1986.

Marín, Manuela. *Al-Ándalus y los andalusíes.* Barcelona: CIDOB, 2000.

———. *Individuo y sociedad en al-Ándalus.* Madrid: Mapfre, 1992.

Martín Merás, Luisa. *Cartografía marítima hispana: La imagen de América.* Barcelona: Lunwerg, 1993.

Mehrez, Gamal. "Todavía las 'cartas de tijera.'" *Al-Andalus* 16 (1951): 221–23.

Menéndez Pidal, Ramón. *Poesía árabe y poesía europea: Con otros estudios de literatura medieval.* Madrid: Espasa-Calpe, 1955.

Menocal, María Rosa. *The Arabic Role in Medieval Literary History: A Forgotten Heritage.* Philadelphia: University of Pennsylvania Press, 1987.

———. *The Ornament of the World: How Muslims, Jews, and Christians Created a Culture of Tolerance in Medieval Spain.* Boston: Little, Brown and Co., 2002.

———. *Shards of Love: Exile and the Origins of the Lyric.* Durham: Duke University Press, 1994.

Meyerson, Mark D. Introduction to *Christians, Muslims, and Jews in Medieval and Early Modern Spain: Interaction and Cultural Change,* edited by Mark D. Meyerson and Edward D. English, xi–xxi. Notre Dame: University of Notre Dame Press, 1999.

Minnis, A. J., and A. B. Scott, eds. *Medieval Literary Theory and Criticism, c. 1100–1375.* Oxford: Clarendon Press, 1988.

Monroe, James T. *Hispano-Arabic Poetry: A Student Anthology.* Berkeley: University of California Press, 1974.

———. "The Striptease That Was Blamed on Abū Bakr's Naughty Son." In *Homoeroticism in Classical Arabic Literature,* edited by J. W. Wright, Jr., and Everett K. Rowson, 94–139. New York: Columbia University Press, 1997.

———. "*Zajal* and *Muwashshaha:* Hispano-Arabic Poetry and the Romance Tradition." In *The Legacy of Muslim Spain,* edited by Salma Khadra Jayyusi, 398–419. Leiden: Brill, 1992.

Moran Cruz, Jo Ann Hoeppner. "Popular Attitudes towards Islam in Medieval Europe." In *Western Views of Islam in Medieval and Early Modern Europe: Perception of Other,* edited by David R. Blanks and Michael Frassetto, 55–81. New York: St. Martin's Press, 1999.

Morrison, Karl F. "Interpreting the Fragment." In *Hermeneutics and Medieval Culture,* edited by Patrick J. Gallacher and Helen Damico, 27–37. Albany: State University of New York Press, 1989.

"Mujeres y salud: Prácticas y saberes." *Dynamis* 19 (1999): 17–400.

Muñoz Fernández, Ángela, and Cristina Segura Graiño, eds. *El trabajo de las mujeres en la edad media hispana.* Madrid: Asociación Cultural Al-Mudayna, 1988.

Murray, Steven O. "Woman-Woman Love in Islamic Societies." In *Islamic Homosexualities: Culture, History, and Literature,* edited by Steven O. Murray and Will Roscoe, 97–104. New York: New York University Press, 1997.

Navarro, Emilia. "Manual Control: 'Regulatory Fictions' and Their Discontents." *Cervantes* 13, no. 2 (1993): 17–35.

Nederman, Cary J. *Worlds of Difference: European Discourses of Toleration, c. 1100–c. 1500.* University Park: Pennsylvania State University Press, 2000.

Nerlich, Michael. *Ideology of Adventure: Studies in Modern Consciousness, 1100–1750.* 2 vols. Minneapolis: University of Minnesota Press, 1987.

Nichols, Steven G., Jr., *Romanesque Signs: Early Medieval Narrative and Iconography.* New Haven: Yale University Press, 1983.

Nirenberg, David. *Communities of Violence: Persecution of Minorities in the Middle Ages.* Princeton: Princeton University Press, 1996.

———. "Enmity and Assimilation: Jews, Christians, and Converts in Medieval Spain." *Common Knowledge* 9, no. 1 (2003): 137–55.

———. "Religion and Sexual Boundaries in the Medieval Crown of Aragon." In *Christians, Muslims, and Jews in Medieval and Early Modern Spain: Interaction and Cultural Change,* edited by Mark D. Meyerson and Edward D. English, 141–60. Notre Dame: University of Notre Dame Press, 1999.

"El número medio de hijos por mujer en 2004 fue de 1,32, la cifra más alta desde 1993," *El País,* June 22, 2005. Available on-line at: http://www.elpais.es/articulo.html?xref=20050622 elpepusoc_2&type=Tes&anchor=elpporsoc.

Oberhelman, Steven M. "Hierarchies of Gender, Ideology, and Power in Ancient and Medieval Greek and Arabic Dream Literature." In *Homoeroticism in Classical Arabic Literature,* edited by J. W. Wright, Jr., and Everett K. Rowson, 55–93. New York: Columbia University Press, 1997.

Olson, Glending. *Literature as Recreation in the Later Middle Ages.* Ithaca: Cornell University Press, 1982.

Pagis, Dan. *Hebrew Poetry of the Middle Ages and Renaissance.* Berkeley: University of California Press, 1991.

Pérès, Henri. *Esplendor de al-Andalus. La poesía andaluza en árabe clásico en el siglo XI: Sus aspectos generales, sus principales temas y su valor documental.* Translated by Mercedes García-Arenal. Madrid: Hiperión, 1983.

Perry, Mary Elizabeth. "Magdalens and Jezebels in Counter-Reformation Spain." In *Culture and Control in Counter-Reformation Spain,* edited by Anne J. Cruz and Mary Elizabeth Perry, 124–44. Hispanic Issues, vol. 7. Minneapolis: University of Minnesota Press, 1992.

Perry, T. A. *The* Moral Proverbs *of Santob de Carrión: Jewish Wisdom in Christian Spain.* Princeton: Princeton University Press, 1987.

Phillips, William D., Jr. *Enrique IV and the Crisis of Fifteenth-Century Castile, 1425–1480.* Cambridge: The Medieval Academy of America, 1978.

Poovey, Mary. *A History of the Modern Fact: Problems of Knowledge in the Sciences of Wealth and Society.* Chicago: University of Chicago Press, 1998.

Quétel, Claude. *The History of Syphilis.* Translated by Judith Braddock and Brian Pike. Cambridge: Polity, 1990.

Reynolds, Dwight F., ed. *Interpreting the Self: Autobiography in the Arabic Literary Tradition.* Berkeley: University of California Press, 2001.

———. "Music." In *The Literature of Al-Andalus,* edited by María Rosa Menocal, Raymond P. Scheindlin, and Michael Sells, 60–82. Cambridge: Cambridge University Press, 2000.

Rodríguez, Juan Carlos. *Theory and History of Ideological Production: The First Bourgeois Literatures (The Sixteenth Century),* translated by Malcolm K. Read. Newark: University of Delaware Press, 2002.

Rodríguez Puértolas, Julio. "Jews and *Conversos* in Fifteenth-Century Castilian *Cancioneros*: Texts and Contexts." In *Poetry at Court in Trastamaran Spain: From the* Cancionero de Baena *to the* Cancionero General, edited by E. Michael Gerli and Julian Weiss, 187–97. Tempe: Arizona State University Press, 1998.

Rosen, Tova. "The Muwashshah." In *The Literature of Al-Andalus,* edited by María Rosa Menocal, Raymond P. Scheindlin, and Michael Sells, 165–89. Cambridge: Cambridge University Press, 2000.

Roth, Norman. "Jewish Collaborators in Alfonso's Scientific Work." In *Emperor of Culture: Alfonso X the Learned of Castile and His Thirteenth-Century Renaissance,* edited by Robert I. Burns, SJ, 59–71. Philadelphia: University of Pennsylvania Press, 1990.

Rowson, Everett K. "Two Homoerotic Narratives from Mamlūk Literature: al-Safadī's *Law'at al-shākī* and Ibn Dāniyāl's *al-Mutayyam.*" In *Homoeroticism in Classical Arabic Literature,* edited by J. W. Wright, Jr., and Everett K. Rowson, 158–91. New York: Columbia University Press, 1997.

Rubert de Ventos, Xavier. *Nacionalismos: El laberinto de la identidad.* Madrid: Espasa-Calpe, 1994.

Ruiz Montejo, María Inés. "La temática obscena en la iconografía del románico rural." *Goya* 147 (1978): 136–46.

Said, Edward W. *Orientalism.* New York: Vintage, 1978.

Sánchez Albornoz, Claudio. *España: Un enigma histórico.* Buenos Aires: Sudamericana, 1956.

Scheindlin, Raymond P. *The Gazelle: Medieval Hebrew Poems on God, Israel, and the Soul.* Philadelphia: Jewish Publication Society, 1991.

————. *Wine, Women, and Death: Medieval Hebrew Poems on the Good Life.* Philadelphia: Jewish Publication Society, 1986.

Schimmel, Annemarie. *My Soul Is a Woman: The Feminine in Islam.* New York: Continuum, 1999.

Sells, Michael A. *Desert Tracings: Six Classic Arabian Odes by 'Alqama, Shánfara, Labíd, 'Antara, Al-A'sha, and Dhu al-Rúmma.* Hanover: Wesleyan University Press, 1989.

————. "Love." In *The Literature of Al-Andalus,* edited by María Rosa Menocal, Raymond P. Scheindlin, and Michael Sells, 126–58. Cambridge: Cambridge University Press, 2000.

————. *Mystical Languages of Unsaying.* Chicago: University of Chicago Press, 1994.

————. *Stations of Desire: Love Elegies from Ibn 'Arabi and New Poems.* Jerusalem: Ibis, 2000.

Serés, Guillermo. *La transformación de los amantes: Imágenes del amor de la antigüedad al siglo de oro.* Barcelona: Crítica, 1996.

Shepard, Sanford. *Shem Tov: His World and His Words.* Miami: Ediciones Universal, 1978.

Siraisi, Nancy. *Medieval and Early Renaissance Medicine: An Introduction to Knowledge and Practice.* Chicago: University of Chicago Press, 1990.

Solomon, Michael. "Calisto's Ailment: Bitextual Diagnostics and Parody in *Celestina.*" *Revista de estudios hispánicos* 23 (1989): 41–64.

————. *The Literature of Misogyny in Medieval Spain: The* Arcipreste de Talavera *and the* Spill. New York: Cambridge University Press, 1997.

————. "Towards a Definition of the Popular Medical Treatise in Late Medieval and Early Modern Spain." In *Textos medievales y renacentistas de la Romania,* edited by María Teresa Navarro, John J. Nitti, and María Nieves Sánchez, 183–93. New York: Hispanic Seminary of Medieval Studies, 2002.

Stetkevych, Suzanne Pinckney. "Intoxication and Immortality: Wine and Associated Imagery in al-Ma'arrī's Garden." In *Homoeroticism in Classical Arabic Literature,* edited by J. W. Wright, Jr., and Everett K. Rowson, 210–32. New York: Columbia University Press, 1997.

Stone, Gregory B. *Death of the Troubadour: The Late Medieval Resistance to the Renaissance.* Philadelphia: University of Pennsylvania Press, 1994.

Sturges, Robert S. *Medieval Interpretation: Models of Reading in Literary Narrative, 1100–1500.* Carbondale: Southern Illinois University Press, 1991.

Tiffany, Daniel. "Lyric Substance: On Riddles, Materialism, and Poetic Obscurity." *Critical Inquiry* 28, no. 1 (2001): 72–98.

Tolan, John V. Introduction to *Diálogo contra los judíos,* by Pedro Alfonso de Huesca, iii–lx. Huesca: Instituto de Estudios Altoaragoneses, 1996.

————. *Saracens: Islam in the Medieval European Imagination.* New York: Columbia University Press, 2002.

"El Tribunal del Real Protomedicato en la Monarquía Hispánica, 1593–1808." *Dynamis* 16 (1996): 17–259.

Turner, Howard R. *Science in Medieval Islam: An Illustrated Introduction.* Austin: University of Texas Press, 1995.

Vallvé Bermejo, Joaquín. "Una fuente importante de la historia de al-Andalus. La 'Historia' de Ibn 'Askar." *Al-Andalus* 31 (1966): 237–65.

Vance, Eugene. *From Topic to Tale: Logic and Narrativity in the Middle Ages.* Minneapolis: University of Minnesota Press, 1987.

Van Gelder, Geert Jan. *God's Banquet: Food in Classical Arabic Literature.* New York: Columbia University Press, 2000.

Wack, Mary F. *Lovesickness in the Middle Ages: The* Viaticum *and Its Commentaries.* Philadelphia: University of Pennsylvania Press, 1990.

Walsh, Timothy. *The Dark Matter of Words: Absence, Unknowing, and Emptiness in Literature.* Carbondale: Southern Illinois University Press, 1998.

Walther, Wiebke. *Women in Islam.* Montclair, N.J.: A. Schram, 1981.

Weir, Anthony, and James Jerman. *Images of Lust: Sexual Carvings on Medieval Churches.* London: B. T. Batsford, 1986.

Whetnall, Jane. "Songs and *Canciones* in the *Cancionero general* of 1511." In *The Age of the Catholic Monarchs, 1474–1516: Literary Studies in Memory of Keith Whinnom,* edited by Alan Deyermond and Ian Macpherson, 197–207. Liverpool: Liverpool University Press, 1989.

Whinnom, Keith. *La poesía amatoria en la época de los Reyes Católicos.* Durham: University of Durham, 1981.

Whitman, Jon. *Allegory: The Dynamics of an Ancient and Medieval Technique.* Cambridge: Harvard University Press, 1987.

Williams, David. *Deformed Discourse: The Function of the Monster in Mediaeval Thought and Literature.* Montreal: McGill-Queen's University Press, 1996.

Wittkower, Rudolf. "Marvels of the East: A Study in the History of Monsters." In *Allegory and the Migration of Symbols,* by Rudolf Wittkower, 45–74. Boulder, Colo.: Westview Press, 1977.

Women and Work in Spain: From the Middle Ages to Early Modern Times. Edited by Marilyn Stone and Carmen Benito-Vessels. New York: Peter Lang, 1998.

Young Gregg, Joan. *Devils, Women, and Jews: Reflections of the Other in Medieval Sermon Stories.* Albany: State University Press of New York, 1997.

Yovel, Yirmiyahu. "Converso Dualities in the First Generation: The *Cancioneros.*" *Jewish Social Studies* 4, no. 3 (1998): 1–28.

Zemke, John. *Critical Approaches to the* Proverbios morales *of Shem Tov de Carrión: An Annotated Bibliography.* Newark, Del.: Juan de la Cuesta, 1997.

Zumthor, Paul. *Speaking of the Middle Ages.* Translated by Sarah White. Lincoln: University of Nebraska Press, 1986.

Zwartjes, Otto. *Love Songs from Al-Andalus: History, Structure, and Meaning of the Kharja.* Leiden: Brill, 1997.

Index

JEAN DANGLER
is associate professor of Spanish at Tulane University.